Winter Sign

The University of Minnesota Press gratefully acknowledges the generous assistance provided for the publication of this book by the Hamilton P. Traub University Press Fund.

Winter Sign

Jim dale Huot-Vickery

University of Minnesota Press
Minneapolis
London

Published by the University of Minnesota Press
111 Third Avenue South, Suite 290
Minneapolis, MN 55401-2520
http://www.upress.umn.edu

Printed in the United States of America on acid-free paper

Library of Congress Cataloging-in-Publication Data
Vickery, Jim dale.
    Winter sign / Jim dale Huot-Vickery.
        p.   cm.
    Includes bibliographical references (p.   ).
    ISBN 0-8166-2969-2 (alk. paper)
    1. Natural history—Minnesota—Superior National
Forest Region. 2. Winter—Minnesota—Superior National
Forest Region. 3. Vickery, Jim dale. 4. Human ecology.
I. Title.
QH105.M55V535   1998
508.776'7—dc21   98-26190

The University of Minnesota is an equal-opportunity
educator and employer.

10 09 08 07 06 05 04 03 02 01 00 99 98
10 9 8 7 6 5 4 3 2 1

For her

"I am the Witness," he said. "To witness was my path of knowledge; to tell you impeccably what I witness is my task."

—Nestor, in *The Second Ring of Power*
by Carlos Castaneda

Contents

Acknowledgments

I extend thanks, of course, to the deer, wolves, fox, eagles, and all our wild relations who allowed me glimpses, sometimes tragic, of their lives.

Among my own kind, a special *merci* goes to *mon avant*, Anna Shallman, who helped evoke *Winter Sign* in countless ways. Foremost, perhaps, was her partnership on QUEST-SEA, our thousand-mile canoe expedition from the Quetico-Superior of northeastern Minnesota to Hudson Bay of the Arctic Ocean in 1996. The journey enlarged my geographical sense of Hocoka and inspired me to focus on *Winter Sign* with unbending intent.

Larry Rodich, known to friends as Ish, provided moral and technological support including a solar-powered laptop word processor. Ranger Jeff Field, known in Apostle Islands National Lakeshore as 243, helped with computer program conversions and, over the years, friendship, humor, and the more serious business of rangering together on Lake Superior.

For my listening pleasure, which I indulged while writing *Winter Sign*, I'm indebted to native and eclectic musicians I never met: Paul Horn, Steve Halpern, Loreena McKennit, Peter Kater, Bruce Cockburn,

R. Carlos Nakai, Gabrielle Roth, Douglas Spotted Eagle (including the Indian Creek Drum Group and Linda Dee of Dine' Nation), Bill Miller with his powerful "Wind Spirit," among others. Their music carried me into harmonies of word, theme, and sound that helped move *Winter Sign* in a soulful direction.

Other assistance, no less worthy, came from Anne Swenson and friends at the *Ely Echo*, Arlene Krunkkala and Kate Furness of the Ely Public Library (and unknown assistants throughout Minnesota), from Bear and Rosemary McCoy at Winton's Fat Chicken Feed Store, Carl Karasti, Eiji Okamoto, Dirk Hanson, Ron Brodigan, Ann Mayo, and the many wildlife biologists and naturalists I've explicitly cited. J. Parker Huber, editor of *Writing Nature*, provided generous Sacred Green Space—as he called it—when it was most needed. Simon Bourgin of Washington, D.C. steered me away from other book projects and encouraged this one with faithful correspondence. Anne LaBastille, Adirondack author and friend, insisted I keep writing during my darkest night. Todd Orjala and Laura Westlund, editors at the University of Minnesota Press, honored me by nurturing this project, while copy editor Renie Howard helped bring it to fruition.

To all: *mes amitiés à.*

Introduction:
A Path with Heart

The overall sign—after twenty-three years in the North Country—seems as clear as a crystal of snow:

We are hunted and haunted.

Winter hunts us with its cold and haunts us with its beauty.

Such is winter a mistress to reckon with: white wicked yet alluring: to be avoided even as we embrace her. And so it is we move between soul and soul, our own and that of a season, hoping the two flow together into something we can live with. Like all love-hate relationships, we twist and turn, sigh with pleasure or cringe in pain, yet we are taken by winter in the end.

We have no choice.

We can only surrender, as I did.

The snows came, darkness deepened, deer hunkered down, and wolves moved tenaciously across the face of the land.

And my spirit sang:

Sing it now, oh Earth, sing your snows and winds. The howling, the feel, the crystal sting. Take me now, if you must. Take me now with your cold song: your bright and shining whiteness.

Or let me go.

It was a heart song, rooted in the Quetico-Superior of northeastern Minnesota, that has known no end.

To find the Quetico-Superior, you can target North America along the southwest shore of Hudson Bay of the Arctic Ocean where the wide mouth of the Nelson River flows into the sea. Up the 410-mile Nelson or, as the Cree natives called it, the *Kisiskatchewan* ("rapid current"), is Manitoba's Lake Winnipeg: 250 miles long north to south.

Here terns call in summer as formations of white pelicans soar against blue sky.

Below is blue water that can be followed south beneath autumn's geese past the mouths of Belanger River, Poplar River, and Berens River. There's the Bloodvein, Sandy, and Black rivers. At the southeastern end of Lake Winnipeg is the mouth of Winnipeg River up which— past *Chute de Jacques* (now Lamprey Rapids), Boundary Falls, Tetu Lake, and the Dalles—is Lake of the Woods (Lac des Bois) into which, a hundred miles to the south, Rainy River flows.

Up the Rainy is some of *mon pays*, my country, where rock and water characterize a land I call home.

It is an ecosystem of pine trees, birch, poplar, cedar, and fir. It is a land of eagles, wolves, black bear, ravens, moose, white-tailed deer, and fox. The rock is hard and old, its granite the heart of a mountain range once as high, geologists claim, as today's Himalayas. No more. Now—abraded by prehistoric glacial ice and known as the Canadian Shield—the great peneplain is relatively gently rolling, smoothed into ravines and ridges or, up close, fractured into blocks and crags, spotted with glacial erratics, or given over to the waters of lake, river, and stream.

It is among these waters I live.

Called the Quetico-Superior (for Ontario's Quetico Provincial Park and northeastern Minnesota's adjacent Superior National Forest), water in this bioregion is everywhere. Besides the lakes and rivers there are marshes, bogs, ponds, and swamps. If water is not already on the ground, perhaps leftover from melted glacial ice, it's coming down.

From dewdrop to stormy downpour, from fog to frost, from mist to winter's incessant snow and blizzards, the circle of gathering, flowing, and evaporating water is complete for whoever wanders this way.

Not surprisingly, it is snow that so readily comes to mind.

Winter, in the Quetico-Superior, is the longest season. At approximately 48° north latitude and 92° west longitude, snow can come in mid-October and stay, deepening unto spring thaw, until early May. Almost seven months. (The other seasons, a mere two months each, come and go in heated and berried flash.) It is snow and ice, then, that made and mark this land. We who live here year-round, who the French-Canadian voyageurs would have called *hivernants*, are essentially winter people. We know parkas, mukluks, mittens, snowshoes, skis, and sled dogs. Snow sparkles gold on cloudless winter mornings. There are shell-pink sunsets. Stars glimmer among northern lights. Gone is July's humid green lushness, the stifling noons and blood-thirsty bugs: the ticks, mosquitoes, blackflies, and deer flies.

Instead there is the cold air, the crystalline snow, and that bright and shining whiteness.

Sounds beautiful. And it is.

For those of us who know this land, however, beauty is only part of the winter story.

There are those long nights, those we rarely speak about, that surely and irrevocably shift the soul.

Nights like wolves—hungry—moving through heart shadows.

And I've finally begun to understand.

No matter how beautiful the country, how rich the winter with sparkling shine, where there is life and light, upriver or down, one finds death and darkness. There is a shadow world. What stands to reason yet bows to soulfulness comes screaming at us when we least expect it.

Some of us try to avoid this little unpleasantry, or think our luck is equal to the journey, yet the dark side of things will come, yes it will, to balance the sheets, teach us lessons, and keep us on our toes.

Should I have been surprised by this?

If I came to the woods of the Quetico-Superior, as I did, to live in a cabin as near to nature as possible, is it not only right I would discover some shadows of things? that I should be taken to the edge, perhaps, of what my heart could stand?

Sign, I learned, embraces all extremes.

I mean many things by *sign*.

There is the obvious meaning, of course, of *track*: what is physically seen, heard, touched, tasted, or smelled. In the old days of frontiersmen, explorers, and voyageurs (and still today among hunters, trappers, and pilgrims of nature and spirit), sign was a track left by something moving through time and space.

"Cutting" sign was reading it:

A grizzly bear hunting marmots in a meadow?

The hoofprints of horsebacked warring Sioux?

A doe with fawn at beach to drink?

A man in boots with puzzled destination?

Tracks, if followed, led a tracker onward, track-to-track, sign-to-sign: closing the gap between tracker, prey, enemy, friend, family, or lover. Sign led to discovery. Whether it was a footprint, old campfire, red blood on the snow, or the sudden appearance of an owl, sign told a story of life and death on the move. There was an art to reading sign. Scouting sign took all that a man *was* and knew. A good tracker on a fresh trail could decipher an unfolding mosaic, daytime or night, yesterday or the next instant, and where, precisely, he fit in.

This was good to know.

It could save his life.

Ironically, sign as track, today as always, is both lasting and brief. An axe-chopped tree, like a chainsaw cut, will last for decades, if not a person's lifetime. So will charred sticks from a campfire or rocks from a tent ring. A deer's hoofprint in snow, however, like a wolf's track, will often be worked by sunshine, wind, and more snow until it vanishes in a few days.

Good trackers, hence, know the age of things: what is fresh, perhaps worth following, and what is old and should be left alone. Nor is every trail a good trail. The difference is sometimes a fine line known only by experience: a slow gathering of knowledge gained by taking a few wrong trails to bad scenes.

Along the way, on good trail or bad, a sign's intricacy
and subtlety must be taken into consideration, as well as
the registrations of a sixth sense: intuition.

What, exactly, is going on here?

There's always more than what meets the eye.

Although there are many other meanings of sign beyond
that of track (like sign as symbol; a motion/gesture expressing an idea; an advertisement/direction mounted on
wood or steel; an indication of disease; or, as a verb, to
write one's name, sign on/up/off, etc.), it's the relation of
sign to experience, intuition, and spirit that most in-
trigues a man like me.

When you nurture openness to the natural world—its
rock, trees, other plants, soil, water, birds, animals, and
the flow of energy among them—and live close to this
confluence for a long time, you come to see sign as delicate as a fox hair stuck to a moist twig, or a downy
feather dropped from a launching eagle over a remote
river, but it can also appear as an unnerving roar of flap-
ping black wings. It might be finding a seagull with a
broken neck, but alive, or seeing a stranger's haunting
stare before a snow-slippery drive, or a doe—never seen
before—stepping up to you on a cabin's starlit deck at a
time of heavy decision.

Sign as omen.

The mind, the gut, the spirit register something the
mind alone cannot comprehend. Sometimes there are
shivers, hair tingles on the back of the neck, or chakras
brim over with energy. Reactions vary. What's going on
is subjective and visceral, a response to the awesome in-

effable, and it arrives like wind or one of those heart wolves when you least expect it.

The unknown touches us.

Whether the experience is felt coming from deep within us, or from the equally unfathomable beyond, mystery seems to brush us and drive home a notion we might readily resist: the wider world, inside or out, can expand into our limited vision and impress itself upon us.

Yes, mystery can—and will—speak.

It lets us know, through its marvelous unfoldings, some good, some terrifying, we are not alone but intricately related to all things.

Inevitably, sign as experience, uncanny event, or spontaneous appreciation can indicate something about the past, present, or future. When future-related, sign can be a portent, premonition, omen: even, possibly, what don Juan Matus, in Carlos Castaneda's controversial books, calls manifestations, gestures, or knocks of the spirit. Infinite energy, that vast array of alignments from which we emerge, in which we live, beckons us. Perhaps such sign gives us direction. It's the flash of insight, the anomalous, the synchronous event, or the bizarre dream whose meaning unravels over time.

We need not agree with, or believe, in the possibility of these things.

What's important is we remain open to them.

I suppose my sensitivity to the wider ranges of sign, from track to emergent mystery, has to do with finding myself at mid-life on two independent but, as it turns out, mutually nurturing trajectories.

The first trajectory is intellectual: a personal study of spirituality in its many forms. This path began with boyhood's Catholicism but, by the time I graduated with a degree in theology from St. John's University in Collegeville, Minnesota, the trail had begun to branch off irrevocably every-which-way. My focus on comparative religions, gardened with independent study, wasn't enough. Whether it was the apophatic mysticism of Meister Eckhart, the Zen of D. T. Suzuki and Thomas Merton, or the visions of Black Elk and Sitting Bull, I was fully engaged and obviously strewn. Yet there seemed to be an ecumenical, common denominator among all the systems, something just beyond the page, the thought, the hunch: an implicit, unifying similarity made increasingly alluring yet hardly more explicable by the work of psychiatrist Carl Jung.

A student of Sigmund Freud, Jung veered away from Freud's obsessive sexual interpretation of human behavior to devote his life to understanding the human psyche in a more soulfully oriented context. How was the ego conscious of itself, he asked, and how did it relate to the much larger unconscious mind? Where do dreams come from? Whence the source of art? of commonly held symbols? myths? fears? fantasies? Jung, who believed personal growth was a circumambulation of the self, postulated a *collective* unconscious: a deep well of knowledge and experience in all of us, regardless of cultural background, that is passed on to us from generation to generation as assuredly as hair and bone.

We're not, his life work indicated, tabulae rasae: blank tablets unaffected, when we're born, by experience and impression. Within us, rather, is the entire milieu of both biological evolution and aeonian psychological, including spiritual, striving. We carry with us, Jung underscored, all past and possibility.

Cultural differences, hence, such as those I'd been studying, were essentially minutiae: ethnic, stained-glass expressions—through language, dress, customs, myths—of a deeper, everlasting global experience and vision.

The shine of light. The glow of energy in its infinite forms.

And what of *nature* in Jung's scheme of things?

"People who know nothing about nature," he wrote late in life, "are of course neurotic, for they are not adapted to reality."[1]

That is one trajectory.

The other has to do with my growing belief we cannot get to know nature, as subject or experience, without investing ourselves. Hence a second trajectory—one I followed diligently and which led to the locus and vortex of *Winter Sign*—combined exposing myself to the natural world and studying the careers of people who dedicated their lives to nature: struggling to understand it, defend it, and write about it.

People like Henry David Thoreau, John Muir, John Burroughs. Men like Bob Marshall, Aldo Leopold, and Sigurd F. Olson. I also tracked Edward Abbey, Rachel Carson, Annie Dillard, Loren Eiseley, Richard Nelson, Anne LaBastille, and Barry Lopez, among countless others of their kind. They'd all stitched together an appreciation of places wild, free, wind-whipped and lonely, where wolves run free as snowflakes fall, where deer bed in starlit peace, or where polar bears roam ice ridges glowing in auroral light.

My naturalists wove a quilt of images, ideas, inclinations, and loves, one which covered me with its threads, its colors, with hope for the world.

As the full import of this concerted movement swelled within me, I wrote *Wilderness Visionaries*, a collection of biographies of wilderness naturalists. It wasn't the academic treatise of Roderick Nash's *Wilderness and the American Mind*, but it was a passionate overview of the major players and what they contributed to North America's wilderness preservation movement.

However, as I noted in *Open Spaces*, my second book, it was my personal immersion in wild country—the touch of boot on rock, the canoe voyages, the years spent in various simple cabins, the handling of wood, the long walks, the sitting beneath pines, the coming of deer and wolf—that mattered most in terms of an education about the natural world. In order to *know* nature, I needed to experience wild places as much as possible and see what they had to say.

Here was the edge.

The wild regions I came to know, some albeit fleetingly, were many.

There were the five years I spent in a north woods cabin near Itasca State Park and the headwaters of the Mississippi River in north-central Minnesota. There was the move to northeastern Minnesota with its Boundary Waters Canoe Area Wilderness, near which, for another five years, I based myself in two Burntside Lake cabins while exploring—by canoe, foot, snowshoe, and ski—

the vast Quetico-Superior around me. Here I retraced Ojibwe and voyageur canoe routes, a challenge I'd continue in the years ahead. I tracked down pictographs, trying to read the land and its early people through the script of red ocher. And I lost Bojo, my Siberian husky, to a wolf, learning in a fierce manner, and perhaps truly for the first time, how wild nature—often from necessity—will sometimes violently strike the loving hand that feeds it.

Along the way, there were also trips and excursions to Alaska's Wrangell Mountains (just prior to much of the region becoming a national park), down North Dakota's Little Missouri River in the Badlands, and into Ontario's Wabakimi-Kopka country. All were my teachers. As a ranger for the National Park Service from 1986 to 1995, I'd visit northern California's redwood forests (patrolling, on foot, a grove of the tallest trees in the world) and, later, live a hundred days a year for eight years, from late May until the gales of autumn, in a cabin on South Twin Island, part of the Lake Superior archipelago known as Apostle Islands National Lakeshore off the coast of Wisconsin.

I called South Twin *Wâbos Miniss*, in honor of the region's native Ojibwe who knew the island as Rabbit Island. I also called the island *Île Jumeau du Sud*, giving the English name of South Twin its French translation; many French-Canadians, after all, had exercised the good sense of marrying the Ojibwe.[2]

Regardless, the island's shores were lapped by blue waters of the largest lake in the world.

It was a rich life on South Twin, and I knew it: the

boating, the sunsets, the people, the constant working of clear water against sandstone, yet I also knew—like my other adventures—it was another circling of a place I really knew was home.

Hocoka.

Hocoka was—and remains—my cabin and land set in the center of the Quetico-Superior twelve hundred miles upriver from the sea. It was here I returned full-time each autumn and hated to leave after ice-out each spring. It was here, not far from Burntside Lake, Sigurd Olson's Listening Point, and the memory of Bojo, that the deer, wolves, and spirit of winter worked me hard and opened my eyes. Year after year during the great swing of seasons, winter after winter, snow falling, snow melting, fourteen winters in all, I came to see what for me was an abiding truth:

Hocoka was my path with heart.

It is in this soulful journey that *Winter Sign* is rooted.

What follows, of course, must be a mosaic.

It is a mix of Quetico-Superior winter ecology, personal observation and experience (anchored with journal entries launching chapters), and the mystifying—essentially spiritual—matrices in which I found myself. When due, I credit information and annotate widely, thus grounding as much as possible what is otherwise a highly subjective journey. What's important, yet can only be implied, is the flow among all elements. The dance. Landscape and human: outer and inner: the objectivity of science and the rich resonance of the individual soul. Along the way, as with all of us, what seems to run parallel as independent and distinct intersects, at times, into startling, if not sustaining, synergisms.

Here are the flash points in our lives.

Here are our deep and abiding stories.

My stories, I'm inclined to say, are given here like the tracks winter arrows leave when, shot, they glance— snow crystals flying, sparkling—off rock.

CONTACT

We need another and a wiser and perhaps a more mystical concept of animals. Remote from universal nature, and living by complicated artifice, man in civilization surveys the creature through the glass of his knowledge and sees thereby a feather magnified and the whole image in distortion. We patronize them for their incompleteness, for their tragic fate for having taken form so far below ourselves. And therein we err, and greatly err. For the animal shall not be measured by man. In a world older and more complete than ours they move finished and complete, gifted with extensions of the senses we have lost or never attained, living by voices we shall never hear. They are not brethren, they are not underlings; they are other nations, caught with ourselves in the net of life and time, fellow prisoners of the splendour and travail of the earth.

—Henry Beston, *The Outermost House*

In the Western world, in the biological sciences, we have an extraordinary tool for discovery of knowledge about animals, together with a system for its classification; and through the existence of journals and libraries we have a system for its dissemination. But if we are going to learn more about animals—real knowledge, not more facts—we are going to have to get out into the woods. We are going to have to pay more attention to free-ranging as opposed to penned animals, which will require an unfamiliar patience. And we are going to have to find ways in which single, startling incidents in animal behavior, now discarded in the winnowing process of science's data assembly, can be preserved, can somehow be incorporated. And we are going to have to find a way, not necessarily to esteem, but at least not to despise intuition in the scientific process, for it is, as Kepler and Darwin and Einstein have said, the key.

—Barry Lopez, *Of Wolves and Men*

A Necessary Violence

Snow: 0° F: Barometer Rising

Strange. Another dream.
  It woke me from an evening nap:
  Five wolves running along the lake's shoreline
toward the cabin.
—journal, Hocoka, Winter

The Smith & Wesson .357, stainless steel with black rubber Pachmayr grips, lay holstered in a desk drawer by my left thigh.

The gun was out of sight, out of mind.

During summers, from May to October, I often wore a revolver as a National Park Service ranger in the Apostle Islands of Lake Superior, but on January 30, midway between ranger seasons, the gun in my cabin at Hocoka was more of a forgotten bear precaution than anything else.

Still, the gun was loaded with .357 hollow-points: bullets designed to expand on impact.

Outside, beneath clearing skies, at least six whitetail deer fed from a scattering of corn, oats, and molasses I had gotten in the habit of feeding them. It wasn't enough food for the deer to survive on but perhaps enough to help them get through the cold heart of winter. Solo, the whitetail matriarch, was around with twin fawns, Blacky and Moon. Shy, another doe, always alone, who liked to sniff the air for scent, was also near the cabin, as were White Eyes, the largest buck, and Ruff, a feisty fork-horn who often cocked his head with a seemingly quizzical "What's up, Mr. Cabin Man?" when he saw me.

Ruff, in midwinter, was generally a loner.

Several other deer, recent area arrivals, meandered around the edges of things, nudging into Solo's territory.

This was my thirteenth winter in wolf country, yet wolves, like the gun, were not on my mind this afternoon. With wolves I was drawing a blank. I hadn't seen fresh wolf tracks for ten days, not since I'd skied in moonlight to the northeast end of the lake where I'd found the tracks, the wolves probably nearby, possibly watching me.

If I had learned anything about *Canis lupus lycaon* over the years, it was that wolves don't miss much. Paying attention means food, for it's the wolf's business to notice prey sign, hunt its maker, and kill what can be killed. Sharp senses also help wolves steer shy of people with harmful intention.

I didn't have harmful intention that night on skis, nor did I ten days later as I sat at my desk in midafternoon.

Wolf legs, moving, kicking up snow in wads of fluff.

Suddenly, as I stood to file papers, I saw a fleeting movement out the kitchen window. Was someone coming? I walked to the window and saw a deer moving quickly across a path leading away from the cabin. The deer seemed restless, aroused somehow beyond a deer's normal nonchalance and patient fluidity of motion. Curious, I went into the lakeside room of the cabin and looked out the front picture windows. Another deer was running on the snow-covered lake by the canoe landing, where the deer came ashore to stand among woodpiles.

Both deer were mobile radar for me, their agitation indicating something was up, and as I scanned around, still wondering if I had company, two deer bolted past the corner of the cabin right in front of me.

A wolf, gray with streaming tail, was behind the last deer, chasing it: both wolf and deer in full run: the wolf bearing down, closing in, closing in, down to a deer trail skirting the lake cove. The wolf lunged, brought the deer down, and both skidded behind a balsam fir. The deer began to bawl over and over, likely calling its mother who, if alive, was probably nearby.

In years of observing deer I had never heard this bawl, a plaintive cry of fear and trauma.

I had an urge to run outside and scare the wolf but, no, I resisted. It was too late. Not only might I have an injured deer on my hands but I would be interfering with a wild process.

Yes? I wondered. No.

No? Yes.

I wavered. Then the bawling stopped.

Ohh man.

My heart pounded as I grabbed binoculars and looked down at the wolf and deer, seeing little but shades of fur behind balsam. In moments the wolf left the deer, trotted into a wooded ravine at the tip of the cove, and came out onto the lake. I saw it clearly: could have shot it if that was my way. It didn't seem aware of me as it meandered around, ate snow, then gazed north past a granite ledge below the cabin. Soon it trotted to the other side of the cove, climbed Rainbow Ridge, and moved out of sight.

The wolf never gave me a glance.

I had thought wolves usually eat their kills on the spot, so I was surprised when the wolf disappeared up the ridge.

I looked down at the deer that lay alone by the fir. Which deer was it? I would go see. But was it wise to walk up to a fresh wolf-kill? There was violence in the air, scattered blood on snow, and large predators—like the 90- to 100-pound male wolf—get possessive about their meat.

Were more wolves around?

I went to my desk, got the .357, and headed down the slope.

The deer, apparently a yearling, was sprawled on buckled legs. Its right rear haunch was wet with blood. More blood oozed from slash marks on the deer's neck. Yet the deer—not Blacky or Moon—was alive. It held its head up: dazed eyes: looking around. It had difficulty determining what direction I approached from.

Should I shoot the deer, and put it out of its misery?

I had never shot a deer. I had never killed anything with that .357.

I stepped closer onto the skid-trail of blood. The deer stood up, twirled around, and fell. It tried to stand again and fell forward, breathing heavily.

Stress.

Shock.

Shoot it?

Let nature take its course?

Was this any of my business?

Yes, it had become my business, as friend and woodsman Art Madsen later pointed out, but I decided to back off, give the wounded deer space, and, never faced with this before, give myself time to think.

I also wanted intelligent opinion.

I returned to the cabin, got my Karhu skis, and skied a mile of trail and snowy roads to a neighbor's home to use her telephone. No one was home. I entered anyhow. I phoned two acquaintances at Ely's International Wolf Center but they were out. I called them at their homes: no answer. I called the local Department of Natural Resources: no answer, and a DNR friend at his home: ditto.

I finally reached Al Heidebrink, a state game warden, which was good, for by now I was concerned about shooting a deer out of season. Al spoke with a voice of doctoring calm.

He said I could go ahead and shoot the deer. He also reminded me, and he did this gently, of something I knew: wolves have been attacking and killing deer for thousands of years and I *could* let nature take its course.

Uh-huh.

Just before Al hung up he said he'd never heard of a wolf dragging down a deer and leaving it alive next to some guy's cabin.

I left my neighbor a note and skied toward home, working up a sweat, trying to decide what to do. The sun was low in the western sky, day aging, running out of light. As I approached the cabin I saw the deer's head still up.

Was nothing or everything expected of me?

What were my instincts saying?

Would the composite spirit of the deer, those I had been feeding and befriending, linked to me by trust, understand if I used the gun?

I asked the Great Spirit, from which all life flows, what I should do.

I asked for a sign.

I got my gun and went out on the deck, started down the steps toward the deer, and, for the first time since I built the steps years earlier, I slipped on ice, fell backward, and caught myself with my right arm, jarring my shoulder but breaking my fall. I got up, took a deep breath, and headed toward the deer. Despite the slip, a possible sign, I'd decided to shoot.

I would kill the deer quickly and end its suffering.

But as I approached, the deer stood up on wobbly legs. I stepped closer and the deer moved off the trail. It wove slowly among trees, leaving me a poor shot with a handgun. I moved again, trying to get a good look at the deer in dusk's fading light. The deer stopped, swayed on its legs, then kept going.

Okay. If I had to stalk the deer, in effect hunting it, the situation had gone from mercy killing to hunting, and the deer wanted to live.

Two signs: the slip on the step and now this.

Again I backed off.

Still, I was curious if the deer would collapse from exhaustion so I walked up past the cabin to trails the deer seemed headed toward. White Eyes, the old buck, stood on a high ridge, watching me: his silhouette sharp and bold in the crepuscular light. I walked deeper into the woods but didn't find the yearling.

Perhaps it would regain strength by resting, slip out of its shock, and live, or it would die of blood loss on its own terms.

Or the wolf would return and kill it.

I walked back to the cabin, hoping I'd done the right thing, which, essentially, was close to nothing at all. There was just enough twilight left for me to split wood. As my axe bit into birch, the air taut with the wake of violence, Anne, whose phone I'd used, arrived with a friend. I explained what happened, showed them where the wolf had attacked the deer, and said I was going to track the yearling in the morning.

"Seven-thirty," I added, looking at the clock. "Would either of you like to come?"

I didn't sleep well that night for I felt the presence of pain. I had my own aching tension, of course, but the worst pain lay alone in the dark woods.

For years the deer around me—Solo, Ruff, White Eyes, Shy—had been with me through good times and bad, their beauty like family lifting me up, coming to me in sun and shadow, all brown-gray gifts of forest. They shared the land. They shared my journey. Now one of them bled in cold beneath stars.

Some people, I knew, would judge me soft (I mean, fella, what's the fuss?), yet I tossed and turned in the loft, my eyes closing and opening, looking into my own night, down my own wintry scope of things, Orion up, cold creeping into bone, awaiting unfolding dawn.

Morning arrived beautifully with calm, clear skies as the rising sun shone a golden glow on sparkling snow.

As usual, I fired both woodstoves and brewed strong

Colombian coffee, dripping it into a black mug with a howling wolf etched white on its side. I looked at the steaming mug, then outside: no deer. Understandable. The ridgeside was a sea of scent: alarmed deer, wolf, fresh blood, me: a vortex of smells, a mixed juice of tension, evoking collision recent and near.

When Anne arrived we began tracking. Again I had my gun. The deer's trail of hoofprints and flecks of blood, bright red on white snow, led up a draw, leveled off, then sloped down toward Lund's Cove. We tracked slowly at first, walking on opposite sides of the trail, but when the trail leveled I took the lead.

A raven, riding a breeze, flew in circles in front of me.

Downhill now, stepping slowly, quietly, my eyes scanning the ground . . . the deer.

It looked dead and for a moment I felt relief. Nature had run its course. The deer lay in the middle of the trail where other trails converged. Its neck and head were stretched out on the ground uphill toward me. Its eyes were closed. Behind her, for I could see now she was a doe, was a patch of snow red with blood and smeared with hair.

Had the yearling crawled a few feet, harassed by the raven, before death?

Abruptly, in one fluid motion, the yearling looked up and straight into my eyes.

I had come.

I stepped closer, wondering if she would run, but although she tried she couldn't stand on her legs, couldn't even clear her chest off the ground. She had been in shock, bleeding and crippled for sixteen hours. I thought of the probable pain, the raven overhead, waiting, and I knew the wolves would be back, perhaps ripping into the deer before killing it, as they sometimes do.

Enough.

"It's okay," I said softly to the yearling, then cocked my gun and aimed it at her forehead. Her eyes were clear and soft, resigned yet aware in our mutual recognition of imminent death. She never took her eyes off mine as I apologized in my heart. A connection was made, some heightened pact deep and everlasting, one we alone would know, as I followed through with what I hated to do.

I fired and her head went limp.

I fired three more times for I wanted to ensure death.

I holstered the gun, knelt on one knee for a moment to honor the deer and our critical juncture, then walked to the yearling and touched her ears as her life slipped away. I caressed the limp body, looked at the wolf wounds, then rolled the deer on her side and straightened her legs.

Those legs, once so fast, and once too slow, would run no more.

Just like that, death came home at the touch of my hand and blood soaked into the land.

I wasn't surprised, a day after I shot the yearling, to find myself skiing a trail: striding, poling: gliding on snow: no better place to go than the far, most wild, end of the lake.

My heart was heavy. I knew theoretically as well as anyone else that wolves must kill in their life-death dynamic with deer, and I knew the very beauty and fleetness of deer have been shaped by their predators.

But why my lured intervention in such an intimate, violent, and fatal way?

And why does it take death sometimes to bring us into the light and heat of who and what we love?

Two autumns earlier I watched my mother die of cancer. Now I had killed one of the deer whose beauty sustained me through a winter of grief.

A fresh wound felt ripped open.

I skied to the shore of a small island where I often go to think things over. I jabbed my poles in the snow, took off my skis, and leaned against a pine's trunk. Sunlight warmed my face but the wolf came back to me now, racing around the cabin's corner, a gray rushing canine blur, and I heard the deer bawling and saw its eyes as I pulled the trigger. Over and over: wolf, deer, shot. It felt so sad, so inexplicable, and I couldn't hold back the uprush, the surge of welling sorrow, the tide that rises with its own truth, and I wept.

I wept for the yearling that did nothing to deserve such a violent, painful ending, and I wept, I suppose, for all sentient life surrendered to stars: the mothers and fathers, the children and the lonely, the deer and wolves and birds, on and on, everything woven in a mortal web alive with radiant whiteness.

"Oh, James," my mother had said on her deathbed, "you've always been so sentimental."

I still wasn't sure as I skied home whether I'd done right or wrong by shooting the deer. I never would be; here sorrow would abide. There was a gray area inside me now, a span of possible scenarios, and as thoughts came and went—the shoulds, coulds, and maybe nots— it seemed important I follow through on the killing.

I visited the yearling daily.

Ravens arrived immediately, a raucous flock of six or seven that flew off in a black burst of wing and call whenever I approached. Within two days they ate the yearling's eyes and followed the flesh of a bullet's exit wound into the rib cage, exposing bone. Soon, after a night of northern lights, a pack of wolves arrived.

At first I heard them howling among ridges in darkness, then, in daylight, I found their tracks and scent marks surrounding and claiming the kill. Skies grew cloudy as the wolves feasted and dragged the carcass to my summer footpath. The head was carried off. Bones were crunched and splintered. Within four days of the shooting, the carcass was eaten, tugged and twisted into a tangle of spine, fur, and skin.

The yearling was becoming raven and wolf. It was flying and flowing back into the pulse of the land. It was wings circling in the sky. It was starlit motion of limber wolf legs. It was tracks in the snow.

Nothing went to waste.

I watched this transformation even as the other deer, scattered by the violence, returned to the cabin.

They forgave the gun.

If we must die, I thought to them, this is how it will be: quick.

Shy was missing but Solo, Blacky, and Moon were back, and Ruff again with his "What's happening?" One day Blacky, Moon, and Ruff chased each other playfully—back and forth, twist and turn, back and forth— as I watched. I would see more of this play, this fawn and fork-horn feistiness, in the days ahead. Here was sign of

a new peace upon the land, and in me, and as days
turned into weeks, as winter with its bright moons
waned toward spring, the killing of the yearling seemed
to recede like an intense dream.

But why had the wolf left the yearling alive?

Here was the crux. Here was the lasting question.

One friend suggested the wolf might have been a
young one without an adult's honed killing techniques.
Someone else suggested I might have somehow frightened the wolf off; but, no, this wasn't apparent. The
wolf *might* have thought the yearling was dead when it
stopped bawling or, at least, it knew the yearling was seriously injured. Couldn't the wolf have returned with its
scattered pack to follow blood on the tracks?

How far, after all, can a lame deer go as it stiffens in
cold?

I saw how far.

Yet even as I rehearsed these scenarios, some true in
part no doubt, I sensed another possibility—*Come deeper,
now, come deeper*—as to why the wolf left the yearling
alive. It was an undercurrent, a pulse, I was aware of all
along.

It is the story that counts.

For years I had watched wolves and deer around me,
and had, to some extent, romanticized wolves in my
writing as symbols of wildness roaming freely with cun-
ning and nerve. Wolves had become an indelible part of
my life on the edge. But their killing of deer, with its
blood, bawling, and viscera, a necessary violence, a
fierce interface, had always gone on beyond me: around
the point, over the ridge. There was always visual dis-

tance, hence, as with most people, a circumstantial emotional insulation.

Certainly I had never shared in a deer-kill like part of a wolf pack hitting on its main prey.

This, of course, would no longer be.

For perhaps, in order to more fully know wolves and the whitetail deer around me, the time had arrived on a sunlit January day to be led by a wolf more deeply into the heart of the matter.

Hocoka

Stars: 16° F: Barometer Falling

*Saw a bald eagle twice on Monday, at first flying
past the cabin southwest to northeast, then later
overhead right above the cabin's southeast corner:
it headed out over the lake ice and up against gray
sky to land in a large white pine at the tip of the
island.*

*Why is it so many North American native peo-
ples felt seeing an eagle was always a good sign?*

*Eagles have been considered sacred messengers.
They carry the heart's prayers to the Great Spirit
then return with potent gifts of clarity and vision to
be used for the good of all people.*

*Thus light, with eagle as intermediary, passes
through us into the world.*
—journal, Hocoka, Winter

The heart of the matter, its
soul, what my French-
Canadian forebears and métis cousins called *âme* (which,
ironically, also means bore of a gun), was rooted in a
place that came to be known as Hocoka.

"Everything the Power of the World does," Black Elk
(*Hehaka Sapa*), a Teton-Dakota (Sioux), once said, "is
done in a circle."

Everything tries to be round.

Life and death, Black Elk explained,[1] is a circle. The
four directions form a circle, as do the seasons. The sun

and moon, themselves round, move in circles. Wind whirls. Birds' nests are cyclical. In Black Elk's days, hoops and shields were round. Even tipis, themselves round and coning upward to a vent, were arranged in a circle.

"In the middle of the circle," according to Short Bull (*Tatanka-Ptecila*), another Dakota, "was a place called Hocoka, the center."

It usually was a place of fire.

When I first came to the land, hungering the heat of contact, I did not come alone.

Her name was Chris.

It is she I met on the shores of Burntside Lake in 1981, canoed with in the Quetico-Superior,[2] shared values and libraries with, and whom I married on a fine June day in 1983 near a gnarled jackpine on the shore of a pond in the Boundary Waters Canoe Area Wilderness. Inevitably, it was Chris who brought my attention to Short Bull's words and reminded me that the Dakota's ancestors, the Woodland People, had preceded the Ojibwe on the land we were about to call home. If we needed a name for our new place in the world, we might consider Hocoka. The word would form its own kind of circle, returning eastward through dimensions of culture and time. Although the Dakota had moved out onto the plains, a word, at least, could come back.

We wouldn't steal linguistically from a culture so much as honor it.

And so we did.

It was the idea, anyhow, that mattered. Ideas counted for a lot in 1983 when Chris and I were young, brave, and driven by dream.

We wanted to live close to the land. We wanted to feel its wild rhythms, its seasonal circles, and hear what the wind, stars, and snow had to say. We wanted to feel a time that once was known to many. We wanted to keep our water needs simple, fetching it through ice if necessary, and we wanted to burn wood for heat. A cabin, not a house, was called for, and in its lamp-lit warmth, as the deer browsed outside and wolves howled, we wanted to find something—touch it, know it—that our modern culture had turned its back on.

We weren't rejecting a way of life: we were embracing an older one to bridge with the new.

We wanted natural ways and natural beauty.

There were things, we figured, to learn.

Had not ways of being been forgotten? We would rediscover them.

Might we not complete a few circles of our own?
Possibly.

Hocoka, then, became more than a borrowed name for a geographical place. It referred to an axis, a center, of many journeys. Some journeys would be to distant places. Others would be to the far reaches of heart. Mind would be part of the adventure. So would soul. The important thing was to have an anchorage, a base, a home where one might live one's days and harbor one's hopes while becoming more deeply acquainted with a wild world.

We recognized Hocoka, our wild world, when we saw it after a relatively short but persistent land search.

Using Les Scher's *Finding and Buying Your Place in the Country*[3] as a guide, we began tracking available land and cabins in the hinterlands around Ely. We checked on a large house along Highway 1 south of town. Too big. Too close to a road. There was another house and barn with meadow further south. No. The house was again too large, bigtime unfinished, and we foresaw no need for a barn.

A favorite site (which I can still walk to any time I want) curved around the shore of a beaver pond. A stream flowed into the pond from the north where another beaver pond—with large grassy meadow—was home to heron and mallard. Downstream the water let loose over rocks and small waterfalls of splashing water to a long lake flowing into the Boundary Waters Canoe Area Wilderness. The building site itself had a stand of red pines through which breeze soughed and sighed, the sound of needles sweeping air scented with resin. A rock point with several jackpines was covered with pine needles, blueberries, and bearberries, altogether a mat of growing and decaying life through which jutted bare rock and, to the west, gave way completely to sloping granite angling down into water.

What a place, we agreed, to sit and ponder.

We could build a main cabin back by the pines. I could build a writing cabin closer to the pond, perhaps on exposed bedrock by the jackpines for a panoramic view to the west with its sunset colors and reflections. Or perhaps I could even build a writing cabin on the rock bluff with elevated view a short way down the shore.

I imagined friends coming, perhaps discussing wilderness issues, philosophy, and literature in cozy chairs by a woodstove, or even outside around a campfire beneath stars.

Perhaps we'd pass a pipe.

On the dreaming went as we searched for a place to live, buy, cast our luck.

Scenery was important, of course, as was price. Exposures and services, possible jobs, and quality of community life all counted. The place had to be forested for firewood and, ideally, rich in wildlife. A short walk in wouldn't hurt, and we could survive comfortably without electricity, plumbing, and telephone.

There was one thing, however, we could *not* do without:

Water.

Not water in well, pipes, and showers but water to immerse ourselves in all the way. Water to swim in. Water to float on in a canoe as gold sunset light silhouetted islands and loons yodeled in distant coves. Water where walleyes circled in dark shadows. Clear water to drink. Water to hear as it slapped rock shores on windy days or spent itself in slosh until settling silent: reflecting shoreline pine or gold of autumn birch. Water on which the moon would sparkle its silver, and water from which fog would drift like smoke. Water that would freeze and crack in winter's cold: to skate, ski, and snowshoe on: water covered by snow and undulating drifts over which wolves might wildly pass.

For this we needed substantial water, more than the sheltered intricacy of a beaver pond, and although I've walked back to that pond many times since—seeing fox, beaver, herons, ducks, woodcocks, and once finding a

deer antler half-buried in needle duff—Chris and I let
the pond dream go.

Then came a warm summer day when the time was right
to check on land I'd heard about from a friend, Anne
Wognum, publisher of the *Ely Echo*.

I'd worked for Anne a couple years, writing features
and profiling interesting folk, and through Anne I'd
learned her sister had twenty-eight acres of land for sale
on a small lake I call Otter (*Loutre* in French, *Nigig* in
Ojibwe) about eight miles out of Ely. The land, like adjacent lakeshore, had been in the Wognum family for
generations and divided among the children. Most of it
was sold except for the parcel owned by Adela, yet the
going price was simply too high for Chris and me to
take seriously.

We decided to take a look anyhow.

Using a simple, penciled map Anne gave us, we drove
out into the country, parked as close to the lake as we
could, walked an old railroad spur to the lake's southern
shoreline, then bushwhacked along the shore from point
to point until we found the cove we were looking for.

Offshore like ships, as we rounded the last point,
were two large islands forested with pine. Beyond, seen
down a channel, was a cluster of smaller islands that gave
way to more water.

*Such blue beauty of water and sky framed by gray of rock and
dark green pines.*

Beyond was a bay we could not see.

The lake, we noticed on a map, was a little more than
a mile long and a half-mile wide. It had seventeen islands
or more depending on whether you counted exposed

rock reef. Its elevation of almost fifteen hundred feet made it a true headwaters lake. No other lakes, rivers, or substantial streams flowed into it.

It was downhill all the way to the sea.

We headed south, scrambled along a rugged shore, then found a small draw that led up a rock slope. We climbed past sumac, small aspen, blueberries, and clumps of juniper to open ledge-rock. There, about forty feet above the water, we turned to look at the lake.

We had found Hocoka.

Below us, as we looked east, shoreline pine and fir opened out onto a small bay of wind-moving water. To our left was one of the lake's large islands, while to our right a rock ridge, about eighty feet high, which we later named Rainbow, ran perpendicular to the ridge we stood on. Straight ahead, beyond the bay, the lake coved into a rugged shoreline where a narrow channel led out to open water. Even the open ledge-rock on which we stood sloped gently and was easily large enough for a cabin.

The place was perfect.

By being tucked in a bay, it felt sequestered and isolated without a building in sight, yet with its elevation and southern exposure it felt spacious, light, and worked by circulating wind.

A large rock ridge behind the cabin site would break winter's coldest northwest winds, leaving the spot in an eddy of calm.

Juneberry bushes, we noticed, had recently dropped their white petals. Young pines were growing among birch, willow, and alder down by the lake. Patches of sarsaparilla fringed scattered boulders. Pink corydalis

bobbed in passing breeze. There were starflowers, wild
lilies of the valley, twinflowers, and moccasin flowers
pink and delicate in the damp shadow of labrador tea.

There was sign of deer which, in this country, meant
wolves.

How the heart leapt at such beauty.

How the heart longed to extend its joy into future
days and the swirling myriad of seasons.

Soon, then, a baptismal swim, a windfall of negotiated
price, and Hocoka was ours to homestead.

The landscape alone was intriguing from the start.

The rock on which Hocoka's cabin was to sit—where
Solo roamed ridges, moose occasionally crashed
through brush, and where wolves howled in moonlight
beneath stars—was some of the oldest exposed rock in
the world.

Half the earth's age, geologists say: two to three billion years old.

I liked to think about that as I gazed around at the
land's ridges, ravines, and boulders for the first time. The
jagged chunks of granite toothing toward sky. The scattered cracks a walker or snowshoer could fall into where
bones might rot like branches among leaves. The delicate moss and lichens attached to the rock's wet, sloping
slabs.

This was very different from the flat dirt fields of the
Red River Valley where I grew up (same latitude straight
west), but similar to the old, exposed rock of Québec
where some of my Huot ancestors lived two hundred
years or more in the country of the Abenaki (Algonkin,

Ojibwe, and Cree peoples), all sharing the same forest, water, and rock that was as hard and old as rock gets.

Was I unconsciously lured to the Quetico-Superior, I asked myself, because it had some of the same rock structure as Québec? Was there some kind of rock-crystal psychic connection?

Or was it that the age of both areas was so truly amazing, hence alluring, like sign of safe, home bedrock, familiar ground, found in the roaming white-out of time, human evolution, and technology's blizzard?

Apparently much of the Quetico-Superior's rock, particularly its greenstone, was formed during the diastrophic upheavals of the Archeozoic era.

It was the earliest time, the primordial time, when volcanic lava licked up and out beneath water and land as the earth's shell cracked from inner heat. It was a time when mountain ranges rose and stretched from Canada's Hudson Bay south into northeastern Minnesota. Skies were dark then from volcanic eruptions and ashfalls as the hot, liquid rock, glowing orange in night darkness, snaked through cracks, faults, anything giving way.

The volcanic violence eventually stilled. Water and wind weathered the mountains. Slowly they were washed away in rivulets of water, stream, river, waterfalls—particle by particle—all washing away in the great unpeopled silences: washing away into adjacent seas.

Yet the *base* of those mountains, as hard as rock gets, remained through time, despite the great weathering. This base, an upland core of enduring rock, now known as the Precambrian Shield or Laurentian peneplain, stretched from central Canada to its southwestern tip underlying Hocoka, northeastern Minnesota's Iron Range, and Duluth.

It is this rock that gives the Quetico-Superior its stark, granitic character.

There are only a few other places in the world where such old rock stretches exposed to sunshine and human glance: in Africa south of the Sahara, northeastern South America, Australia, Scandinavia, some North American mountain areas, and deep in the Grand Canyon.

By the Paleozoic ("ancient life") era, five hundred million to two hundred million years ago, the land of today's northeastern Minnesota, Hocoka's ground, experienced slow but persistent and dramatic change as North America was washed with repeated invasions of shifting, shallow epicontinental seas. The seas might have been caused by the slow sinking of continents relative to sea level, with no change of ocean volume, or they were caused by the uplift or subsidence of large portions of the ocean's floor.

No matter.

Geologists, too—trained and paid and doing their best among peers—still guess.

According to George M. Schwartz and George A. Thiel in *Minnesota's Rocks and Waters*, the Precambrian Shield was "the first large part of North America to be more or less permanently elevated above the level of the sea."[4] If so, the shifting epicontinental North American seas sloshed at the shield's shores. The seas came and went, then, as rain washed the bare rocks, frost and ice chipped away rock particles, and more rain came, washing, eroding, baring the land I came to call home.

By two hundred eighty million years ago, organic life began to flourish in the subtropical climate of Minnesota. Insects with two-foot wingspans buzzed the shield's edges. Dinosaurs roamed most of the state. By the Cenozoic ("recent life") era, seventy million years ago, aquatic life patrolled the zone where land met sea. Proving this, a crocodile skull was found in an open-pit mine dump near Coleraine on the Mesabi Range in 1967. Shark teeth, too, were found, and other evidence points to a lush terrestrial floral community.

But then came a deep, hard cold of an imposing kind.

As the top of the earth tilted away from the sun, or as the earth varied in solar orbit, climatic changes beginning two million years ago accelerated cooling during the Pleistocene ("most new") epoch to create glaciers. (This as primitive peoples, the *australopithecines,* evolved on the plains of Africa.) The North American glaciers formed in northern Canada east and west of Hudson Bay, and expanded outward, moving back and forth across the face of the land.

Continentally, all of northern North America was covered by ice except, perhaps, extreme northern Alaska and the Yukon River Valley. All of the United States north of the Ohio and Missouri Rivers was covered by ice, as far east as Long Island and west to the foothills of the Rocky Mountains. Altogether about four million square miles of North America were covered by ice up to ten thousand feet thick. Ice lobes passing and rasping across northern Minnesota reached as far south as present-day Illinois, Kansas, and Nebraska during some of the last glacial movements.

Each ice advance, as many as nine (and taking only

five thousand to ten thousand years to develop), was followed by a warmer interglacial period, some only ten thousand years long, others lasting one hundred thousand years with weather more mild than ours. Bison, musk ox, mastodons (large, shaggy elephants), and reindeer roamed the ice-free land. But the ice would return, indomitably, nudging all life back to the south as the glacier's snout—building and moving over more time than a person can conceive—plowed and gouged everything out of its way.

The last glacial period in northern Minnesota and adjacent Wisconsin began about seventy-five thousand years ago: the Wisconsin stage of the Pleistocene epoch. Three glaciers from northern Canada converged on northern Minnesota to extend a lobe of ice as far south as today's Des Moines, Iowa.

The ice advanced, stopped, retreated, then advanced again at least several times.

When the glaciers advanced, growing larger every year, the snow that fell simply didn't melt. It was continual winter as snow accumulated in snowfields thousands of feet deep.

"The weight of the snow," Schwartz and Thiel explain, "compacted the bottom layers into ice, and gradually under the increasing pressure of the snow the ice spread out in all directions over the land. As the thick ice sheets moved, they scraped off great quantities of rock and soil. They carried along everything from huge boulders to fine dust, freezing everything they touched into their vast, icy bases. As the glaciers advanced, the rocks over which the ice moved were scoured and striated, and the larger boulders incorporated in the ice often gouged large grooves in the bedrock. The rocky basins of many of Minnesota's lakes near the Canadian border were scraped out by this process."[5]

Places like Shagawa Lake, Bass Lake, Little Long, Fall, the bays of Basswood, Cedar Lake, Agnes, Quetico, Saganaga, Knife, and countless more, even Otter Lake whose shores of a cove I know well. The lake basins, like the ridges, generally ran southwest to northeast, marking the passage of great ice, the durability of the land, and the overall lay of the North American continent southwest and west of Hudson Bay.

The Mankato substage of Wisconsin glaciation came to an end approximately eleven thousand to sixteen thousand years ago. As global climate steadily warmed, continental ice receded back past the Quetico-Superior until, by eight thousand years ago, the snout of the melting glacier was approximately three hundred miles northeast of Minnesota. In only two thousand more years the ice retreated to the Québec-Labrador plateau and, relatively soon thereafter, settled in a vestigial mass on top of Greenland.

Sea levels, meanwhile, rose about 360 feet from the abundance of glacial meltwater.

What remained at Hocoka, and its much larger Quetico-Superior sphere, was the bare Precambrian (or Canadian) Shield with its granite cliffs and ridges (some two hundred to four hundred feet above surrounding lakes), erratically scattered glacier-dropped boulders, primitive plant forms like lichens, and flowing water.

Especially the flowing water.

For if the Ice Age left anything it was as much a liquid legacy as a tale of hard rock.

Rocky basins, brimming with water, overflowed into lower basins (and still do). Streams and rivers carved permanent channels. Curtain Falls on Crooked Lake was formed, as were Pipestone Falls and the rapids of Newton Falls. The Kawishiwi River found its bed, as did the Vermilion, Burntside, Granite, and Basswood. All formed a vibrant, flowing web called—by cartographers and geologists—the Upper Watershed of the Rainy River.

Watershed size?

About ten thousand square miles.

While draining much of today's northern St. Louis and Lake counties, the watershed gathered unto itself even the smallest of waterways: the Horse River, Pony, Moose, Maligne, and Little Indian Sioux to name a few. All flowing, like Hocoka's water, into the Rainy.

And *where* did the Rainy River flow?

West to Lake of the Woods, northwest to Lake Winnipeg, up Lake Winnipeg's 250-mile length, then northeast via Nelson River to Hudson Bay.

This was the flow of the land, and I liked it.

It suited me fine.

I could, come some twilight, toss an eagle feather into Hocoka's brown water and it was theoretically possible for it to float into the polar bear country of Hudson Bay and there fuse with the full sweep of the Arctic Ocean.

The feather, like myself someday, would take a journey among rock and water clear to the sea at the tail end of a long scope of time.

The image humbled a guy. It put me in my place.

The cabin itself, at least at first, was a simple, frame 12 x 24-foot building bought from a neighbor a half-mile away and floated piecemeal to Hocoka.

Unquestionably piecemeal. I ripped the cabin apart.

The situation was this:

Hocoka did not have good, straight pines for log building, nor did the land have road access. Don Markwardt, an Iron Range engineer who had the old cabin, did not need it sitting in front of the picture windows of his *new* cabin. Chris and I needed a shelter while building the cabin of our dreams: something stouter than a tent but not costing a helicopter to move. When Don mentioned he'd sell his old cabin for several hundred dollars, even skid it on red pine logs down to his lake landing, the deal was clinched.

But how to move the cabin to Hocoka?

I wasn't much of a mathematician but I did know I had a problem. There were a good 2,640 feet between Markwardt's landing at the southwest end of the lake and the site where, come 1983, I wanted the cabin to be.

The traditional way of moving buildings across water, or along a lakeshore, is to wait until winter when ice is solid enough to support a flatbed truck or skidder. The method, however, is (1) expensive and (2) rather dangerous, seeing as how ice sometimes has an unpredictable propensity to break under extremely heavy loads at the most inopportune times.

Regardless, you couldn't count on good ice.

A winter could go by and a building might be sitting come spring exactly where it was seven months earlier when the geese flew south.

Same address.

Gossip of the township board.

My solution, albeit labor-intensive, was simple. I removed the cabin's roof shingle by shingle, board by board, and rafter by rafter, pulling nails like a crazy man beneath October sun. I was going to dismantle the walls, too, but when friends arrived on an appointed day to help barge the lumber, I set aside hammer, prybar, and crowbar and reached for my Jonsereds chainsaw. No time left but *do* time. Using studs as vertical guides, I cut the cabin walls and floor into eight-foot square and eight-by-twelve-foot sections.

For someone like me, who knew little about carpentry, this was brave stuff. True wood-butchery. Feature newspaper material. All kinds of photo opportunities went to waste as we loaded the pieces of what had been a cabin onto a canoe barge, paddled northeast to Hocoka, unloaded, then returned for more.

The ploy wasn't all that preposterous.

An old photo in Kenneth G. Roberts and Philip Shackleton's *The Canoe* shows a native couple barging a farm wagon and household belongings straddled across a pair of birchbark canoes on Leech Lake in northern Minnesota. Woodsman Calvin Rutstrum once barged lumber from an old schoolhouse near Sioux Lookout, Ontario, to his wilderness cabin in the same manner as the Leech Lake people.

So precedent had been set.

My own barge was a woodbutcher's best effort. I borrowed two seventeen-foot aluminum canoes, bought two four-by-eight-foot sheets of inch-thick plywood, rounded up six eight-foot two-by-fours, and six four-inch bolts. The innovative result was amazingly stable and buoyant. One barge load consisted of the cabin's entire floor plus a corner wall section, and the canoes still had six inches of freeboard.

My work, of course, had barely begun. Heavy wall

and floor sections had to be carried uphill to the building site (where I'd already made a dozen concrete footings, barging buckets of sand for the mix), walls had to be re-assembled, and the roof had to be rebuilt. There were steps to build, windows to place, doors to haul (and hinge), and stovepipes to snug together.

Steady work, little pay.

The scheme, however, worked.

Instead of waiting for questionably thick ice in March to move the beginning of a home by skidder or truck with luck, the old cabin was Hocoka's nest by Thanksgiving.

And the champagne tasted fine.

Once the cabin shell was up, we still had the logistical problem of hauling in a constant stream of more build-ing supplies, food, clothes, tools, mail, books from our old cabins, propane gas tanks, laundry, buckets of sand for more footings, furniture, woodstoves, and whatever we felt worth the haul.

At first we used the barge, then, in winter, when we parked a half-mile from the cabin, we used snowshoes to pull small red plastic sleds. For the bulkier, heavier stuff, like boxes of files and one-by-six-inch tongue-and-groove pine siding, I pulled a wooden toboggan. I'd load the toboggan, sling a towline around my chest, make sure my snowshoes were secure, yank, and pull. Just like a beast of burden. I'd drag for a while, rest, catch my breath, unzip my parka to let cool air in, then keep going.

With the heaviest loads on the coldest days, I'd choose a tree shadow across the snowshoe trail ahead, aim for it, reach it, rest, then choose another shadow.

It didn't take long to see living without a road was going to be a mixed blessing.

Chris and I had our reasons, though, for not rushing to build a road all the way in, a cumulative decision with karma I was to live with throughout the years ahead. For one thing, we couldn't *afford* a road. With limited money, the thought of buying gravel was like seeing ourselves standing by a swamp and throwing thousands of likely borrowed silver dollars into the water one at a time. Filling wetlands with gravel and money. This image and associated attitude would come to haunt me, evoking social disapproval, yet Chris and I had a more important reason than money for choosing what we did.

We wanted, to the best of our ability, to walk gently on the land.

Hands off.

Saws, bulldozers, and trucks dumping gravel ran against this romantic grain.

Wasn't such environmental impact precisely what we were trying to avoid, in part, by our choice of lifestyle? How begin a soulful, landward journey by killing acres of woods for a roadway?

Nor were we interested in improving property values.

There was still another consideration.

Chris and I wanted to preserve Hocoka's sense of remoteness.

Although only seven raven miles from Ely, Hocoka was on the outer perimeter of human development. The Boundary Waters Canoe Area Wilderness, part of a 2,485,176-acre international wilderness system larger than Yellowstone National Park, was a mere half-mile of lake away. To the northeast, then: wild nature. To the

southwest and south: Ely, Duluth (one hundred miles
distant), and Minneapolis–St. Paul (250).

Hocoka straddled these two extremes yet it was to
the north we looked and yearned.

We could, at first, see no buildings from our land. We
saw no cars. The only motor traffic was the lake's occasional motorboat, snowmobile, or, overhead, airplanes.
Their scarcity lent Hocoka, in terms of sonic values, an
ambience of the far north. Silence and solitude, as near
complete as in the heart of Quetico Park, were the norm.
They helped Chris and me see—along with the ridges,
woods, and wolves—that if we wanted a semi-wilderness
experience, as we did, Hocoka was the perfect place to
hunker down.

It was a compromise, yet here, on the northern
perimeter, we could discover what it was like to live on
the roadless edge.

Getting two woodstoves to Hocoka from the end of the
road was a challenge solved by musher Dave Olesen,
sled dogs, and, indirectly, Japanese adventurer Naomi
Uemura.

The stoves were heavy so we asked Dave Olesen
for help. Dave, who would later race Alaska's Iditarod
several times and homestead a cabin, with Kristen
Gilbertson, near Hoarfrost River at the east end of Great
Slave Lake in Canada's Northwest Territories,[6] was the
chief dog-handler at the Minnesota (now Voyageur)
Outward Bound School south of Ely. When we explained we needed to move a cast iron Jotul woodstove
and a Monarch cookstove, he asked us to pack a trail
about four feet wide from the parking area to the lake.

From there he and the dogs would handle it. Agreed. Chris and I snowshoed the trail countless times, back and forth, packing and widening, and Dave arrived on schedule.

With him were three Outward Bound instructors, ten freight dogs, and a most unusual sled.

"It's a *kamotik*," Dave said while muscling the dogs into harness.

Turns out the small *kamotik*, designed low, wide, and strong for freight, lashed together Eskimo-style to absorb shock, had just been built by famed Japanese explorer Naomi Uemura then staying at Outward Bound. Uemura was studying Outward Bound's winter outdoor programs to possibly apply methods to programs designed and promoted by himself. In his free time, he split wood for the school in a manner amazing students: he'd stand a dozen or more pieces on end then hustle from one piece to another splitting each with a single blow of the axe. He also built the *kamotik* using sled features he'd noticed in Greenland before mushing solo from Ellesmere Island to the North Pole.

Uemura, in Japanese eyes, was more than an explorer. He was a hero. As Eiji Okamoto, himself from Japan, later explained to me, all of Japan admired Uemura's focus, drive, and outstanding accomplishments. Born in Hyogo, Japan, in 1941, Uemura attended the University of Meiji (when he started mountain climbing) and, in 1966–68, climbed his first two major peaks, Mount Kilimanjaro in Africa and Mount Aconcagua in South America. Later in 1968 he rafted 3,750 miles down the Amazon and climbed Alaska's Mount Sanford. He scaled the world's highest peak, Mount Everest (29,028 feet), in

1970, Mount McKinley (Denali) later that year, then began studying dogsledding in Greenland in 1972. Soon he mushed 1,875 miles of Greenland's northwest coast, then, in 1974–76, mushed seventy-five hundred miles from Greenland to Alaska along the shore of the Arctic Ocean.

There was absolutely no moss on this man who loved winter and preferred traveling alone.

In 1976, Uemura climbed Mount Elbrus in Europe, followed, in two years, by the North Pole dogsled trip and a traverse, north to south, of Greenland. Again, in 1979–80, he climbed Everest and Aconcagua. In 1982 he mushed in Antarctica. His goal in the winter of 1983–84, while pausing at Outward Bound and building the *kamotik*, was to return to Alaska and become the first person to climb Denali alone in winter.

This he did.

Unfortunately, on the way down from Denali's summit and after radioing a passing airplane of his success, Uemura apparently fell into a crevasse. His body, despite searches by students of Meiji University, was never found.

Uemura's *kamotik* was wider than we expected.

Once the cookstove had been dismantled, and pieces lashed to the sled, ten dogs and five people pulled, pushed, and guided the sled down the packed trail toward the lake. A sled with ten eager dogs pulling it, however, doesn't go exactly straight. One of the *kamotik* runners would edge out over the side of the trail about every fifty to seventy-five feet, causing the sled with its heavy load to veer off into deep snow and get bogged down. The dogs, disgusted, would glance back at us like "Let's get this show on the road." People pushed, Dave hollered, the dogs pulled, the sled would slide back up on the trail then, a few moments later, veer to the *other* side of the trail where, sure thing, it would plow into deep snow and stop dead.

A half-mile of this wore us out, although when Dave and dogs reached the lake, they surged ahead.

Running, I couldn't keep up, surrendered, and just let the outfit go.

We caught up to Dave and dogs at Hocoka. Again they were bogged down—cookstove teetering—along a steep path that led up from the lake to the cabin. By now we had the method down, knew what to do, so we all pushed the sled in unison, Dave barked instructions, the dogs grunted and pulled like the freight champions they were, and the *kamotik* inched forward until that heavy stove slid to the front door of its new home.

The next trip, for the heavy but narrow Jotul stove, was easier. Soon both stoves were wrestled into place, stovepipes were assembled, and fires lit.

Heat.

No: more than heat.

Hot heat. Those stoves were dreams sustained by flame.

They were hearts, like sparks, held together in hope against the Arctic's deepest, most penetrating, chill. Two stoves burning: two hearts glowing. Dreamtime. The beginning of a life in woods with all glory to see, feel, and imagine. A home. Hub. Anchorage. *Fire.* Warmth to read by. Heat to write in, keep a journal, take notes: remark

on life. *Flame.* Birchbark kindling crackling at touch of
wooden kitchen match. Boiled water for strong coffee.
Tea water. Hot chocolate. Fried breakfast eggs with
ham. Baked turkeys. Warm morning face water. Dish
water. Simmering beef stews. Oven pizzas. Soup. Fried
steak. More black coffee. Warm beds. Waves of warmth.
Fresh baked bread. Firelight on wood walls. Midnight
fire crackling. Morning's flush of a stoked fire's rush.
Fried sausage and pancakes with pure, stove-warmed
maple syrup.

Chunks of aspen, birch, black ash, maple, occasionally oak, this connection too, knowing a wood's worth as
flame. Finding the trees, cutting them, thanking them,
hauling them, splitting chunks, swinging axes, feeding
wood into fire's insatiable maw.

Sizzling bacon.

Yes, more than heat.

Heat: stomach: passion: heart.

Without the heat, on the most basic of levels, Chris
and I would have simply frozen. No fire no life. Yet with
the heat of Jotul and Monarch, brought to us by the
strength of dogs, friends, and Uemura's skillful hands, we
had Hocoka: a warm home of our own, however rustic,
where we could laugh, watch, eat, host, sleep, wonder,
cry, learn, love, hope, dream, and talk God.

By the end of our first winter, the only thing missing at
Hocoka was a black cat I called Rip.

Her formal name, as Chris originally pointed out, was
Fatima, African for woman, yet with her Persian blood,
gold eyes, jet-black fur, stubby door-chopped tail, and
propensity to sleep most of the winter, she reminded me

of a feline Rip Van Winkle who could sleep forty years and still surface with a cat's proverbial nine lives.

Rip had been a kitten with Chris in Minneapolis–St. Paul then settled with her in a backwoods cabin between Burntside Lake and Coxey Pond where I engaged them both. I found Rip quiet, independent (she'd swipe at a hand when she felt like it), prankish (walking willy-nilly across a page's fresh ink or, worse, bringing home the scent of skunk), warm (purring up to your lap, again when she felt like it), and intelligent (knowing when Chris and I were leaving and swatting us with cold glances of scorn).

In time I also called Rip Swivel Ears and Black Banana: terms, really, of endearment: but it was Rip, or Ripper, that remained her name until that dire night in the end.

Her biggest fear, I think, was to be left behind, to be cast adrift at sea, yet as a superb mouser she needn't have worried. Rip was a working part of the family. Where Rip lived, mice didn't, at least not for long, and so it was never questioned that Rip would join Chris and me at Hocoka.

It was a bright winter day, veering toward spring, when Rip saw Otter Lake for the first time. She had ridden with me in my pickup from Chris's old cabin, preferring the top of the seat behind my head. Although panting from the pickup's twenty miles of motion, she hadn't become sick; instead she had gazed out the glass, more curious than afraid, and when Chris carried her down the first part of the trail she was docile and willing. We reached the lake and looked out at the packed snowshoe trail leading northeast to Hocoka.

You couldn't see the cabin from where we stood and the bay, for a cat, was far away.

Carry Rip further?

Put her down and let her follow?

Rip squirmed.

Chris set her on the packed snow and, to our surprise, Rip took off in front of us. She led the way. She'd never seen the lake before, or its cove with cabin, but there Rip was, up ahead, just a black fuzz-ball on brilliant white snow: a small golden-eyed period of hope strutting off—like Chris and me—into Hocoka's wide, welcoming world.

Solo

Cloudy/Snow: 40° F: Barometer Unknown

Saw a wolf three days ago: Hub's cove.

Solo here today, looking haggard: limping. Stiff rear haunches. I saw her fawns Blacky and Moon first, by deck, then Solo appeared below. Blacky trotted down to her and licked her face and neck, and she licked him in return.

Moon joined them but, nonchalant, stood nearby.

Hard to see Solo in poor shape, susceptible to the wolves.

Who knows?

Perhaps she pulled a muscle running from the wolf of a few days ago, slipping on ice.
—journal, Hocoka, Winter

It's hard to say exactly when Solo first came into my life at Hocoka as part of its wide, welcoming world. As the land's whitetail matriarch, Solo was to stay with me so long—through all the years and changes—that her origin became obscure.

Like her species, *Odocoileus virginianus borealis*, she seemed to step out of the far reaches of time and mystery.

Perhaps she was the fawn I stumbled upon my first spring at Hocoka. I was walking the path out to the driveway, meandering among fir, small swamps, and black ash, when I saw a doe standing bolt upright in front of me. Her head was straight up, her neck swelling as she inhaled air, her body taut. I stopped. In a moment the doe snorted and was gone.

I stepped forward.

There on the path in front of me, with white spots running along its brown, curving back, was a fawn curled up on spindly legs. Its eyes were wide open looking at me. "You don't see me," its demeanor seemed to say. But I could, plain as day, and I walked up to it. I could have picked that fawn up and held it in my arms as the thought crossed my mind. Instead I feasted my eyes and looked around in the greening forest for the doe.

Gone. At least out of sight.

I decided to get a photo of the fawn, turned around, went back to the cabin for a camera, and hiked back out to the fawn.

The fawn was gone.

Or perhaps Solo was behind the snorts I heard in night woods. Or the twigs cracking when I stepped outside the cabin beneath stars.

Or she was the deer I saw on Rainbow Ridge, early on, on a bright and shining winter day. I'd been skiing the lake, tracking wolf sign, and was headed back to the cabin when I noticed a deer on the side of the ridge.

A doe, caught in mid-stride, was watching me pass. I stopped, stared back, and locked her gaze.

She and I in day's last light were linked by the visage of wolves.

The doe spooked when I nudged a ski tip forward.

Then she turned, lunged forward in deep snow, and

fell to her chest. *Now,* I thought. *Right now is when a wolf would make its kill: then and there.* But the doe, still strong, still pulsing with heart, muscle, blood, and life, gained her footing and was gone.

Or, better yet, perhaps Solo was the deer—silhouetted—I saw appear on the lake ice during a thick snowfall: stepping, in what appeared slow motion, out of the whiteness like an apparition coming to browse on the mists of time. With the white, snow-covered ice beneath her, and the snowflakes swirling around her, she seemed to float in a cloud as a faint presence, almost a shadow, yet solidifying, legs moving, head up with chest toward me: coming closer like a visitor in a dream: arriving with a sacred softness as if our meeting was a shaping, crystallizing destiny.

She stepped closer.

And she was alone.

Almost mythical, then, Solo began.

Despite my journals and phenological note-taking,[1] I somehow failed to note the precise instant Solo walked into my life. Her appearance was not so much when I first *saw* her as when I identified her among a composite of impressions: when she began to stand out with familiarity and distinction. From that day—December 6, 1985—onward, I would look and listen for her, wonder about her whereabouts when she was gone, miss her when she seemed overdue from one of her little tramps, then be delighted when she'd show up again.

It was always that way with Solo.

A little circle going on.

Sometimes I'd even start thinking she might be dead,

possibly killed by passing wolves, and I'd step out of the cabin, walk around a corner or down a trail, and there she'd be: standing and staring at me, watching me come, wondering perhaps what was taking me so long with the grub.

"Belle wâwashkeshi," I'd say in a mix of French/Ojibwe as I greeted her: "Beautiful deer."

And I'd thank her for coming back.

I couldn't help it.

Over time, and of all the deer, it was Solo who emerged at the forefront of Hocoka's whitetail life. Not only did she have the most fawns from year to year, often annual twins, thus carrying on her kind, but it was her territory Chris and I had inadvertently chosen to inhabit. This we discovered when Solo appeared to linger longer and longer in the vicinity of the cabin. When we realized Hocoka was really *Solo's* home, and that her movements might merely be orbits in and out of sight, we also realized her lineage preceded us on the land and, in all likelihood, would outlast us.

Chris and I were the visitors.

There was more to Solo's growing prominence over time, however, than mere propinquity, for by seeing her most winter days, and watching her closely, the landscape of other deer, rock ridges, pines, lakes, wolves, ravens, eagles, fox, and even winter itself, seemed to open and expand through her. Solo became a kind of prism: a reflection of what was around. Her senses became, in part, extensions of our own. The more we watched the more we learned. In time I seemed to glimpse in Solo the ecological integrity and wild beauty of all whitetails and, by association, the instinct, intelligence, and equally wild beauty of their primary Quetico-Superior predator, the wolf.

This was important to me.

It was at the fierce interface of deer and wolves, after all, that I was to intersect the heat and heart of Hocoka.

Time and again Solo led the way.

Time and again she became my teacher.

For this reason—in an otherwise inexhaustible sea of possible trails—I began tracking her more thoroughly, paid close attention, and made it my business to learn as much about whitetail deer as I could.

The trail was like snow coming down, falling, falling, coloring my surroundings and enriching much of what, inevitably, was yet to come.

The Ojibwe, I quickly learned, called deer trails *omonsom*, and it's apparent from the evolutionary record that whitetails approached the Quetico-Superior on those trails soon after glacial ice nosed north. On a continental scale, whitetails—or their genetic ancestors—had roamed North America's woodlands and prairies for millions of years.

Biologists seem fairly certain about this.

Whitetails, now found in all forty-eight contiguous states and eight Canadian provinces, are a descendant of ungulates (hoofed quadrupeds) going back to the Eocene geological and evolutionary epoch thirty-six million to fifty-eight million years ago. Of the order Artiodactyla (even-toed), the family Cervidae, and genus *Odocoileus* (exclusively American), the whitetail's earliest alleged ancestor was the Eocene genus *Diacodexis,* a rabbit-sized artiodactyl with double-pulled ankle bones, long legs, and a gait adapted for running.

Descendants of *Diacodexis,* during the Miocene thirteen million to fifteen million years ago, grew in size, developed tusks and permanent giraffe-like protuberances or horns, then, by the Pleistocene a million years ago, became the antlered deer as we know them.

Or close enough, anyhow, to count.

Just to keep things complex, and as Rollin H. Baker notes in a related study of whitetail origin, classification, and distribution in the anthological whitetail bible, *White-tailed Deer: Ecology and Management,*[2] no fossil forms have been found bridging the deer with permanent horns with today's deer, like Solo's mates, that annually shed their antlers. No one understands this. Antler growth requires much nutrition, evokes a high annual energy toll, and it seems to biologists that keeping horns, rather than dropping antlers every year, would be the way to go.

Another evolutionary mystery surrounds whitetails. While sharing woodlands and prairies in the Pleistocene with such hoofed neighbors as mastodons and mammoths, why is it that *deer* survived the trials of the Ice Age, when the great glaciers came sweeping down from the far north, while so many other ungulates didn't?

Regardless, today there are four worldwide subfamilies of Cervidae, seventeen genera, at least thirty-seven species, and 190 subspecies of deer. Whitetails are divided into thirty subspecies in North and Central America, ranging roughly over three million square miles from sub-equatorial South America (approximately fifteen degrees south latitude) up through the United States and the Quetico-Superior to near treeline in Canada (approximately sixty degrees north latitude). North of Mexico, there are seventeen subspecies of whitetails. Of them all, *Odocoileus virginianus borealis,* or northern woodland whitetails, Solo's kind, is the largest in size and range: ranging from the Atlantic Coast of New England north into Québec, over into Ontario, then west through the Great Lakes states to near the Minnesota–North Dakota border.

Northern woodland whitetails abut Virginia whitetails (*O. v. virginianus*) and Kansas whitetails (*O. v. macrourus*) to the south, Dakota whitetails (*O. v. dakotensis*) to the west, and caribou to the north.

Total whitetail population?

Current estimates vary from fifteen million to twenty million whitetails in North America, with densities on average of eight to thirty deer per square mile. (This is arguably down from an estimated prehistoric population of twenty-four million to thirty-three million. One estimate of forty million for a prehistoric whitetail population is described as "not unrealistic."[3]) Leonard Lee Rue III, in *The Deer of North America,* argues for a current North America whitetail population of 19.5 million.[4]

Deer, then, long ago and now: almost everywhere.

As the largest subspecies of whitetails north of Mexico, Solo's kin—particularly the bucks—grow to awesome size. A mature buck will stand forty inches at the shoulder, be about sixty to ninety-five inches long, and weigh three hundred pounds or more. The all-time weight record is 511 pounds, a buck shot by Carl J.

Lenander Jr., in 1926 near Tofte, Minnesota, along the north shore of Lake Superior. Amazingly, the record was matched in 1981 by another Minnesota buck, shot by George Himango, an Ojibwe, hunting on the Fond du Lac reservation.

Less is known about large does although, generally, they're 35 to 40 percent smaller than bucks.

Large or small, whitetails have roamed close to the hearts and stomachs of Native Americans and Canadians for as long as elders, historians, and biologists can remember.

One Ojibwe myth, about the first man and woman, has an Adam-like young native and Mani, his mate, banished from a garden paradise by *Matchi-Manitou* (Bad Spirit). The young man is given a bow and arrow and told he'll find deer which he is supposed to shoot for food, now that he needs it. Mani is to prepare the meat and make clothing and moccasins from the hide.[5] Although the story has Christian mythological overtones, it was true in a fundamental way.

Natives—whether Mohawk, Huron, Fox, or Ojibwe—depended upon whitetails for much of their meat.

Richard E. and Thomas R. McCabe, in "Of Slings and Arrows: An Historical Retrospection," have documented at least forty-seven Native American and Canadian tribes who subsisted, at least in part, on whitetails.[6] Approximately 2.34 million natives lived in an assumed three-million-square-mile range of whitetails north of Mexico until about 1800. There might have been thirty million whitetails at the time, or forty million. No matter, really, the number, although natives must have eaten prodigious amounts of venison. Assuming the average native ate two pounds of meat a day, their total consumption of whitetails possibly approached 427 million pounds a year.

Computing whitetail ages, sex, actual meat yield (minus bones, fur, etc.), anywhere from five million to six million whitetails were likely killed annually.

Food, however, was just part of the attraction.

Natives made a variety of clothes from the deerhide: shirts, sashes, moccasins, shawls, breechclouts, skirts, robes, mittens, and headwear. A complete wardrobe for men or women might require six to eight deer, fewer for children. Hide was also used for blankets, pipe pouches, shields, storage bags, harnessing, wrist guards, arrow quivers, rugs, snowshoe netting, drums, thongs, bow-strings, lodge and tepee coverings, bow-wrappings, saddle pads (out west), balls for games, and what might be called buckskin hands of honor.

According to ethnologist Frances Densmore, when Ojibwe wanted to summon men from scattered villages to discuss war or matters of similar urgency, a messenger was sent with a life-sized hand made of buckskin and filled with moss.[7] The hand was smeared with red paint to indicate blood. Tobacco was tucked in a wrist opening. If sent to warriors, the fingers of the hand were curled around a pipe. If a receiving warrior smoked the pipe, he acknowledged willingness to respond to the summons.

Such a hand was also used to seal agreements with the U.S. government when the hand was placed on a pile of goods being given to the Ojibwe. Apparently the buckskin hand symbolized the honor of the tribe.

Still other parts of whitetails were used.

Thread, string, and fishnets were made from sinew.

Deer bones were used to make hoes, hide fleshers, arrowheads, hooks, clubs, and arrow straighteners. Flutes, bracelets, and beads were made from tibia and ribs. There were instances of spoons, clothespins, and bull roarers made of bone. Antlers were used for spear points, arrowheads, points (the tines) on war clubs, knife handles, flaking tools, combs, and needles.

Deer fat was used as food seasoning, a preservative, and for tanning hides; also for tallow, lubricant, hair oil, and as a skin protectant. Teeth were used as pendants, game pieces, and for shelling corn. Hooves were used for rattles, armlets, and, boiled, for glue. Deer hair was used in embroidery, as moccasin insulation, and for decorative roaches (tufts of fur worn on the head or around the neck). Deer heads were sometimes used as masks in ceremonies or part of a hunting decoy disguise.

Obviously, whitetail uses went far beyond meat. They were seemingly infinite, limited only by imagination. Even there—in myth, story, faith—whitetails were thought to imbue speed, agility, and potency in romance. A number of tribes had whitetail clans who called upon the deer's mystical and all-pervasive influence for community well-being.

Even some burial mounds, in which various native peoples placed their dead, were shaped like whitetails.

Yes, *wâwashkeshi* was everywhere.

Although native peoples occasionally kept deer as pets,[8] most deer—when needed for food—were wanted dead.

Solo's kind were killed with a variety of weapons: bow and arrow, spear, atlatl (in very early times), knife, guns (acquired through fur trade with Europeans; a rifle sometimes cost thirty deerskins), hatchets, snares, and clubs. Methods of killing deer included still-hunting, stalking (sometimes in disguise or on snowshoes), fire drives or surrounds, pitfalls, drives to enclosures and funnel traps where deer were killed at close range, jacklighting (approached at night in a canoe with a light suspended above the bow to mesmerize or blind deer), drives over cliffs or into water, running to exhaustion, poisoning, and luring with antler rattles: whatever worked.

Most hunting was communal, involving groups, and although it bore great prestige (second only to warfare and sitting on council) it was usually hard work and never considered sport.

Men did the vast majority of hunting, while women, if they went along, drove the deer, dressed carcasses, and helped lug it all back to camp.

Lone hunters could be very effective.

Ethnologist Johann Georg Kohl tells of an Ojibwe who killed fifty-five deer with sixty bullets in six weeks.[9] William J. Warren, also an ethnologist (and mixed-blood of English-Ojibwe descent), tells of No-ka who allegedly killed, in one *day*, sixteen elk, four buffalo, five deer, three bears, a lynx and, for good measure, a porcupine: all near the mouth of Minnesota's Crow Wing River.[10]

Other historical records indicate that each native hunter killed an average fifteen to thirty deer a year.

Successful subsistence hunting couldn't, of course, be taken for granted, and rarely was. Whitetails were scattered unevenly throughout their range and, during extremely severe winters, native people starved to death. Starvation was an old bad song that came around too often to arrogantly count on comfort. Deer meant food, clothes, life, and, because many native people believed deer (like other animals) had souls (whose presence or absence was due to the Great Spirit), whitetail abundance or scarcity was viewed as a reflection of a hunter's or tribe's spiritual integrity.

Gratitude nurtured prayerful approaches to killing, atonement with dead deer, and group ritual expressing appreciation for deer-as-gift.

J. Owen Dorsey, for example, in an 1884 monograph for the Smithsonian Institute's Bureau of Ethnology, tells of a native clan of the Omahas called the Deer-Head Gens.[11] The clan's members couldn't touch the skin of any deer. Unlike the Ojibwe, Fox, Abenakis, and other natives who relied heavily on deerskin for clothing, the Deer-Heads couldn't even make moccasins of deerskin. Nor could deer fat be used for hair oil.

Deer-Heads could, however, eat deer meat.

Smart people.

Names for men reflected the clan's close association with deer. There was Little-Hoof-of-a-Deer, Dark-Chin-of-a-Deer, Deer-Paws-the-Ground, Deer-in-the-Distance-Shows-Its-Tail-White-Suddenly, and He-Who-Wags-His-Tail.

One name meant a fawn isn't killed by a hunter.

Respect for deer among the Deer-Heads began at an early age. Five days after a child was born, he or she became the centerpiece of a traditional ceremony. A decoration, in dark red, was painted on the baby's face while along the back, painted with tips of fingers, were rows of red spots designed to imitate the spots of a fawn.

South and east of the Deer-Heads, in central Florida, the Timucua people expressed appreciation of deer in a way that spoke for many other natives.

They embodied thanksgiving in ritual.

Each year, in late winter as spring approached, the Timucua stuffed a large buck's hide with special roots, put garlands on his antlers, neck, and body, then hung the decorated deer on a post or tree. This they did with parade, music, and song. As the deer hung with its head and chest facing sunrise, the Timucua chief prayed more deer would inhabit the land for the good of his people.

Everyone saluted the sun after the prayer, returned to their homes, and the buck was left on its perch as winter waned, the sun veered high and hot, and—in time— another winter approached more surely than a strong hunter's next breath.

Although whitetails like Solo ranged widely throughout North America, as native dependence and homage attest, they were relative newcomers to the Quetico-Superior as I began to share their shores.

As the last ice age receded ten thousand to thirteen thousand years ago, it left a peneplain of exposed granite with little soil for plants other than lichens and mosses. Caribou, eating moss, were likely among the area's earliest cervids. As plant life and forest matured, woodland caribou (*rangifer tarandus*) inhabited the region along with other herbivores including moose and, one suspects, some whitetails nudging onto the shield. It was this flow

of caribou, moose, and deer, albeit scant, that varied
from ecosystem condition to condition, leading scientists—on their maps of prehistoric whitetail range—to
crosshatch northeastern Minnesota as a "range discrep-
ancy" area. When conditions favored caribou, it was
they who roamed rock ridges and surrounding forest.
When fire swept the land, as it did some areas every sixty
to one hundred years, it created light, soil, and nutrients
for aspen, birch, and other types of woodland browse
appealing to moose and deer.

The mosaic of vegetation shifted at sporadic intervals.
Some dry periods of frequent fire, hence tender post-fire
browse, lasted hundreds of years.

Then the pines would return: the reds and whites, their
deep-green groves darkening the slopes of gray ridges.

As many as twenty-five generations of white pine
have surfaced in the Quetico-Superior in the last six
thousand to eight thousand years: a long lineage of *Pinus
strobus*, their boughs sighing in breeze beneath blue sky.

Then, again, fire, or devastating insects, or wind-
storms blowing the giant trees down.

The forest was varied, dynamic: a living, pulsating
collage of plants.

"So extensive was natural disturbance," ecologists
Clifford and Isabel Ahlgren say in *Lob Trees in the Wilderness*,[12] "that a true climax or self-maintaining equilibrium
forest has never been a significant part of the [Quetico-
Superior] scene."

When the first Europeans arrived in the Quetico-
Superior, led by Pierre Esprit Radisson, Sieur des Groseil-
liers, and Jacques de Noyon in the 1600s, then French-

Canada's La Vérendryes in the 1730s (passing within twelve miles of Hocoka, their birchbark canoes clipping sparkling water), they found surprisingly little wildlife.

One party of paddlers, led by John MacDonnel of the Northwest Fur Company as late as 1793, ate only fish while traveling from Grand Portage, at the mouth of Pigeon River on the northwest shore of Lake Superior, inland almost three hundred miles to Rainy Lake.

The forest, though, was beautiful. Although woods still occasionally crackled with flame, or smoke from wildfire could be smelled on portages, the pines were big, with crowns high and wide. In some places they completely shut out the sun.

Which, when it came to meat, was the problem.

The mature pine forest, sweeping as it did for hundreds of thousands of acres, shaded the ground and used most of the limited soil nutrients. Moose and deer had scant browse—the forbs, succulents, and tender sprigs of small branches—while the woodland caribou, although they could survive, were relatively few in number.

How beautiful, though, it must have been when a lone caribou, its antlers burnished with the rich gold light of sunrise, dipped to sip the ice-free water at the lip of Curtain Falls.

No more.

The caribou are gone.

Perhaps it's Solo's own whitetail twin that drinks those cool, free waters now.

The change from caribou country to whitetail country was dramatic when it came, and the landscape—at least in the hinterlands of Ely and Hocoka in the 1880s through the early 1900s—must have looked like hell.

Yes, the timber was the best, towns grew, the pay could support a man and most of his favorite vices, and the logging camp food was plentiful, but the land with its felled pines, the virgin reds and whites, with endless rolling ridges and ravines of stumps, cried out *ravage.*

People were cutting pine bigtime.

By 1900, the little town of Winton, Ely's satellite settlement, had six hundred loggers of the St. Croix Logging Company jostling for elbow room when they weren't out in the woods at work. That number doubled in a decade when, come winter, loggers from at least ten camps cut pine as fast as they could. A "Steam Hauler" mounted on runners and half-tracks was used to pull ten to twelve sleighs (each holding up to five thousand board feet of timber) from woods to lakeshores where logs were rolled onto the ice. Another machine, called the "Bull of the Woods," was a sixty-foot long scow that pulled rafts of logs.

Slowly, acre by acre, Ely country's pine forests—in a microcosm of what was happening elsewhere on the perimeter of the Quetico-Superior—were muscled and machined to Winton's mills.

The St. Croix Logging Company wasn't the only outfit to cut forest north and northeast of Ely. In 1898–99, Samuel Simpson of Minneapolis contracted with George Swallow of Milwaukee and Louis Hopkins of Duluth to log and saw at least fifty million board feet of lumber from timber holdings around Burntside Lake northeast to Ensign Lake. Like the St. Croix, the

Swallow and Hopkins Lumber Company worked out of Winton.

At first two hundred men were hired to operate a mill which cut 150,000 board feet of lumber daily. Ten-hour shifts and sawdust about everywhere. A boarding house slept eighty-nine men and anyone they could sneak in. Twenty-five homes went up, replete with running water and electricity. A school was built.

Solo's ancestors, meanwhile, meandered north: following nose and stomach into the good cud cutover country where summer sun baked earth and, with rain, sent forth aspen saplings, birch shoots, and sprigs of cedar: favorite foods.

Swallow and Hopkins had over fifty winter camps, each with a hundred men and sixteen horses. To expedite their annual cut of thirty million to thirty-five million board feet, railroad lines—including the Cloquet near which I live—were built. The Four Mile Portage (later sold to St. Croix) was built. It connected Fall Lake near Winton with Ella Hall and Mud Lakes and, by 1901, Basswood Lake's many miles of shoreline. Railroad spurs were later extended to Gun Lake and Basswood's Pipestone and Jackfish bays.

Timber came from Crooked Lake, Ensign, Wind, Newton, Moose, Basswood, and Knife Lakes, all along the U.S.–Canada border. About six hundred million board feet were eventually cut as Winton's population grew to two thousand before a long decline. Swallow and Hopkins ceased operations in 1915 while the

St. Croix, which alone harvested a billion board feet, folded three years later.

As far as the forest was concerned, and what later became the million-acre Boundary Waters Canoe Area Wilderness, its ecology—in many lifetimes—would never be the same.

A 1948 Forest Service timber survey, for example, indicated that prior to logging, tall pines (reds and whites) covered 334,000 acres. After logging, tall pines remained on 26,560 acres, or about 8 percent of the original tall pine forest. Logging, in other words, removed *92 percent* of the mature pines. Almost one-third of Superior National Forest's border lakes country was cut, mostly its central portion (south, southeast, and southwest of Basswood Lake) with smaller tracts east and west.

Where cutting was done, trails, camps, logging roads, and railroad spurs remained. Stumps, like those charred black by slash wildfire still visible in the woods of Hocoka, were scattered throughout the landscape.

And where did all the lumber from virgin timber go?

Some was used locally, of course, but most went south to growing cities: Omaha, Kansas City, St. Louis, Des Moines, and Minneapolis–St.Paul. What happened to some of Ely-Winton's surrounding forests was the tail end of a timber-harvesting phenomenon that, by 1932, totaled 67.5 billion board feet from throughout Minnesota.

Enough wood was cut to cover the entire state with a solid slab of wood over two feet thick.

The forest that returned, meanwhile, consisted—and still consists—primarily of aspen, birch, balsam fir,

spruce, and not (relative to their original abundance) red
and white pines, although many stands remain.

The change affected shrub and herb growth with related changes in wildlife. Gone were the caribou, the last
one seen near Burntside Lake north of Ely around 1915.
In their place came whitetail deer, arriving noticeably
about 1890. Plant and animal diseases changed (whitetails, for example, carrying a brain worm that killed caribou). Nonnative plants were introduced accidentally
and deliberately. By the early 1980s, when I was situated
on Burntside Lake, met Chris, and began the move to
Hocoka, environmentalists were busy debating how the
area's changes affected definitions and understanding of
wilderness.

Could a forest, essentially on a boreal rebound, be
truly considered wild?

Solo probably thought so.

Her kind, after all, had their predators over the eons:
essentially any animal wanting and eating meat: and this
hadn't changed much.

Among those predators in the Quetico-Superior, as I
settled at Hocoka, were the occasional cougar and pe-
ripheral coyote, some bobcats and lynx, the opportunis-
tic fox and bear, and, foremost, the wolf.

I knew little about cougars or bobcats in those early
days. The only cougar I'd ever seen, outside of a zoo,
was dead, its head cut off near a barbwire fence of a
farmer's pasture near boyhood's Red Lake Falls. And only
once, north of Big Elbow Lake near the headwaters of
the Mississippi River, southwest of the Quetico-
Superior, had I seen a bobcat (*Lynx rufus*). It flashed

across a leafy logging road in front of me. I might have heard other bobcats near Big Elbow—wailing like terrified babies in the dark—but those strange sounds came screeching out of the night silence into which they promptly returned.

My lack of experience with bobcats wasn't unusual. Few people, even among those who have spent many years in the woods of northern Minnesota, have seen bobcats or their sign.[13] The large cats, weighing twenty to forty pounds and occasionally up to sixty pounds, are—like lynx—simply rare. They're also extremely secretive, evasive, silent: preying primarily on snowshoe hares with which they share population cycles.

Bobcats will, however, as biologists know well, sometimes kill and eat deer: fawns, does, even large bucks. They hunt, often at night, by hiding and pouncing on a deer, thus ambushing it, or they stalk a deer quietly, wait their moment, then leap on a deer's head and shoulders. They'll cling with claws and rip the deer's throat open or break its neck by twisting the deer's head around and snapping it back.

For this reason, perhaps, some early French trappers called both bobcat and lynx *loup cervier*: the deer wolf.

Bobcat deer-kills, at least in the hinterlands of places like Maine, can be extensive. One study came up with thirty-four whitetails killed by bobcats: one was a fawn, eight were yearlings, and the other twenty-five were adults over two years old, including twenty bucks.[14] This is less likely to happen near the Great Lakes where bobcat deer-kills are more rare. Although a study of bobcat stomach contents at northern Michigan's Cusino Wildlife Experiment Station once revealed contents of

20 percent to 76 percent deer meat, the highest percentage was during, and after, human hunting season. Thus most of the meat was likely carrion. In a separate study, Michigan's El Harger tracked bobcats over five hundred miles during fifteen years yet only found four instances of bobcat-deer predation. Three of the dead deer were fawns less than a year old. The other kill was a 120-pound buck.

Not surprisingly, bobcats—wherever they are—appear to make deer nervous.

When a bobcat passes by, whitetails have been known to stamp their forelegs on the ground, snort, and watch, watch, watch. They don't trust bobcats. Not one hundred feet away. Not two hundred. Not until a bobcat is over three hundred feet away, the distance of a football field, will a whitetail's eye and nerve let *loup cervier*—whether deer-slayer or scavenger—go.[15]

The same caution was shown toward another whitetail predator that made an early appearance at Hocoka: the red fox. Although only three feet long and weighing up to fourteen pounds, *Vulpes vulpes* was good at taking what he could get, including an occasional fawn.

Hocoka's deer seemed to know this.

They didn't trust fox.

They took careful notice when a fox passed in the distance or was seen scurrying on its trails in search of meat.

When a fox was far away and relatively indistinguishable, the deer would watch the fox until its identity was certain or, equally important, its trajectory of direction posed no threat. Perhaps it was the distant, canine motion that alarmed the deer: the shape and sight of an animal meandering through the landscape. Once a fox was identified, however, especially up close, deer had mixed reactions. Some would snort warnings to other deer, and leave the scene, while other whitetails—as I saw Solo do—stood their ground.

They'd even sometimes stamp their hooves, agitated now, and step *closer* to the fox, pestering it with large presence until the fox was driven away by all the attention and commotion.

This, of course, would never happen with black bears, a more formidable whitetail predator occasionally visiting Hocoka: browsing Juneberries, sniffing birdfeeders, or coming up on the cabin's small deck. *Makwâ*, as the bear was known to Ojibwe (male bear: *nabek*; female: *nojek*), doesn't get pushed around by anything or anyone unless they've a mind to. As a whitetail predator, however, black bears are generally too slow to give deer fair chase. Hence bears, essentially herbivores, catch and kill deer opportunistically when they can, especially fawns in spring.[16]

And in winter?

Bears hibernate: sleeping the sleep of the deep.

It was a rare occurrence for me to see a bear track in snow, a sign of restless passage.

Beyond doubt, then, it was the wolf—as the primary predator of Quetico-Superior whitetails—that Solo and kin had to watch out for: *Canis lupus lycaon* with, possibly, genetic influence from *Canis lupus nubilus*, the old Great Plains wolf. Whether howling on distant ridges, or crossing the snows of winter lakes, it was the wolf, alone or en masse, that could readily take deer down, as I saw that sunlit January day.

Along the way, feared or loved, wolves lent wild soul to the country.

Fortunately for me, much was known about north-eastern Minnesota wolves when I began to share their space. Studies by Sigurd F. Olson in the 1930s, Milt Stenlund in the 1950s, and, more recently, by biologists Rolf Peterson, Mike Nelson, and particularly L. David Mech, presented a fairly uniform portrait of the wolf. I learned, for instance, that although wolves were once the most widely distributed mammal in the world, their viable North American range (outside Canada and Alaska) had been reduced to my home ground. A few wolves were showing up in northern Wisconsin, Michigan, Montana, Idaho, and Wyoming, but otherwise Hocoka was in the heart of wolf country.

Population estimates for Minnesota wolves hovered around twelve hundred, then, as the years passed, rose to 1,750.[17] Of this number, approximately two hundred wolves roamed Voyageurs National Park, the Boundary Waters Canoe Area Wilderness of Superior National Forest, and adjacent corridors and perimeter areas. Although the population of this core group dipped sharply in 1969–77 as a result of a series of severe winters, it stabilized by 1986 at about one wolf every seventeen square miles.

Biologically, adult wolves, usually gray, are about six feet long and stand thirty inches high at the shoulder. Female weights average fifty-five to sixty-five pounds, males seventy-five to ninety-five pounds, with larger sizes (especially in the far north) not uncommon.

Wolves usually form packs consisting of a dominant (alpha) pair and their offspring.

Pack sizes in northeastern Minnesota have averaged four to ten wolves with extremes varying from two to three wolves (not counting loners) to thirteen to seventeen wolves.

Although wolves can travel thirty or more miles in a day, they often spend days going nowhere or cover only several miles. Much of a wolf's time (as high as 62 percent) is spent resting, usually daytimes between midmorning and 6:00 P.M.[18] When wolves *do* travel (approximately 28 percent of the time) they easily trot five to nine miles per hour depending on ground conditions.

Wolves can, of course, run much faster and have been paced by truck at thirty-five to forty miles per hour: about the same top speed of a whitetail.

A midnight wolf, I'd sometimes imagine: running, kicking up snow crust as moonlight glints off guard hairs, ear tips, eyeballs, the faint breath of haste, the scattering of shattered snow crystals, as the great wolf, free in space, lunging—lunging with grace—polices its wild range.

Whether running, trotting, or just nosing around, wolves establish territories—varying in size from 43–318 square miles—which they defend unto death. Boundaries between packs are marked with urine, scat, and, to an extent, by howling. (Visualized from above, territories have been compared to adjacent cells of a beehive: a collage of variously sized, abutting shapes.) There is usually a buffer zone between territories: a heavily scent-marked area where two territories come together and across which a wolf strays at great risk. Wolves will kill wolves from other packs if they invade, even skirt, their territory and, because of this, packs tend to avoid buffer zones where chance of confrontation is high.

Ironically, these buffer zones become relatively safe for whitetails.

I say relatively because wolves, requiring meat to live, are *always* hunting and—although wolves throughout North America prey on elk, caribou, bison, mountain sheep, mountain goat, and musk-oxen—they rely on whitetails for food in northern Minnesota. Can't be helped. There are fifty to one hundred deer per wolf. Moose are harder to kill. One can bet, then, if a deer shows up in a buffer zone, and a wolf catches its scent or motion, the chase will be on.

Motion spurs a wolf and most deer are caught on the run.

When a deer runs away, a wolf rushes it, tries to catch and kill it, or at least test its strength. Most chases last less than twelve hundred yards (although biologist Mech documented an anomalous chase of thirteen miles over a period of two hours: outcome unknown). Healthy deer, given "normal" conditions such as dry ground, usually get away. Debilitated deer, however, such as those that are old, have limb abnormalities, are weak from malnutrition, or are simply tricked or caught at a disadvantage, are quickly brought to bay. Wolves will attack a deer's rump (avoiding flailing hooves) and, when the deer stops, a pack-mate—if a pack's involved—will often grab the deer's head or nose.

Other wolves, meanwhile, grab at flank or neck.

Here again: the fierce interface, the bawling and viscera, the necessary violence.

Apparently wolves prefer to prey on fawns in summer, old bucks during the autumn rut, and, in winter, deer of both sexes five years old or older.

And the howling?

Why do wolves howl?

Many reasons.

According to wolf biologist Mech,[19] wolf howling advertises a pack's presence to other packs up to six miles away, thus announcing—and indirectly defending—territory. Howling maintains group contact when the pack is split, or when it's time to reassemble. Often howling seems to nurture social bonds or merely manifest excitement, as when wolves awaken from rest, finish playing, or for some reason are annoyed. Wolves will also howl in response to strange howls, thus reversing the claim to country or upping an ante of threat.

All true, little doubt, yet I suspect wolves howl for another reason.

Wolves howl for the hell of it: the pure joy and hell of being a wolf beneath stars in open country where deer must die for the howling—the wild song of winter nights—to linger on.

Except for Solo and her fawns, who lived at Hocoka year-round, the rest of Hocoka's winter deer began to gather around the cabin right after the lake froze.

Here was the locus of their winter life and blood—on rocks, trails, glittering lake snow—more here by traditional right than my transient mortal passing.

Freeze-up itself could arrive as suddenly as a subzero

cold front following a blizzard, or it could linger, taking days, held back by gusty northwest winds working channels, stirring water, throwing autumn's last waves against gathering shoreline ice. Although each freeze-up was different, with coves freezing before bays and bays before open water, general freeze-up rarely varied by more than a week.

On average, Otter Lake was frozen shore to shore by November 5.

Come cold night some years, I'd step outside beneath stars and listen to the lake ice cracking and whumping as it thickened. I could also hear ice whumping on distant Kawasachong, other lakes, and probably ponds: a symphony of whumps and whip-cracks, the landscape speaking, freezing, as night unfolded and winter arrived.

At other times, beyond the crackling of my woodstove's fire, I'd hear the ice's high squeals or deep groans, like whale songs, as the granite beneath the cabin rumbled with pressure.

Cooling now.

The top half of the earth was cooling.

Unlike summertime, when sunshine bathes and bakes the northern hemisphere, juicing its verdure, in autumn the earth's northern regions lie back, tilt away from the sun, present an angled face to its radiant source of life and grow darker and colder by the day. By mid-November at 48 degrees north latitutde and 92 degrees west longitude, Hocoka's approximate location (and, coincidentally, that of many biological wolf/deer studies), the sun rises a minute later each morning, veers a low arc of 25 degrees declination above the southern horizon (compared to June's 69-degree declination), then sets a minute earlier each evening.[20] By winter solstice in late December, what sunlight there is essentially strikes Hocoka a glancing blow at 22 degrees and ricochets into space.

Days, hence, are half as long as they are in summer, and considerably less bright, while nights are twice as long.

This makes all the difference in the world.

Winter's night season, with its deep cold demanding and sucking energy, a cold so pure it can freeze flesh in a flash, has arrived for a reckoning.

The deer *feel* this threat, this ultimate climatological challenge, and over the eons, from one generation to the next, they've evolved ways in their northernmost ranges to optimize their chances of surviving killing cold.

It is the onset of hard cold, in fact, that triggers white-tail migration.

Although whitetails are not technically considered migratory mammals, they do move to winter ranges. Deep snow is a consideration in terms of timing, for it can make travel difficult, but it's cold weather (and safe ice?) that usually determines whether deer linger on their summer range or head out.

This truth came home to me early each winter as the deer, alone or in small groups, began to arrive at Hocoka or simply passed through. Whitetail migration was one of the land's salient seasonal pulses. The far north had its caribou migrations, obviously awesome and spectacular out in the open tundra, yet the woods around me in early winter were also alive with moving deer. They were eva-sive, and often traveled at night, but you knew they were there, could see their sign, as they moved to winter homes.

Why, though, move?

According to whitetail biologist John J. Ozoga, only about 10 percent of northern deer range will support deer most winters. Most deer country, come cold, just doesn't have the browse and wind protection to favor life.

"Deer that subsist solely upon natural browse in winter," Ozoga explains, "are generally on a negative energy balance. To reduce their energy expenditure, they must have optimal cover where they can bed comfortably and remain inactive for long periods of time safe from predators."[21]

When deer depart for such cover, striking out on migration to winter yards, they sometimes make false starts. If cold weather turns warm, deer have been known to turn around—*oops*—and return to their summer range with round-trips up to fifteen miles. At other times they *delay* migration for inexplicable reasons. (Still good browse?) Fluctuations in movement seem normal, yet, sure as forty below, whitetails will eventually go where weather, time, and herd instinct lead them.

Migratory distances vary from region to region.

In the southern part of the United States, where whitetails find everything they need in one area, they're nonmigratory. This changes dramatically among northern whitetails where, in Michigan for example, they'll migrate thirty miles. A Minnesota deer, albeit in prairie country, is known to have migrated fifty-five miles. (The all-time whitetail migratory record is seventy-five miles, although a Kansas doe, responding apparently to wanderlust, is documented as having traveled 170 miles.) As for northeastern Minnesota, a 1976 study by R. L. Hoskinson and L. David Mech, using radio-collared deer, came up with average whitetail migrations varying from six to twenty-four miles.

The route is sometimes direct, with deer hardly pausing to eat. At other times they mellow out, take their time, take a month to get to where they're going.

Matriarchal family groups usually migrate together as fawns follow dams (mother does) to traditional winter ranges. Thus fawns, through imprinted memory, learn the way to winter areas time-tested for survival. Orphaned fawns will travel with related kin. Yearling bucks seem to have two choices during migration: reunite with their dams (who drove them off earlier in the year when they delivered new fawns), or link up with the big guys, the older bucks, who form gregarious fraternal groups after the autumn rut.

Less is known about buck migration than matriarchal clan movements. Mature bucks likely migrate alone, often—like most moving deer—under cover of night, while others might migrate in small groups, probably young ones following an older, experienced buck who has already established his dominance and is willing to do so again.

The bucks that arrived at Hocoka, like Ruff, White Eyes, and Dusty, appeared to arrive alone. They came from the northeast, likely the Boundary Waters Canoe Area Wilderness a short distance away, and such a sight, if seen, their coming: heads up, footing sure, and antlers poised for combat. With their charged vitality and edgy attitude, they seemed to know exactly where they were, where they had come from, and what—if they had any say—was going to happen next.

By the time the bucks and migratory does reached Hocoka en masse, usually mid-December, they were already deep into their winter physiological changes.

Their fur coats, for example, had molted.

Biologically, as autumn days become shorter and ambient light diminishes, a deer's pineal gland releases the hormone melatonin (particularly at dusk), which, in turn, modifies the amount of another hormone, prolactin, released by the pituitary gland. The photoperiodic result triggers a deer to shed four or five pounds of summer fur and, during a span of approximately three weeks, grow a new coat. The new hair, unlike summer's solid hair, is hollow and filled with air for insulation. The longest guard hairs are over two inches long with densities of almost three thousand hairs per square inch, or about three million hairs on an adult deer. Beneath the guard hairs, up snug against the body, is a new layer of fine, woolly underhair.

For additional warmth, deer tighten microscopic skin muscles attached to hair roots, thus "fluffing" their hair and trapping extra air for insulation.

Another whitetail physiological preparation for winter, also prompted by photoperiodism, is the buildup of body fat. So imperative is this as an energy reserve against the cold months ahead, that a deer—particularly fawns—will stop growing in autumn and, metabolically, transform nutrients into fatty poundage. Does, especially those without milk-demanding fawns, will put on fat throughout summer and fall. Bucks, too, fatten, although they'll lose 20–25 percent of their body weight during autumn's rut, thus beginning winter almost more debilitated than strengthened.

Fawns have the greatest challenge. Not only must they eat enough their first summer and fall to grow (from six or seven pounds at birth in May-June to almost one hundred pounds by late December), but they must lay-away fat for winter survival.

The equation, really, is simple.

Fat is banked calories. Fat is stored energy. Fat—come February's deep cold and March's general exhaustion—means life.

I had to name the deer as they entered Hocoka's winter sphere.

Although naming deer seemed and sounds juvenile, Bambi-ish, something for humorist Garrison Keillor to poke fun at on a Saturday evening, what was a man to do?

If you speak or write about something, you must (1) point, (2) give it a number (like Aldo Leopold did with chickadee 65290 in *A Sand County Almanac*), (3) use its already existing name, or (4) my option, take a chance on a new name.

A name helped me think more clearly about a specific deer, jot journal notes about him or her, mark my calendar with phenological observations, and say hello come morning, sunset, or whenever our paths intersected. Along the way I kept in mind what Chief Dan George once said about talking to animals:

"If you talk to the animals they will talk with you, and

you will know each other. If you do not talk to them you will not know them, and what you do not know you will fear.

"What one fears one destroys."[22]

Could it be that naming a deer is a show of respect? a manner of paying attention?

Might specific identification be the first step toward intimacy and talk?

I tried naming the deer based on a physical or behavioral characteristic, something true of an individual, something it did, or anything, really, that made an individual's "deerality" stand out.[23]

Deer, one learns, are not *just* deer: look the same, act the same. Like a dog, cat, or any animal, deer have individual traits. Each is a specific manifestation of unique genetic, physiological, environmental, and social alignments.

Solo got her name, of course, from being alone, whether as a fawn left to luck and mercy on a trail, or as the lone, snow-shrouded silhouette stepping toward me on a blessed day.

With Solo's first fawn, however, her name became a misnomer. Moot. Turns out Solo was just too fecund to remain alone for long, no doubt causing buck fights no human saw or dreamt. Over time, and from one winter to the next, Solo had many young: the twins Blacky and Moon, for example, or singles like Scratch and Saut.

I'd often meet the fawns for the first time around freeze-up. I might have caught a glimpse of them as spotted fawns in summer and autumn, with Solo hiding discreetly back in the dense greenery, but not until the bare, cold, season of ice did the fawns, with Solo, slip into Hocoka's more obvious view. The fawns were just learning life. At first they were skittish and afraid of me, their instincts strummed with nervous fear: tail up, bolting off, "I'm outta here": running down the ridge toward the lake or out onto the ice itself.

Tung . . . tung . . . tung, their little hooves went as thin cove ice drummed the perky gait of fawn: *tung . . . tung . . . tung.*

As Solo, meanwhile, stood her ground and watched my every move.

The fawns, seeing this, would return, stand near Solo, and a new acquaintance began.

To name the fawns, as was my way, I'd look at them carefully: their faces and foreheads: buck or doe?: trying to see if there was any swirling fur announcing antler pedicel. And I'd watch how each fawn moved, carried itself, and reacted with Solo or to their mutual surroundings.

Or I'd look for a special incident as the thought of naming arose.

Saut, for example, leapt over a branch of a wind-fallen tree when I asked playfully what his name was. I named him *Saut*, French for leap or jump. Tag, Solo's first apparent fawn, was always tagging along behind her. Moon had an oval face. Blacky's facial fur was blacker than normal, while Bandit's dark facial fur seemed to form a mask around his eyes. Speedy ran among and around the adults—avoiding kicks, scoring food—quick as a flash. Scratch scratched his cheek with his right rear leg at a critical naming moment.

Noticing what was unusual, something original, was part of the fun, and the deer didn't seem to care.

Who knows what, if deer do such things, they named *me*?

Maybe they gave me a number like the National Park Service did in summer.

Worse yet, maybe they called me something I was better off not knowing: a name that would've rasped against my sense of romance or, if deer could laugh, would've had them chuckling and guffawing like a bunch of north woods monkeys living it up at my expense, in more ways than one, back in the bush.

Newly arriving adults, meanwhile, whether bucks or does, were named the same way if they stayed around long enough.

Princess's eyes were narrow like those of an oriental princess.

Cinnamon had an unusual cinnamon color to her fur.

Precious, well, she was just plain precious enough to warrant linguistic affection.

White Eyes had conspicuous rings of white fur graying around his eyes.

And so it went, the deer weaving their web, names surfacing, perhaps all of us little knowing what intricate fate we would share in the days ahead.

Except Solo.

In her forthright gaze, looking as she did from her salient, maternal rule, there seemed a knowledge encompassing the past, present, and what was yet to come. It made me feel a little naked, a little nervous, as if she knew the wolves that passed through the neighborhood were not really the wolves I, unlike her, needed to worry about.

Other wolves in different guises would knock on my door looking for Little Red Riding Hoods of the heart.

To Solo's credit, she kept her distance.

She never, over the winters, let me touch her, nor did she come to me if I was foolish enough to call.

She *would*, however, come to corn: even beseech it with presence and stares on the coldest of winter days.

And, once again, *"Belle wâwashkeshi,"* I'd oblige.

Even without fully knowing why—the pact I was making: a realization that took years to surface—I'd spread a mix of corn, oats, and molasses[24] in several locations: on and near a boulder behind the cabin, beneath a cluster of northern pin oak, on a small, log birdfeeder by the deck, and in several spots between the cabin and lake. Only by spreading the feed in small doses in each area, rather than dumping it all in one place, were the smaller deer likely to get any.

Thus I meddled with nature.

It was a gesture toward whitetail winter survival, however, that developed naturally, perhaps synchronistically, when Solo and her twin fawns, Blacky and Moon, began raiding sunflower seeds from birdfeeders. Then one night, near Christmas, I stepped outside the cabin onto its small deck lit with lamp-glow spilling through windows. Thick snowflakes fell gently out of the darkness. And there were Blacky and Moon, side by side, with snow plastered on their backs and faces.

It was near midnight.

The fawns could have run. Instead they stood still in falling snow and looked at me.

Hey, their shy glances seemed to say, *aren't you the guy*

*with the good stuff? Huh? Huh? How come the birds get treats and
we don't? Why must we keep raiding the feeders?*

Which, by the way, are empty.

Huh? Huh?

Once again: What was a man to do?

Those fawns wanted food.

I opened the shop door, found the sunflower seeds,
and spread some outside in celebration of the holidays.

Blacky and Moon ate.

Within a few days of repeat performances, and as
Solo joined her young at the feeders, I realized corn and
oats were cheaper than sunflower seeds and likely better
for the deer. I bought a fifty-pound sack and sledded it to
the cabin.

Thus began a lot of work.

It was in this way, however, beginning with Solo's
emergence from the crest of an evolutionary whitetail
wave, and my taking her and kin to heart as family, that I
embraced Hocoka's central journey. I became part of a
wild web encompassing whitetails, wolves, and winters.
At first the dynamic merely fascinated me, then it ener-
gized me.

Inevitably, as the lasting snows came, it gave me life.

Snow Wonder

Partly Cloudy: 10° F: Barometer Falling

*Awoke this sunlit morning to thick hoarfrost on all
the trees and bushes, the beauty jerking me awake.*

*As I chored around, I kept glancing out the
windows at the sparkling frost. A gentle breeze blew
loose crystals through shafts of sunlight: sparkles
falling at an angle through sunlit space in front of
the cabin. The sparkling continued for hours, following the sun's westering glow.*

*When I fed the deer and birds, I caught some of
the crystals on my sleeve. They were stellar crystals, perfectly and infinitely formed, either loosened
by breeze from overhead branches or crystallizing
in open sky.*

*Words stop on the edge of such beauty: the
tongue fails, slipping into clichés, although the
heart and poet try: try to describe this glory.*
—journal, Hocoka, Winter

The snow that fell on the
dead yearling, as wolves and
ravens fed, did not obscure the realization there's a deli-
cacy to snow—the unequivocal wonder of it—that melts
the hardest, most hammered, heart.

For if there is magic and challenge in the whitetail's
world, perhaps—as with northern peoples—it rests in
the miracle of a snow crystal. If there is ineffable beauty

in the wolf's universe, as there is everywhere and always, perhaps it blooms in that meteorological instant when water vapor freezes into hexagonal plates, dendrites, and stellar shapes.

Lumped together, crystals form snowflakes, and it is there—coming down, swirling around, drifting—one finds the ageless white edge of winter's mysteriously changing world.

The deer can feel this edge. The marten and wolf can. The fox can as it curls to rest in falling snow: snowflakes settling onto the fox's shoulders, its back, and, beyond, into the fox's fading tracks. Even black bear sleep in response to ice as ravens sweep higher, lower, circling 'round through snowy, eagle-free sky.

Winter is a world, as a native northern Minnesotan, I've known all my life, yet it was at Hocoka where snow truly came home to me.

I began to see cold, snow, and ice in all their power.

In snow's brilliance was the alpha and omega of Solo's life and all her relations. Snow accepted tracks, reflected sun, and responded to the subtlest changes of temperature. Its arrival signaled the beginning of a half-year voyage. Its departure in spring brought great drama, outer and inner, to a close. Snow hid and held. It came in beauty like a shadow of the glacial past. It left only at the touch of spring's sunlight to fill lakes with freshwater.

I was born to snow on a March day and so snow, cold to touch, has always whirled on the outer edge of life's embracing, welcoming warmth.

In time, like the Quetico-Superior's native peoples, I

would number my years by winters known and survived. Winters were chronological touchstones. Almost anyone, after all, can survive summer with its warmth and plenty.

Winter, like wolves, culls the weak.

"I have seen eighty-seven winters," an Ojibwe elder might have said around a lodge fire two centuries ago as snowflakes fell outside in moonlight. "Listen to me. When the snow stops, and the deer flounder, the young must hunt. Now we wait, conserve our strength, and grow determined as stomachs growl. Remember hunger brings vision. Gather firewood for the old people. Leave them the last of the food. Prepare snowshoes, arrows, and, those who have them, guns. The time is coming when we must go and take what we need if given us."

Soon there would be flecks of blood: bright red on white snow near snowshoe tracks.

Bloodshed could not be helped in the northern forests where birch, fir, pine, and cedar wove a home where people needed meat. Fish and wild rice were good. Moose, caribou, elk, beaver, and especially *wâwashkeshi*, deer, were better.

Snow, eternal as fire, was the common element binding people and prey. It was foe and ally. White: intricate: powdery: crusted. Radiant in sunlight: dulling in twilight. Snow—like rain, or the baking of sunshine on musty autumn leaves—was a given, although there was a difference.

Snow lasted half a year. Six months. Six full moons.

The warm seasons, in comparison, were ephemeral. They responded to the hot flashes, the sharpened

seasonal angles of sun, and did not know—like snow—
the implacable endurance of cold, crystallizing space.

Snow, of course, has always been more than what is
gathered from concise dictionary definitions.

Yes, *snow* is a noun referring to intricately branched
hexagonal forms. And true, meteorologically, snow is
precipitation in the form of ice. The physics of a snow
crystal, as Ruth Kirk claims in her book, *Snow*,[1] might
even consist of a hundred million molecules, each with
an oxygen atom at the center of two hydrogen atoms
held by electric charges at 120-degree angles from the
oxygen atom, yet, even as a boy in that world of electric
white, I knew that snow is more than what science
teachers and dictionaries said it was.

Everything always is.

Northern friends and I, aswirl in a world of white,
opened our mouths to catch falling snowflakes on our
tongues. This was joy. We swept arms and legs in snow
to make snow angels. We shoveled snow, and formed it
into balls with our hands to throw impulsively at targets:
girls, cars, trees, girls, each other. We packed it to play
street hockey or, grounded at home, swept snow off
steps. We watched snow fall in the truant light of night
streetlamps and the glow of neighborhood windows. We
watched snow, from the warm side of those windows,
simply fall: a special peace coming down: *School called off?
A whitened, free day falling out of nowhere?* We brushed snow
off bicycles and cars in morning light. We fell in snow:
head over heels. We trudged through snow at 5:00 A.M.
to Catholic mass, sledded on snow, rolled in it, and ate it
for water.

Some dads plowed the stuff.

We rubbed snow on the rosy cheeks of sweethearts, or got it shoved inside our collars just before a kiss.

Inevitably, we grew up to ski on snow. We've walked on it with snowshoes when snow lay deep. Perhaps some of us have even skidded off snow into the ditch, our car's tires slipping, nothing to do but steer into the slide, hands on the wheel, life taking one of its little side-slips over the ice crystals into ditched destiny: a moment of cool, maybe, or solitary panic, but everyone, by god, *should one survive*, is gonna know the reason why.

Snow.

In English, the word comes from Anglo-Saxon *snaw.*

Snow is *schnee* in German. *Chion* in Greek. *Neige* in French. *Gôn* in Ojibwe.

No matter the name, we've seen it swirl in the light of hazy moons. We've rolled snow into snowmen: stuck rocks and sticks in heads for faces. We've studied tracks in snow: *Dog or wolf? woman or child?* We've heard it squeak beneath boots more times than we can count, and we've felt it sting eyes during steep downhill runs. We've camped on snow, stood on its compacted glacial tongues, and watched snow avalanche down slopes.

Perhaps, in some of our most memorable hours, we've even seen snow close up.

There was wonder.

There—whether on ski jacket, parka sleeve, or snow-sugared deer on a snowy day—was beauty sharpened and crystallized into astonishing shape.

We must, then, consider quite closely the crystal.

There are probably hundreds of kinds, yet, obsessive

classifiers that people are, in 1951 the International Commission on Snow and Ice simplified crystal classification (begun in 1681 by Italy's Donat Rosetti) by recognizing seven basic crystal groupings:

Stellar crystals: six-pointed stars radiating out from a center: the classic shape, formed at temperatures between 6.8° and 1.4° F. The branches of a hexagonal snow crystal grow at an angle of 60 degrees to the stem and 120 degrees to each other, reflecting precisely the angle, in a molecule of water, at which the two hydrogen atoms slant off from the oxygen atom.

Plate crystals: hexagonal saucers of different designs, standing solo with no interlocking projections: reflecting prismatic light. They're formed at temperatures between 14° and -4° F.

Spatial dendrites: stellar crystals with feathery projections sticking up at right angles.

Irregular crystals: hexagonal plates joined together in asymmetrical shapes, probably the most common kind of snow.

Column crystals: formed in high, cold clouds, they are hollow six-sided tubes of ice with pointed or flat ends, some one-fourth inch long.

Needle crystals: slender six-sided columns with sharp points on ends, common, often forming conglomerate slow-falling flakes shattering on impact with a hard surface.

Capped columns: a column crystal that has fallen through warmer air where hexagonal plates formed on the column's ends, sometimes called *Tsuzumi* crystals because they resemble a Japanese drum. Capped columns sometimes have a third plate around their middle.

Seven kinds of crystals.

It was a nice try by the International Commission on Snow and Ice but the classification structure didn't satisfy scientists for long.

Having a category like "irregular crystals," snow expert Edward R. LaChapelle explained,[2] was like having a file drawer labeled "miscellaneous": a catchall for everything not fitting elsewhere. For this reason, among others, C. Magono and C. W. Lee in 1966 published a new classification system, this time identifying 101 kinds of snow crystals.

Included are scrolls, pyramids (rare), cups, bullets, plates with sector-like extensions, stellar crystals with needles, side planes, and radiating assemblages of dendrites.

Three-dimensional stuff.

Some of it rimed. Some of it lumped into graupel.

Magono and Lee added "germ" crystals caught in the first stages of formation. LaChapelle liked this. He thought the biggest classification improvement, however, was the category for "broken branches" or stellar fragments which—falling through space: broken edges like prisms flashing flecks of blue, red, green, gold— occur frequently.

Crystal shapes, in whatever form, are perfect manifestations of climatological conditions.

They reflect temperature (32° to -39° F), barometric pressure, humidity, and, some say, velocity of fall. Warm air with much moisture is disposed toward stellar crystals. Cold air with little moisture creates the smaller crystals like plates and columns. All are electrically charged, radiate heat as they form, and create minute convective vortices on their surfaces that help explain symmetrical growth.

Other factors help create snow crystals.

Because crystals usually fall through a variety of atmospheric conditions, a hexagonal plate might extend stellar arms before falling through conditions that form new plates. Updrafts recirculate crystals through clouds; jounced around, crystals thin or thicken with ribs and ridges. Wind rips apart thin stellars. Plates crash into columns. Needle crystals cut dendrites. This gentle havoc we sometimes hear.

Or is that snow striking snowy ground?

Caught in a maelstrom of climatological currents, minute microclimate differences can even cause opposite sides of a crystal to form differently.

Relatively few crystals are truly symmetrical.

Single crystal types fall for short periods. Mixed snowfalls are most common.

And at the heart of things?

Nuclei.

Snow crystals need specks of dust, volcanic ash, microscopic salt flakes, or micrometeorites around which to form. Spores work, as do bits of decayed leaves. Such nuclei are found up to five miles in the atmosphere and, one suspects, much higher.

There is snow on the top of Mount Everest.

Even shattered crystals serve as nuclei around which new crystals grow.

To test this, Vincent J. Schaefer flew a Fairchild plane over Schenectady, New York, in 1946. He dropped six pounds of powdered ice into the center of a long cloud. The cloud changed to snow within five minutes, then disappeared.

This process of crystal parts forming nuclei for new crystals, otherwise known as "splintering," generates most intense snowfalls.

Only recently have scientists discovered new, albeit less aesthetic, nuclei: bacteria. Laboratory cloud chamber tests revealed that two common species of bacteria—*Pseudomonas syringae* and *Erwinia herbicola*—have the best affinity for water ever observed. It's therefore possible that enough bacteria are blown off plants and thrown into the air by ocean waves to account for much of the world's snow.

Regardless of specific nuclei, snow crystals fall to earth in staggering amounts.

In the winter of 1970–71, more than 1,025 inches of snow (about eighty-five feet) accumulated on part of Mount Rainier, setting a record for deep snow. Thompson Pass in Alaska received 974 inches of snow in the winter of 1952–53. In one week in 1959, northern California's Mount Shasta Ski Bowl got 189 inches.

In one *day,* Silver Lake, Colorado, received 76 inches of fresh snow.

So snow comes down.

Fresh snow covers almost one-fourth of the earth each winter. In the Northern Hemisphere, snow falls on half of all land. So much snow falls in the mountains of the American West alone that snowmelt in the Columbia River system accounts for 26 trillion gallons of water come springtime: or, as snow scholar Cullen

Murphy put it, enough water to cover all of Kansas
knee-deep or raise Lake Michigan six feet.[3]

On average, ten inches of snow make an inch of water
and—goes one guestimate—it takes more than one
million crystals to pile snow ten inches deep in a two-
square-foot area.

And if all the earth's atmosphere precipitated as snow,
in a great cleansing washout, all at once?

It would blanket the entire planet with at least an inch
of snow.

Just enough for a deer's hooves to leave drag marks.

In some places, where snow is truly a way of life, it stays
year-round. More than forty-five million square miles of
earth lie under a constant mantel of white.

A Greenlandic myth, arising out of the snow culture
of the *Avanersuarmiut* ("people from the north"), predicts a
crystalline end to the world.

"It will begin," Peter Hoeg relays in *Smilla's Sense of
Snow*,[4] "with three extremely cold winters and then
the lakes, the rivers, and the seas will freeze over. The
sun will cool down so it can no longer create summer,
the snow will keep falling for a merciless white eternity.
Then one long endless winter will arrive and, finally,
the wolf *Skoll* will devour the sun. The moon and stars
will be extinguished, and a fathomless darkness will
reign."

Cool story.

As a boy, walking snow-drifted fields of ancient
glacial Lake Agassiz in northwestern Minnesota, I

would have liked to hear about wolf *Skoll* and the endless winter. I also would have enjoyed meeting Wilson "Snowflake" Bentley of Jericho, Vermont.

Bentley took an interest in snow about as far as it will go.

He was obsessed with it.

Between 1884 and 1931, Bentley shot more than six thousand photographs of snow crystals. Starting at age twenty, he used a velvet-covered tray to catch crystals and a microscope and old large-view studio camera to capture them on film.

His favorite crystals were the almost perfectly symmetrical six-armed stellars.

"I'd love to stay," he once told a host when hearing of a snowstorm and cancelling a scheduled lecture on his hobby, "but I can't afford to miss even one snowstorm."

Bentley, a farmer, was often pictured wearing an overcoat, woolen muffler, and old felt hat. He had a mustache. He lived in three cluttered rooms of a homestead occupied by his married brother and family. It is said Bentley liked to dance and play piano but everyone knew his true love was snow.

He took one hundred photographs of crystals on his sixty-third birthday.

Eventually, time and snow treated Bentley well. In 1931, over two thousand of his best photos were gathered together into a book aptly titled *Snow Crystals.*[5] The book was a track of his love, life, and, more than anything else, established his worldwide reputation as the "Snowflake Man."

He might have enjoyed—who knows?—a good

snowball fight with me on the outskirts of boyhood's Red Lake Falls.

Other snowflake men have ranged from Russia to Japan.

A Russian meteorologist named Shuchukevich, around 1910, spent 176 days studying 246 kinds of crystals. He documented 37 kinds falling on a single day.

Two Japanese researchers, Ukichiro Nakaya and Y. Sekido, while studying snow on the island of Hokkaido, took snow samples during every snowstorm one winter in the 1930s. Even at temperatures below zero, they would catch twenty to thirty crystals on a piece of glass, distinguish their forms, then measure each under a microscope. They repeated the process a few minutes later, then again and again, driven by fascination with ice.

Nakaya eventually collected over two thousand photomicrographs of snow crystals but this wasn't enough. He had to tinker. Get trickier. In 1936 he created the first successful snow crystal in a laboratory's cold chamber, subsequently creating all types of crystals found in the atmosphere.

Snow was, and still is, so much a part of some cultures it's been only natural for a snow-based vernacular to take root and flourish.

Take Alaska's Inuit, for example, particularly those of the Kobuk River region, whose snow words have been passed down through the ages from generation to generation like mother's milk. As Terry Tempest Williams and Ted Major explore in *The Secret Language of Snow*,[6] the

Inuit have at least thirty-nine words for different types of snow.

There is *annui*, or falling snow.

There is *api*, snow on the ground. *Pukak* is unstable snow, actually depth hoar, what skiers call TG (Temperature Gradient) snow: looks like sugar. *Qali* is snow on boughs of trees. *Upsik*—hard, wind-beaten snow—forms firm surfaces for animals and people. *Qamaniuq* is the bowl-shaped snow hollows around the base of tree-trunks. Wind-shaped snowdrifts are *kimoagruk*. *Siqoq* is swirling snow blown in circling, spiral motions, mostly on ridges: what others might call snow-devils. Sun crust, or corn snow to skiers, is *Siqoqtoaq*: formed by warm days when crystals expand and become granular as they re-freeze at night.

There is *mauya*, breakable crust, and *sillik*, unbreakable crust. There is *nutagak*, fresh snow, *milik*, very soft snow, and *katiksunik*, light snow deep for walking.

The list goes on.[7]

Inuit, when it comes to snow, truly speak in specific, beautiful tongue.

Perhaps one of the most beautiful words for snow, however, is the Koyukon *duhnooyh*, an Alaskan word referring to clumps of powdery snow clinging to branches.

"In the old days," Richard Nelson says in *The Island Within*,[8] "pregnant women drank water melted from this snow, so their children would grow up to be nimble and light-footed."

Respect for snow and winter's cold power runs deeply among the Koyukons, Nelson explains. The elders treat cold weather "as a conscious thing, with a potent and irritable spirit. They warn the younger ones to speak carefully about the cold, lest they incite its frigid wrath. In the old days, children were even told not to throw snowballs, because the frivolity or annoyance could bring on bitter weather."

The Russians, too, have known snow and winter for countless generations, and have come up with their own vernacular.

Nast is icy crust on mature snow cover.

Vyuga, myatel, kurritsya, buran, and *pozemka* refer to snow blown around by strong winds in the air or on the ground.

A Soviet tribal hunter of the Altai or Transbaikal, says snow scholar Kirk,[9] would use a single word, *vyduv,* to describe a place that has been cleared of snow by the wind. *Zaboy,* in comparison, is a buildup of snow blown in a depression where it will likely stay well into the summer.

Reindeer escape summer flies in a *zaboy,* and graze in winter in a *vyduv.*

Closer to Hocoka, the Ojibwe of the Lake Superior region have matched anyone with snow words and phrases.

There was, at least in the old days, *sôgipo*: It snows. *Ishpagonaga*: There is much snow. *Bissipo*: It snows in small flakes. *Bidipo*: A snowstorm is coming. *Biwipo*: The snow begins to cover the ground. *Bimipo*: A snowstorm passes by. *Onâbanad*: The snow is crusty hard. *Nin ningwano*: I am covered with snow. *Nin kijobike*: I melt snow for water. *Nin mamitaam*: I walk in snow without snowshoes. And *gijipo*: It snowed enough.[10]

Amen.

Snow crystals, by whatever name, change shape over time, especially on the ground.

Crystals normally tend to round out their form as water molecules sublimate away from appendages, like those on stellar rays, to redeposit in notches between the rays closer to the crystal's center. Or, as scientist LaChapelle says, snow crystals "tend to change so that the ratio of surface area to volume will approach a minimum."[11]

The ideal shape?

A sphere . . . a grain of ice.

Process?

Equitemperature—or destructive—metamorphism.

As the number of snow crystals becomes smaller and individual size becomes larger, snow cover settles. As "firnification" progresses, vapor from snow closer to the ground rises up to colder layers forming new crystals. Some become much larger than the original precipitated crystals.

Cups, scrolls, and columns form. "Sugar" snow is created. If compacted and buried under successive annual snowfalls, grains of such snow bond more closely. Mechanical strength increases. Separate microscopic air bubbles form.

The result, if undisturbed by thaw or evaporation, is glacier ice, which covers 10 percent of the earth's land mass: ice hard enough to move rock, gouge ravines, and dig lake basins as it did, long ago, in the Quetico-Superior.

Although beautiful in form and word, snow in abundance—as I discovered at Hocoka—can be bad news for whitetails.

The first thing snow does is hold visible tracks for even the most inexperienced human hunters to follow. As the snow becomes deeper, a deer like Solo needs to raise her hooves and legs more, drag forelegs through snow, then, once snow is about eighteen to twenty-four inches deep, whitetails must bound: jump: to move around.

This takes a lot of energy.

Worse, snow deeper than thirty inches is generally immobilizing. Deer don't like this. They wallow and flounder in such deep snow, get essentially trapped by countless snow crystals, and thus become vulnerable to the first wolf, loose dog, or other predator that comes along.

Fortunately for whitetails, the progression of deepening snow is usually slow in northeastern Minnesota. Although thaws are possible anytime, winters are marked by long, cold, dry periods of arctic-air-mass weather encroaching from the far north: Nelson River country or, perhaps, the hinterlands of Eskimo Point clear to the Arctic Ocean. Not until this cold air is interrupted with warm fronts coming from the Gulf of Mexico and the Pacific Ocean, creating weather that is cloudier and warmer, do the lasting snows truly begin:

sometimes as early as late October. Twenty or more snowstorms, leaving an inch or more of snow, track through the region each winter. Snowfall depths can reach as high as twenty-eight inches in a single day, as it once did by Pigeon River near Grand Portage on Lake Superior, while total winter snow accumulation can hit 148 inches, about twelve feet total, as it did in the same area in 1936–37.

As ecologist Miron Heinselman explains in *The Boundary Waters Wilderness Ecosystem*,[12] however, average Quetico-Superior snow depths away from Lake Superior are much less. Most of the Quetico-Superior, and particularly its Boundary Waters Canoe Area Wilderness, is far enough away from Lake Superior to escape its snow-generating effect, and the land—like Hocoka—is generally about a thousand feet higher in elevation than the great lake. The result is cooler, drier air and snow-depths ranging from a mere twenty-five inches to an all-time high of 122 inches (tied near Ely in 1995–96). Average winter snow accumulation is seventy-five inches with snow covering the ground approximately 145 days a year, slightly longer near the Gunflint Trail.

Snow settles, of course, as crystals melt, firnify, or generally change shape. The fluff compacts. The resulting snowpack, usually peaking in March somewhere between eighteen and thirty-six inches (yet sometimes as high as fifty inches), is what delivers whitetails their bad news.

They're restricted to trails, can't reach browse without great effort, and usually by March they're burning what remains of their last fat reserves.

Solo and relations have prepared, of course, as best they can.

Their fur has molted, they've migrated to winter ranges, their metabolism has slowed, and they've sought shelter in yards where clans of deer and orbital bucks congregate to make, as a group, their last or enduring stand.

Whitetails, it must be underscored, are on a long, slow starve through winter. The energy balance gets tipped toward the negative as soon as the weather becomes severely cold and the deepening snows make travel difficult. The combination of cold and snow, which is hardest on deer, usually develops midwinter but can begin pronto at winter's onset, say in November, after a subzero blizzard dumps two feet of snow. Regardless, deer lose energy ground (fat reserves) all along the way until by March's deep snowpack the question becomes, What comes first, spring, with its succulent green plants, heavenly abundant, or starvation?

To maximize their chances of survival—when temperatures head for zero degrees, then lower, down to -20° F, then lower yet, to -40° or -50° F (*excluding* windchill), sometimes for days or weeks at a time, with daytime temperatures not even rising to the zero mark—when it gets this cold, deer restrict themselves to their yards, their winter hangouts, and, with their backs to the climatological wall, simply wait it out. Move minimally. Conserve energy. Endure or perish. That equation. For protection they prefer yards of northern white cedar (a favorite winter food), spruce, balsam fir, and, in northern Wisconsin and Michigan, hemlock. Stands of white pine, red pine, and jackpine also sometimes suffice. The important thing is uniformity of trees and a thick canopy of branches overhead: vegetation that will block wind, absorb the heat of sunshine and, at night, retain slightly more of that heat than woods elsewhere.

Studies have shown windflows, hence windchills, in lowland conifer yards can be thirty times less than in mixed stands of trees and up to two hundred times less than in windy uplands.

If deer want bright, daytime sunshine, they know where to find it: the nearest south-facing slope or hillside.

Deer yard populations can be as small as ten to fifty deer or as high as 43,000 (like the Mead Deer Yard of 360-square miles in upper Michigan in 1987). Yard sizes and populations are patchy, varying in shape like wolf pack territories over the years, or like the forest itself with its changing mosaic of trees.

At Hocoka, except when deer gathered for spring migration, the "yarded" deer population averaged six to ten. There were usually two or three matriarchal groups with attached yearlings and fawns, and one or two bucks on the periphery of things.

Stray deer, including old, grizzled bucks, sometimes passed through, as did gypsy does, but they didn't become a permanent part of the yard. Either they were on their way to someplace else, didn't appreciate my company, or Hocoka's nuclear whitetail herd simply drove them off.

Deer yards become more valuable to whitetails as winter progresses.

Trails, for example, become a network of accesses and

exits through deep snow. There are heavily used trunk routes and lesser used side routes. Trails connect sunny spots to bedding sites and browse areas. All of it, one suspects, is memorized, for deer learn how to move fast on these trails: racing down a long stretch or leaping over to an escape route.

Zigzag patterns can be stitched to lead up a ridge, down a steep slope, or anywhere in between.

Besides better trails, deer enjoy group vigilance when congregated in one area. There are more noses, ears, and eyes to detect the approach of trouble. This frees deer to relax more—to eat, rest, sleep, chew cud—which uses less energy. If wolves suddenly appear, deer pass the alarm, flush like quail in a variety of directions, and thus thwart the advantage of predator surprise with multi-directional flight and confusion.

Higher ratios of whitetails to wolves in yards also minimize chances of predation on any single deer.

And if deer die in yards?

At least they die together.

Snow crust changes everything.

By late winter, when hot sunshine (from gains in solar declination) and warming ambient temperatures melt the top layer of snow during the day, the melted snow often freezes during night's cold temperatures to create crust. If the snowpack crusts over, and a period of cold weather returns, the crust becomes a firm surface—varying according to climatological circumstance—providing some animals easy, fast travel while other species break through.

Wolves become especially mobile.

As Mech and L. D. Frenzel Jr. explain in "Ecological

Studies of the Timber Wolf in Northeastern Minne-sota,"[13] wolf mobility—due to firmer snow—generally begins a peak period in late February that lasts into April. Mech and Frenzel note how one wolf (1051) traveled 226 miles from February 26 to April 24; the odyssey began near Saganaga Lake at the north end of the Gunflint Trail, dipped southwest to the Two Harbors area on the northwest shore of Lake Superior, then veered northwest toward Grand Rapids. This was unusual be-havior, of course, for the wolf was probably dispersing into new territory (or simply stricken with wander-lust?[14]), yet the implicit point is that such a journey would likely have been impossible without firm snow.

At first, deep snow hinders wolves at least as much as deer. Slowly but surely, however, and until snow be-comes dense enough to hold a running deer, wolves gain the advantage.

The reason is weight-load on track.

A wolf's splayed paw can get twice as much support from firming snow, in relation to body weight, as the hoof of a deer. A relatively thin or weak crust, holding wolves but not whitetails, epitomizes this. Wolves can frolic and hunt at will. If deer, disadvantaged by break-ing through snow crust and bogging down, are further weakened by malnutrition, they're even more jeopar-dized: wolves will sometimes kill more deer than they can eat, keep going, then, if necessary, return to what the scavengers have left behind.

Thus snow, whether at Hocoka or its outlying regions, is often winter's arbiter of what lives, what dies, who goes where, and sometimes why.

Vapor-to-crystal-to-ice.

It is a wonderful process evoking beauty, joy and, as with the yearling, sometimes tragedy. Nor has snow gone unnoticed by many of North America's great writers.

For Thoreau, snow was the "great revealer." On it he read tracks of animals and people around Walden Pond. Poetically, snowflakes were chariot wheels fallen from a battle in the sky.

Thomas Wolfe, writing in *The Web and the Rock,* described a snowstorm that came howling down across the hills, sweeping in from the Smokies:

"By seven o'clock the air was blind with sweeping snow, the earth was carpeted, the streets were numb. The storm howled on, around houses warm with crackling fires and shaded light. All life seemed to have withdrawn into thrilling isolation. A horse went by upon the street with muffled hoofs.

"George Webber went to sleep upon this mystery, lying in the darkness, listening to that exultancy of storm, to that dumb wonder, that enormous and attentive quietness of snow, with something dark and jubilant in his soul he could not utter."[15]

Naturalist John Muir, who once studied snow crystals with a hand lens on the slopes of California's Sierra Nevada Mountains and Mount Shasta, wrote a chapter on snow in *The Mountains of California.* He noted how six-rayed crystals glint and chafe against each other in their fall through frosty air, breaking up into fragments.

Dry snow, he said, was "rolled over and over, beaten against rock ridges, and swirled in pits and hollows, like boulders, pebbles, and sand in the pot-holes of a river, until finally the delicate angles of the crystals are worn off, and the whole mass is reduced to dust."

For Farley Mowat in *Snow Walker,* snow is "the invitation that glows ephemeral on a woman's lashes on a winter night . . . It is the sweet gloss of memory in the failing eyes of the old as they recall the white days of childhood."

Even Loren Eiseley, archeologist, essayist, and philosopher, wrote of snowflakes in *The Immense Journey.* They were apparitions from a shadow world beyond nature. His insight began one night as temperatures rose and needle crystals gave way to large flakes "floating in like white leaves blown from some great tree in open space."

Eiseley switched on his car lights to examine a single crystal on his sleeve before it melted.

"No utilitarian philosophy," he observed, "explains a snow crystal, no doctrine of use or disuse. Water has merely leapt out of vapor and thin nothingness in the night sky to array itself in form."

Eiseley found this amazing, as must we all.

The process of crystallography might be understood, but there is no logical reason for the existence of a snow crystal. They come to us magically, mysteriously, and always wrapped in beauty. Because of this, whether snow falls on the lashes of a beautiful woman, on the ground beneath night sky, or on the backs of deer and wolves as they go about their way, we're left with an abiding sense of wonder.

It's an awesome sense, a bitter-sweet resonance, strong enough to soften the edge of darkness and melt the hardest heart.

Singing Snowshoes

A Few Stars: 35° F!: Barometer Falling

Snowshoed up Rainbow Ridge midafternoon,
partly for the balmy joy of being outside in sunny
breeze.

Snowshoed back down to the lake then east-
northeast along the shore to Wolf Point, but no fur-
ther: the snow past Wolf Point was a six-inch
covering of dark gray slush.

When I turned to come home, backtracking,
I faced the sun's low, gold light. Sun setting: bright.
A strong wind out of the west blew across the sur-
face of the lake, sending fine hissing sheets of snow
toward me, swirling wafts of crystals flowing and
swirling and finely hissing as they passed me, light
and crystal in winded motion, starting afar and
sweeping past: windwaves of icy bright.
—journal, Hocoka, Winter

As Solo and the other deer adjusted to the wonder and rigors of winter snow, heeding the call to migrate or yard up and hunker down, I took to snowshoes.

They were the only way, sometimes, to travel.

Either snow was too deep to walk in or skis sank too far, and so, if I wanted to go winter's pathless way, really step out into the wild—track wolves, deer, and their weaving mystery—there was often only one choice.

My French-Canadian ancestors called them *raquettes*.

Their Ojibwe neighbors and cousins called them
agimag.

And as I strapped on my snowshoes, fingering the stiff
leather and buckles with cold fingers, I'd often think of
Kagagengs (Little Raven), a hundred-year-old Ojibwe
storyteller of Lake Superior's Keweenaw Bay many
moons ago. Although ethnologist Johann Georg Kohl
wrote about Kagagengs in *Kitchi-Gami: Life among the Lake
Superior Ojibway,* too little has been passed down through
the ages about the old dreamer.

We do know this, though:

He was born in the mid-1700s at Lac du Flambeau,
Wisconsin, which he always—no matter how far he
went—considered home. He didn't move north to Anse
Bay of the Keweenaw until there was a Catholic Mission
there. It's hard to tell from the scant record if he went
there to try saving his soul or whether he was tracking a
woman. It was there, anyway, he met Kohl, who dogged
him with an ethnologist's curiosity. Kagagengs liked to
collect herbs, Kohl said. Meeting someone, he'd use the
salutatory *Bojo* (hello: good day), probably a mix of the
French *Bon jour* and Ojibwe *Boozhoo,* L'Anse being *métis*
country.

Kagagengs looked old, wrinkled, dark, and smoke-
dried.

He also had a good sense of humor.

As the self-proclaimed best hunter of his tribe, he said
he once killed eleven hopping squirrels with one shot.

"Not a soul believed this," Kohl said.[1]

Somehow, I seemed to know Kagagengs and where he
stood.

Whenever I went snowshoeing, it was easy to imagine him next to me as he wrapped a second blanket around his shoulders before tightening the rawhide laces of his own snowshoes. Thus Kagagengs lived on in my winter mind. He, too, had snowshoed to water holes. He, too, had snowshoed to woodpiles or gone snowshoeing for its sheer sunlit pleasure. He had seen one hundred winters, had walked the treacherous ice of Lake Superior and inland lakes countless times, and had rejoiced in a century of Aprils.

April, Kagagengs knew, was the month of the moon for getting rid of snowshoes. With snow melting and easy spring coming, snowshoes weren't needed anymore.

Yet it was not April for that old man when I snowshoed with him. The frequent gray skies, thickening ice, and deepening snowdrifts would have reminded him— and all snowbound natives—that it was, indeed, winter: *bibôn*: with its bottomless cold, short days, long nights and, forever it seemed, snow.

It was time for *anishinâbe*, the people, to wear snowshoes, not break them.

Hard work, this figuring. On some days, if Kagagengs concentrated hard enough, he could recall the open, crystal clear waters of Lake Superior, the dancing flecks of sunlight on waves, and the gales that could swamp canoes and drown warriors. He liked to think about it, talk about it, but it took so much mental energy. Most days, as when he snowshoed with me, his whole life, his hundred years, seemed the story of something else.

Snow.

Frozen water.

Winter, after all, lingered on. And on. And on. Its

whiteness blinded and brittled. There were days, sitting outside in sunshine, when all Kagagengs could see were shadowy figures shuffling among the brightness surrounding his birchbark wigwam. Of course, he was an old man, eyesight failing. It had been a long time since he'd seen individual snow crystals, countless crystals, settle on his deerhide leggings and jacket sleeves. A long time since he had watched snow in the moonlight . . . large flakes drifting down, spawned by passing clouds.

Kagagengs had liked that.

As my Kagagengs finished lacing his snowshoes, and stood to face wind, perhaps it crossed his mind that two hundred miles west of where he stood, other Ojibwe, in today's Minnesota, were dancing.

They were *celebrating* snowshoes.

As many as ten men, all wearing snowshoes, might have been stomping and leaping around two upright poles from which dangled another pair of snowshoes. Known as the Snowshoe Dance, it was performed at the falling of the first snows of winter.

Craziest thing.

Yet there was reason for celebration and thanksgiving.

Without snowshoes, the people would have perished.

Food and snowshoes were closely related among North American natives wherever snows were deep and lasting.

Cold, snowy winters over much of the continent meant hunger, and hunger—like necessity—spurred invention.

Although anthropologists suspect snowshoes were developed in north-central Asia about five thousand years

ago, Native Americans either invented them indepen-
dently or brought them nomadically from the far northwest. Any natives crossing the Bering Strait between
Siberia and Alaska fifteen thousand to eighteen thousand
years ago likely had some version of snowshoes with
them. Invented or refined, the evolution of snowshoes
was one of the most important steps forward in human
foot travel and unique to the northern hemisphere.

The use of snowshoes apparently evolved on only
three continents: in Siberia, northern Europe as far west
as Norway, and North America.

"Its invention," K. Birket-Smith observed as early as
1929, "meant nothing short of a cultural revolution in
the boreal regions."[2]

Canada's Chipewyan, for example, learned how to
survive by bending the bush to make ends meet.

Their inhospitable wintry range extended from
Churchill, Manitoba, on Hudson Bay in the east, north
into the Northwest Territories almost to the Arctic
Circle, west to the shores of Great Slave Lake, and south
to central Manitoba and Saskatchewan: five hundred
miles east to west and six hundred miles north to south.
Big country. Known as the Barren Grounds, it was—and
remains—a merciless land of glaciated rock and boulder-
strewn river valleys. Highland areas have little or no
vegetation. Valleys are dominated by lichens and
mosses.

Summers are short: winters long.

It was perfect caribou country and a land met best on
its own terms.

Those terms were law for the Chipewyan for almost a
thousand years, ever since they apparently left the cradle

of Pacific Athapaskan peoples to migrate eastward around 1000 A.D. They became known as Caribou Eaters in the Barren Grounds. Cree called them Chipewyan, meaning "pointed skins," a reference to the dangling point on the back and front of the caribou skin ponchos of the men.

The Chipewyan called themselves "Dene," or "humans," and grew to a population of about thirty-five hundred people.

Caribou and snowshoes were their lifelines to survival.

Although Chipewyans killed many caribou in summer, winter was the season of reckoning. If meat became scarce, as it often did, Chipewyans would turn to berries, mosses, rose hips, and, under severe conditions, to their caribou clothing.

Cannibalism—known and feared—was the last resort.

To ward off such dire straits, Chipewyan pitched winter camps on the northern edges of forest where they tracked caribou. Hunters used snowshoes of birch and *babiche*: thin, dehaired strips of caribou skin. Men made frames. Women laced the *babiche* into place with eyed needles. The results were snowshoes that hunters could run with. They'd jog along for hours at a pace faster than they could walk. Caribou, once found, were tracked and harried until they floundered exhausted in deep snow.

Then hunters would kill them.

Moose, too, were killed this way: pursued to death.

But moose were rare in Chipewyan country.

Things weren't much different in the relative Banana Belt of northern Wisconsin and Minnesota, among Kagagengs's people, who also had real need for snowshoes come wintertime.

Snowshoes were as necessary for travel in winter as the birchbark canoe was in summer.

This Kagagengs knew and, in his wise heart, he also knew it was right for his people.

Called *agimag*, Ojibwe snowshoes were made from *agimak* (ash wood) and rawhide webbing. The frames, of various forms and sizes (averaging a foot-and-a-half wide and five feet long, depending on the nature of snow and terrain), were kept in place by crossbars called *okanik*. Between the crossbars, thin leather cords were passed around the frames and woven into meshes closer in front and back than in the center of the snowshoe. The foot rested on a strong, elastic cross-cord of leather called a *bimikibison*, and was held in place by a band, strap, or walking thong, and an *adiman*, a heel-band keeping the foot from slipping backwards.

Snowshoes were often painted red, black, blue, almost any hue.[3] Colored tassels, *nimaigan*, were sometimes attached to the frames.

What color, then, flashing at the bottom of vision, sparking the white of snow, as an Ojibwe hunter, like Chipewyans to the northwest, ran down game. Elk were particularly susceptible to being chased. They broke through snow-crust while a snowshoed hunter, like a light wolf, glided over snow with relative ease.

Hunting tales, as a result, were near incredible.

Ethnologist Kohl was told about an elk chase by a hunter along the south shore of Lake Superior:

"He had been running [apparently on snowshoes] for

half a day behind an elk, and several times he had nearly caught it. But, he said, he did not wish to kill it, in order to save the trouble of dragging it home. Hence he sat down several times at some distance from the exhausted brute, gave it time to collect its strength, and regained his own wind also. After a few minutes he would begin his extraordinary chase again, and arranged it so, that the brute was driven nearer and nearer to his hut. At nightfall he had it near enough to his camp, so he went up, drew his knife, and killed it."[4]

Kohl confessed he would never have believed this story had he not heard of similar feats elsewhere and among other native peoples. People who relied on foot travel were good at it, he explained, whether it was speed, distance, or endurance. Food was procured this way, and in an emergency, a runner could be sent on foot or snowhoe to a distant village for help.

In some parts of Ojibwe country, snowshoes were made from long boards cut into the rough shape of a fish. An eye, or *oshkinjig*, was cut so the toes could move up and down. An outline of the foot was chiseled out of the board so the foot would fall back into correct position. Thus a man—hunting deer, woman, or vision— could get around over soft and watery snow.

He could also cross swamps.

Like the Ojibwe, the types of snowshoes used by the distant Nunamiut Eskimos of interior Alaska depended not only on terrain—whether a country was rolling tundra, rocky or forested—but also on the age, sex, weight, and activity of the snowshoer.

A large man traveling in woods might need snow-shoes six feet long and a foot wide. A child's first pair was usually a foot long by five or six inches wide. The most common size was four to five feet long and about nine inches wide.

Historically, before the first heavy snows of late fall or early winter, a Nunamiut man, like a Chipewyan, either made a pair of new snowshoes or repaired his old ones. The making of winter traveling equipment was the main chore—besides hunting—of the head of the house. Usually a father made snowshoes for a son in his late teens or early twenties, taking pride in skilled work.

The process was ageless:

A straight-grained birch tree was felled with a jade adz, preserved frozen or soaked in water until use, then the wood was divided into sections. Each was split into four equal pieces that were whittled into narrow strips. When the green strips were properly shaped, the ends of two strips were tied together, the middle was held apart by two sticks, and the fronts were bent upward by tying them in place with strong cord. After the frames dried three or four days, they were webbed in triangular patterns with rawhide line from cow caribou.

Rawhide line from bull caribou was laced lengthwise while line from bearded seal was laced crosswise for the foot.

There were two basic types of Nunamiut snowshoe frames. Pointed snowshoes were preferred by men because they could run faster on them. The Loucheux type, or rounded-front snowshoes, were used by women because the pointed models caught on their long parkas.

Men only used the rounded snowshoes when walking in brushy country.

Although the Nunamiut depended on snowshoes, most Eskimos didn't need them. They used sleds, or the snow on lakes and tundra became crusted enough to provide firm footing.

There were, however, other Alaskan peoples who used snowshoes.

The Kuskowagamiut of southwestern Alaska needed snowshoes for traveling in wooded country along the lower Kuskokwim River where snow was soft and loose. The only time they needed snowshoes on adjacent tundra was in spring when snow crust wouldn't bear the weight of a person.

Eskimos from the Bering Strait to Point Barrow used crude snowshoes for walking on new ice. Richard K. Nelson, in *Hunters of the Northern Ice*, described the snowshoes as "two feet long with a rudely constructed oblong frame, and webbed with widely spaced leather thongs."[5] Besides their use on thin ice, they helped a man get to where he needed to go over soft snow and the rotting ice of spring.

The Chilkat, too, needed snowshoes to travel inland in winter, when they traded goods with people of Alaska's interior. Their snowshoes were made of light maple or birch heated over a fire, shaped, then webbed with the universal rawhide. They were usually four feet long, ten inches wide, with rounded toes turned up at the point and, in back, a pointed heel.

Historians and anthropologists don't say much about that pointed heel, which works like a canoe's keel to keep the snowshoe straight. It drags in the snow, centers the movement forward, and helps balance a man or woman in situations calling for grace.

Even the Tlingit of Alaska's panhandle used snow-shoes, although more as a convenience than necessity. The panhandle's dense vegetation, with its 250 days or more of rain a year, made *summer* travel into the interior almost impossible. Winter's snow, however, when a man or woman could walk on it with snowshoes, offered hunting and trading options.

Snowshoes were not restricted to these scattered Eskimos, Chipewyan, Ojibwe, and other cited peoples. They were found among *all* Native American groups from California to Maine wherever snow was lasting.

Daniel Sutherland Davidson, in an extensive 1937 anthropological study, *Snowshoes,*[6] cites 158 North American tribes that used frame or wooden snowshoes.

The Plains tribes, for example, made three different kinds of snowshoes: the common "Michigan" type with rounded, slightly upturned front and pointed heel, like mine; a snowshoe with both ends pointed for travel in open, flat country like wind-whipped prairie, a style Chris preferred; and the oval "bear-paw" used by women but favored by men only for wooded and brushy terrain.[7]

Further west, a half-dozen native tribes in California used a widespread style of crude snowshoe for getting around when, otherwise, they couldn't. It was a simple hoop with a few cross-ties of grapevine or rawhide. There was no netting, no provision for heel play, and no keeling tailpiece. Modoc used them. So did Yurock men, along with knee-length buckskin leggings, when they headed into hills to hunt.

On occasion, too, Shasta hunters used snowshoes when they found elk too large to snare. The hunters chased the elk down in snow and killed them with arrows.

Elsewhere in California, Karok people made snowshoes out of hazelwood with iris-cord netting and buckskin ties for the feet.

Every condition, it seemed, like every need, had its winter shoe.

Less is known about East Coast tribes.

Although Iroquois of New York, Vermont, and southeastern Canada's Québec are known to have used snowshoes of hickory frames laced with strips of rawhide, sometimes snowshoeing as far as fifty miles a day, little else is known about East Coast snowshoes.

"The problem," Bill Copeley has explained, at least in reference to New Hampshire, "is that most of the New Hampshire Indian population died or migrated north before whites settled the area, so there is great scarcity of written documentation by their contemporaries."[8]

Copeley nevertheless figured that because the Abenaki tribes who lived in New Hampshire (and further north) shared most facets of Algonquin culture, including periods of deep winter snow, they likely used snowshoes.

An exception to the scant written documentation about East Coast snowshoes came from the pen of naturalist and artist John James Audubon. In *A Moose Hunt* (1833), he tells of a trip he made on foot hunting moose in early March near the Schoodiac lakes of Maine. He and companions traveled fifty miles the first day on a

horse-drawn sledge. The next day they *walked* sixty-two
miles. On the third day, they walked thirteen more miles
on snowshoes.

There, deep in Maine's snowbound backcountry, they
met a native of the Passamaquoddy tribe, named Louis.
He had, Audubon wrote, "abandoned the wandering life
of his race and turned his attention to farming and lum-
bering . . . Here we saw the operation of making snowshoes, which requires more skill than one might
imagine . . . The men generally make the bows to suit
themselves, and the women weave in the threads, which
are usually made of the skin of the Caribou Deer."[9]

Sign of snowshoes, then, from Maine through northern
Minnesota to Alaska.

Yet snowshoes, once so necessary, slowly lost their
grip on the native soul, the backcountry winter need,
when other means of survival and locomotion arrived
with Euro-American peoples. First came guns, which
shortened distances between hunter and prey. Then
came roads, cars, and snowmobiles.

Even among die-hard woodsmen and trappers, it was
Polaris, Ski-Doo, and Arctic Cat, not any diminishing of
snow, that changed the backwoods ways of the world.

It was left to the old men, the Kagagengs of the native
world, to remember the ancient ways as Chris and I did.
Snowshoeing—along with splitting firewood and fetching water through lake ice—tied us to the land. It also
wove our movements into the past and back again.
Whenever we headed out on snowshoes across the lake,
along Otter's shores, or into the snows of Hocoka's
adjacent woods—following dreams, nurturing hopes,

heeding our call—our steps echoed the steps of all native peoples and woodsmen who once had to get around in deep snow.

There was no difference.

The connection was complete.

And maybe the old storyteller, Kagagengs, knew this as he ended his outdoor hours with me, untied the rawhide lacing of his snowshoes, then leaned them against his wigwam as snow shone beyond. Perhaps he even remembered a Menominee song he used to hum called *Singing Snowshoes*.

In it, a man has a pair of snowshoes which, as he returns from the hunt, fly ahead of him, singing like birds. The snowshoes keep flying, winging, flitting forward, leading the way, until they suddenly swoop down the smoke-hole of the hunter's lodge.

It was a happy song, a homeward song.

The Challenge

Cloudy: 28° F: Barometer Falling

Ruff returned today after a two-week absence.
Looking fit. He challenged Dusty to a flailing
brawl which I broke up.

Both bucks were on rear legs striking at each
other.

Later in the day, as Ruff ate stray corn in front
of the cabin, Dusty came down the trail: his ears
back, fur all fluffed out, and looking for a fight.

Ruff took him on.

Both bucks stood on their hind legs, struck each
other with forelegs, and Dusty—hit in the
mouth—was driven off. He moved his lower jaw as
if hurt, testing it, then stood off to the side.

Ruff soon walked slowly north on the trail into
the woods, with Dusty following. Both bucks had
their ears laid back.

—journal, Hocoka, Winter

A buck once sang me a homeward song, and challenged me, in a way I'm not likely to forget.

At first, as he came straight across the lake cove toward the cabin, I thought the buck was Ruff.

It was early December, the buck was arriving at Hocoka about the same time Ruff would have—migrating right after freeze-up and rifle season—and he was good size.

He had four tines on each antler.

Strange, I thought. *Ruff's already been an eight-pointer.*

I had one of Ruff's old antlers on my windowsill. I picked it up and looked at the date etched on its side. He'd been a fork-horn six winters earlier. *Huh.* What would he be by now? A twelve-pointer? But there a buck was: an eight-pointer coming toward the cabin like he knew where he was going and late for breakfast.

His beams and tines were thick, the base a shiny chocolate brown, the whole rack held above a full, muscled body.

But which buck was it?

He didn't look old, or young, but strutting in quintessential prime.

Kagagengs, as hunter, as a man who also saw beauty, would have smiled at the approaching whitetail.

"*Wâwashkeshi,*" he might have said.

Morning, meanwhile, snowed.

Music added to the moment.

Just before I spotted the buck along the lakeshore, I'd turned on an old Yorx tape deck powered by a small solar system. The rich voice of Loreena McKennitt's *The Visit* filled the cabin with winter song. I'd turned, looked east out the picture window, and had seen the buck. Sure thing. He'd outlasted the wolves and bullets. As light snow fell, the buck came straight across the cove. Home-coming? *Riding music now: rising.* Up came the buck from the lake, straight uphill to the old feeding area in front of the cabin.

He scanned the ground, sniffed some yellow deer piss

on snow, licked the tips of stiff, straw-colored spears of grass, and looked around.

Nice.

If it *was* Ruff, he had arrived back at his winter territory after a migration from a place he alone knew.

Cold weather. Time to move. Hesitant starts. Then go.

Maybe the rut was over. Maybe it wasn't.

Thus this buck arrived this once.

The buck had me nervous by twilight.

He hung around the cabin all afternoon and into twilight's feeding time. Fine. But when I began to spread some corn, and walk the path to the westward boulder, the buck blocked me. He stood in the middle of my path, seemed to spread his legs and drop his head, then looked up at me before dipping his head again as if showing me his antlers.

As if he possibly had an ornery problem with me broaching his space.

"Ruff?" I asked.

The buck stepped toward me.

Whoa.

He was fearless.

Instead of bolting at my close presence like a wild buck would, certainly skittish Ruff, this buck had no apparent caution. Still, I needed to get past him to get at the boulder where I usually sprinkled feed. I stepped ahead on the trail.

The buck—bold—didn't budge.

We were close now, too close, and it made me think about those antlers and a buck's unpredictability during rutting season.

Bucks in general, by this date, had been earnestly seeking does in estrus—ripe for mating only twenty-four hours a year. So intent is the stalking of receptive females, the obsessive focus on sex: sex: SEX, plus the constant harassment of other bucks with like lust, that bucks almost stop eating and lose weight, burning fat in a frenetic arousal of higher heat. That heat spills over into a bad attitude, a horny careless edge, a hormonal willingness to test the shapes and strengths of things in a way bucks know at no other season.

Theirs, come rut, is a fighting spirit.

I'm fit, I'm ready, they seem to pose, except to does, *and I aim to be trouble until you and any other dissonance clears out of my face.*

Get it?

Besides fighting over does and related sexual territory, bucks will engage just about anything that rubs their belligerence the wrong way. Even humans, normally feared, can be a little too much for a buck's patience. As long as a buck's testosterone flows, which is about as long as bucks wield antlers, they will occasionally, and unpredictably, take people on.

It's their call.

"No buck," Leonard Lee Rue III underscores in *The Deer of North America,*[1] *"is to be trusted during the rutting season."*

I thought of this as I looked at the buck in my path, his antlers hard and sharp enough to give a guy in a parka at least good bruise.

Was it time for a new Jim lesson? some little jump of life out of the unexpected? some new textbook anecdote about a guy who got nailed feeding his pet buck? I didn't know what to think. The buck was larger than I was, acting out of context, and the only way I'd test his intent would be to walk right up to him, get in his face, and provoke either charge or flight.

Just like another buck.

The option didn't excite me.

I backed down, turned around, and brought corn to the front of the cabin for all the buck's sweethearts.

Late twilight, and the buck listened to my every move.

I'd look out the window and there he'd be: looking back.

I'd step outside, grab an armload of firewood, glance across the snowy top of a woodpile, and there he'd be: looking at me from the far side, his chin high, eyes alert, rack ready for peace or war.

I felt watched, surrounded, encircled.

Every move tracked. Every path covered.

Was a showdown coming, or would the buck just keep me hostage to my imagination?

When I was forced to sidestep the buck the next morning, as he again blocked my path and followed my every move, I had to consider the possibility the buck was sick or, more likely, acting from his center of hormonal belligerence and a potential aggression I had little experience with.

I thought fast.

A certain amount of aggression, I knew, is normal in bucks and, for that matter, all whitetail deer. They establish a dominance hierarchy through self-assertion with mature bucks—because of size and physical strength—at the top. When it came to food at Hocoka, whether the small amount I rationed or what grew abundant and wild all around, the larger, stronger deer usually crowded the young ones out.

This dominance dynamic has been studied at considerable depth by whitetail biologists, notably John J. Ozoga who roams widely in whitetail literature. Ozoga and assistants once studied aggressive, or agonistic, whitetail interactions at the Petrel Grade deer-yard in northern Michigan after fresh browse was felled by loggers in a conifer swamp.[2] The researchers spent ninety-seven hours during seventy separate periods observing 417 whitetail interactions as the deer essentially competed for food. Their aggressive body language (con-. firmed by my own observations of Solo and relations) seemed to form a chain of actions ranging from a threatening "ear drop" to "flailing."

The ear drop was a flattening of the ears along the back of the head and neck of an annoyed deer: first aggressive sign.

Next came the "hard look" or stern stare of an aggressive deer toward another, usually meaning "Get outta my face and space." If these threats didn't work, an aggressive deer sidled toward the other deer or rushed it altogether, sometimes snorting. This, according to Ozoga, worked 24 percent of the time to settle a dominance situation, as the charged deer ran off. If the charged deer stood its ground, however, or got caught off guard, the aggressor would strike out with a hoof or both hooves, often hitting the other deer. If the charged deer fought back, both deer stood on hind legs and flailed front hooves at each other.

Thump . . . thud . . . thump.

The flailing matches, never lasting long, were relatively rare (settling 4 percent of confrontations) but could be injurious. Even a strike by a single hoof might occasionally be lethal. Ozoga suspected a fawn with a broken back, found dead during his study, was possibly struck by a hoof.

The idea behind whitetail aggression, of course, when sexual competition isn't involved, is to drive competitors away from food. Hence the stepladder of signals and body moves. The resulting hierarchy has bucks 2.5 years old or more on top. Prime age bucks will dominate older, perhaps enfeebled, bucks.

Bucks, in general, dominate does. Does dominate fawns. Buck fawns dominate doe fawns.

Ranking lowest are small doe fawns.

"Although the frequency of threat posturing tends to increase among hungry deer towards late winter," Ozoga summarized in *Whitetail Winter*,[3] "the frequency of potentially injurious (and energetically costly) strikings and flailings decreases as winter progresses."

The established hierarchy, in other words, bears a survival advantage as it develops. Individual deer come to recognize each other as winter veers into its hardest, most demanding, months. Social rank is known. Confrontations, already settled, need not escalate into conflict, and although deer remain aggressive—keeping each other in place—they more frequently do this with mere ear movement or eye glance.

Precious energy can be conserved for true moments of peril.

Even as I reflected on Ozoga's work, however, with its scientific methodology and analyzed data, I suspected there were exceptions to normal whitetail hierarchies.

I had heard and read, for example, that does will even drive their *own* fawns away from food. My own observations indicated otherwise. During the thousand or more hours I watched Solo and her kind, Solo never drove her fawns away from food, or struck them, unless she became so worked up fending away other deer she struck her fawn in the melee by mistake. Or she'd raise a leg, preparing to strike, then catch herself as if *Oh yeah . . . it's you.* She normally shared food with her fawns, eating together cheek-to-cheek, sometimes letting the fawns eat first, and she drove away other does, yearlings, and fawns so her own young could score more corn.

This was particularly obvious one evening when I put corn out for Solo's fawns, Blacky and Moon, who were standing near a boulder behind the cabin. Off to the side was a new doe. Solo came up through the woods, walked past her fawns, and charged the strange doe: chasing her up over the ridge behind the cabin.

The hour was late and, as Solo bounded on top of the ridge, her body was silhouetted against the glow of the setting sun.

Perhaps only by watching a whitetail matriarchal group for a very long time might this doe-fawn dynamic become apparent.

Or perhaps Solo's situation was special.

I also noticed another exception to general knowledge about whitetail hierarchy. On a number of occasions, Solo seemed to have inherent top rank at Hocoka by mere right of year-round territorial occupation. Her proprietary status seemed recognized. Although not always the case, even migratory bucks larger than Solo often acquiesced to her dominance when they arrived and she confronted them.

They backed off.

It's possible such bucks had once been Solo's fawns so simply recognized their once-dominant mother.

Regardless, dominance among whitetails is different than leadership.

Mature does like Solo lead their family groups, with satellite matriarchal clans, while aggressive bucks—like the one trailing me—often find themselves avoided and alone.

I had to keep in mind that although doe and buck aggression is identical most of the year, bucks become increasingly belligerent as rutting approaches and arrives. Contact between bucks escalates from bluff and shove to all-out hostility.

Almost anything is possible when testosterone's flowing:

Bucks will crash into each other full-force and head-on.

They'll sometimes gore each other from the side or rear.

Once in a great while they'll fight each other to exhaustion and mutual death.

Occasionally they'll charge their reflection in large

glass windows or, as happened in Oregon, the reflective side of a car.

Deer kept as pets are no less rambunctious and unpredictable. Perhaps even more so.

John Madson[4] tells a story of a farmer who raised a whitetail buck in Michigan, allowed him to roam because of his docility, then put him in a pen near some dogs, hoping the dogs would absorb the buck's odor and stop hounding deer. Smart move? The buck charged the farmer and knocked him into a snowdrift where the man, grabbing the buck's antlers, yelled for help.

Two men beat the buck back with a wooden beam and pick handle.

Hoping to calm the buck down, the farmer put two does in the buck's pen. The buck injured one doe and killed the other. Soon the farmer put a spike buck (two years old with a pair of unbranched antlers) in with the rogue buck, which promptly killed the unfortunate newcomer. Finally a buck the rogue's size was put in the pen. Equal battle? The rogue buck killed his match. Not until the rogue's antlers were sawed off, altering the buck's testosterone level, did he calm down.

In another incident involving an allegedly tame deer, a 240-pound nine-point buck attacked his owner, Tyrie Boyer, on a private game preserve near Williston, Florida. Boyer was taking photos when the buck charged. The buck gored him in the left leg (five puncture wounds), right leg (three wounds), and gashed his left arm.

The buck didn't stop his attack until Boyer killed him with a belt knife.

Bucks will also turn their antlers against predators and sometimes kill them. In one instance, noted by biologists Michael Nelson and L. David Mech,[5] a nine-point buck killed a wolf in Superior National Forest on a winter day. Apparently the buck was being chased by two wolves but was cut off by two more wolves. Surrounded, the buck fought back. The buck gored a seventy-five-pound female wolf and punctured its rib cage, which filled with blood. The wolf died. The three other wolves killed the buck and apparently ate most of the carcass.

They left the bloody antlers alone.

For good reason, then, I was leery of the buck following me around Hocoka.

Soon an afternoon came when I went down to my winter trail, my *bibôn-mikanâ*, to cut some brush. December's snow was deep in the swamp so it was time to clear a path for skis and snowshoes. Like the nature of many winter trails, the *bibôn-mikanâ* was a shortcut un-usable in summer. The brief warm seasons meant pond water, peepers, and mallards crashing up through branches of black ash in excited, quacking fret. Bounded by granite ridges, the swamp's east draw trickled into the lake cove by the cabin. Alders. Willows. Small edge cedar. Swamp grass. Scattered living and dead black ash. It all belonged to fecund summer and autumn mornings of leafy gold, until the hard colds came. Then, with a solid layer of ice and deep, smoothing snows, I could get in there: nip some brush, cut windfalls, shovel snow into hollows, and improve my passage.

The buck watched me as I left the cabin, put on my snowshoes, and, with nippers in hand, walked away.

Reaching the middle of the swamp, I began to cut alders and throw branches aside.

Something behind me.

I turned and there the buck was.

He had followed me from the cabin. Seeing me leave, he had tracked me. A wild buck, whose kind had recently been hunted and shot by people, and he had trailed along behind me, approached me from the rear, and now stood a short charge away. I could have smacked him with a snowball. I'd had fawns and foxes follow me before, but never a buck in its prime on a winter afternoon.

Had I lured him with thrashing of nipped branches?

Hearing me, did he think I was another buck rattling antlers for a little rowdy action?

He stepped toward me.

The trail was narrow. I was on snowshoes. I would not be able to outrun this deer.

"No," I said to the buck in a stern voice. "No! We don't need this."

I stepped behind a couple trees.

The buck came closer.

I whacked a small tree trunk with the nippers, attempting a show of force. Size: strength: weapon: dominance. And I instantly knew I'd done the wrong thing. Another buck, welcoming a brawl, would have brandished the same signals.

Quietly, I squatted down on my snowshoes.

"No," I said again, although gentler.

And the buck, who I still thought might be Ruff,

looked off to the side—just a knowing glance away, breaking eye contact—as if it finally understood me. He stepped into alders and balsam fir at the edge of the swamp, climbed the side of a rock slope, and began to browse.

I stood, snowshoed to the far end of the winter trail, and nipped more brush. This time I was quieter . . . sticking the cut branches in mounds of soft snow.

He's back.

I turned, spooked now, for the buck was back on the trail a short distance behind me.

"No!" I repeated, using the repertoire that worked.

The buck, again with that knowing glance, stepped off the trail and climbed a snow-covered bluff. He was higher than me now. He could see me well. He watched me, I'm sure, as I judged my trailwork finished and snowshoed back to the cabin.

Taking his own shortcut, the buck was waiting.

He was waiting at the cabin for some twilight feed. Suppertime.

Although the buck had blocked my path at feeding hour before, it wasn't because he didn't want food. No, watching him now, he seemed if anything *eager* to eat, nudging out most of the other deer, even bossing Solo. Food wasn't the problem. No sign here for corn to stop. Clearly the buck was hungry, lean, wanting more. He couldn't get enough corn no matter how many deer he drove away, or how much ground he hogged.

This, I suddenly realized, is maybe why he'd blocked my path.

Perhaps he wasn't asking for a one-on-one showdown

to determine who was going to get good sex among does in the backyard, but that I was just a vessel.

I was merely the man with the goods.

Perhaps all the buck really wanted was first crack at what was in my little white bucket.

Or so the story, on a superficial level, might have gone if not for what happened a few days later.

It was getting late in the afternoon when I noticed a deer walk up to the birdfeeder by the deck. The feeder, just a small square of plywood nailed to the flat end of a short, vertical log held upright with stones, was pecked and licked clean. The deer saw me move and looked at the window of the cabin door. I looked back, puzzled, for the deer wasn't familiar.

Definitely not Solo. Not White Eyes. Not Princess, Scratch, or, clearly now, jaunty Ruff.

Then I noticed the bloody pedicels.

The bold buck had dropped his antlers.

It was *Dusty*.

A wave of something—tenderness? cherished memory? fondness for the beauty of a pleasant surprise?—washed through me in a rush of recognition.

Dusty had been an orphan fawn several winters earlier. He had just shown up at Hocoka one day. No dam. Out of place. Small and scrawny compared to Scratch, Solo's fawn. Dusty hung around, unconnected: lost and chased and bullied at feedtime. Soon he took a liking to Solo and Scratch. They, too, chased Dusty away from the corn. He hung in there, though, staying on the periphery of Solo and Scratch's action, and eventually they became a threesome.

Dusty's bonding was tolerated.

The next summer, when Solo was nursing a new fawn, Dusty and Scratch—driven away by Solo—were inseparable. They were two yearling bucks browsing their buddy way through an infinitely wide world of stomach, sense, and destiny. Keeping each other company. Watching each other's flank. By an August afternoon, when they snuck up behind me as I hammered deck nails, each buck had spike antlers sheathed in velvet.

Dusty, I noticed, was still scrawnier than Scratch.

This did not bode well for him the following winter.

I saw him chased away from what little feed there was. I saw him silhouetted in cold moonlight . . . nuzzling around snow for the last crumbs of corn or oats. I saw him just stand there, off to the side and, by February, his ribs were clearly showing.

Dusty was starving.

He was in that last long haul of a severely cold winter when, for a whitetail, what came first was either spring and fresh browse or death.

"Dusty," I'd say, "you're going to make it."

Sometimes, when circumstances allowed, I'd position myself between him and healthier deer so he'd get some corn.

"You're going to make it, Dusty."

And he *had* made it.

Seeing him now by my door—recognizing the mule ears and sharp, intelligent glance: adding his years and size—I suddenly felt honored and ashamed.

Honored by the sheer core gift of his sentient presence.

Ashamed of my forgetfulness.

Honored Dusty remembered me better than I remembered him, and that his trust lingered longer.

Ashamed of my fear: my edgy alarm.

Hadn't an old friend merely come around to say, in part, "Remember me?"

And hadn't Dusty's return affirmed a place which, woven together by winters, whitetails, and the wild passing of wolves, I'd come to love very much?

Yes, I had to say. *Yes.*

Heaven help me.

Hocoka had me now.

Dusty and Solo and the cold and the snow: the long nights and Kagagengs, the snowshoes and skis: the .357 handgun in my desk drawer and the wolves howling on distant ridges: it all had me now, challenged me fully, with a beauty and mercy I was just beginning to see.

BLOOD ON THE TRACKS

What do we ever know that is higher than that power which, from time to time, seizes our lives, and reveals us startlingly to ourselves as creatures set down here bewildered? Why does death so catch us by surprise, and why love? We still and always want waking.

—Annie Dillard, *The Writing Life*

The plants, rocks, fire, water, all are alive. They watch us and see our needs. They see when we have nothing to protect us, and it is then that they reveal themselves and speak to us.

—Morris E. Opler, *Memoirs of the American Folklore Society*

Your observation, to be interesting, i.e. to be significant, must be subjective . . . Senses that take cognizance of outward things merely are of no avail.

—Henry David Thoreau, *Journal*

An Ancient Tension

Cloudy: 30° F: Barometer Rising

Ruff here today, as he usually is, but this time around noon he bedded down behind the cabin. He chose the top of the granite knoll just beyond the large fir. He curled up once, nose tucked in his belly, otherwise rested head up, his eyes sometimes closed.

Never saw Ruff with closed eyes before.

It was different yesterday.

All the deer were spooked by something about sunset. Ruff ran past the picture windows left to right, and Solo broke into a run up toward the cabin and past the southeast corner. Moments later I saw a group of deer disappear in the woods by the ravine connecting ash swamp with lake cove.

Wolves? I wondered.

—journal, Hocoka, Winter

Yet deeper, toward blood on the tracks, and Solo, like a rifle scope, stood aimed and alert.

Her tail flicked nervously.

With her back to the cabin, her neck upright, and ears locked forward, she watched something I couldn't see, something through the thickly falling snow across the cove, something in the woods of the slope along Rainbow Ridge.

Something I was missing at my cabin table.

It was midday.

Silence, like soft snow falling, swirling: all around in the blanketing whiteness: another three inches on January's midwinter snowpack.

Morning's low of 1° F had inched back up, beneath clouds, to 27° F. The barometer was falling.

Next to Solo was a fawn. She, too, had stopped feeding to stare across the cove. The fawn raised a front leg and stamped it on the ground. Not hard, this time, from dire threat. Just enough this day, this moment, to somehow be noticed: seen, perhaps, or heard, or felt as tremors rippled out from hoof contacting frozen ground . . . tremors telegraphing other deer something was up, amiss . . . needed attending to.

Trouble was on the move and all deer better pay attention.

I stopped what I was doing and, as had become my way, looked more closely, for I had made a deal with the deer. Whether they knew it or not, I'd help with nutritious food and hunting season protection, be a kind of steward, a friend, live at peace among them, if they'd be a prism to the landscape.

And the deer were. I'd see them from my trails as I passed to and fro. I'd see the deer out the windows as I did tasks or sat in chairs, comfortable next to my stove. I'd see deer through a picture window by my desk. They slipped by in mirrors or—also reflected—on glass of favorite framed photos: Solo once moving through a June-green patch of blossoming bunchberry flowers with white bracts: *Cornus Canadensis* cast among moss, wintergreen, and pine needle: the image of Solo superimposed on a photo of another season like a faint memory, fleeting wind whisp, of another life.

I'd see the deer as I skied, snowshoed, chored around.

Even at night, while lying in the loft with its open window, I heard deer pass by the back side of the cabin, their hooves squeaking on compact snow in the cold of midnight darkness.

Deer everywhere like living land breath.

Deer circling me, entering me.

It wasn't so much they visited my world as that I lived in theirs. I had moved into their stream of time and created an eddy around which they adjusted, flowed, continued their indomitable being while accepting me and my implicit pact.

I looked, now, through their prism:

Thick, swirling snow whiting out the island and lake in the distance. Fresh snow on pine boughs, billowing, weighting the dark branches down. More snow on aspen and birch branches, on the ice of the cove, on fir, hazelnut, maple, and oak.

And snow, like deepening sugar, on the heads and backs of deer.

Still, their focus:

That radar lock-on so telling, the gift of sharp sense, the visual sensitivity to motion, smell as sensitive as a wolf's and, possibly, hearing eight times better than mine: that tightening of identification, the aiming, no question now, just the standoff: that watching that goes on watching because life depends on it.

My cabin and movements seemed of little concern to Solo and fawn. They might have flinched at a gunshot but they wouldn't have looked away.

I scanned the ridgeside with binoculars.

There.

Two wolves, one behind the other, meandered along the face of the ridge about halfway up. The wolf in the lead, with furry white facial mask, looked strong, large, healthy as it plowed fresh snow with its chest, following an old deer trail with a foot of new snow in the past month—or more, couldn't tell—the wolf placing each paw carefully, wasting no effort, angling uphill now, past pine trunk, knoll, snowbank.

Breaking trail.

The wolf in the rear, same brown color, looked thin, tired, its fur tufted, matted, mussed, all strength conserved, pausing to look around, conserved for the work of moving ahead, prowling, hunting, seeking what it needed at minimal expenditure.

Huh, I thought: Wolves on Rainbow Ridge.

The wolves walked slowly, sometimes slipping into full view as they looked across the cove or wove among balsam fir and brush.

If they saw the deer, they seemed to take no further interest as they switchbacked up the ridge and disappeared from sight.

The fawn looked away into the swirling light of distant lake then back at the ridge. Solo flicked her tail and, in one motion like two wings of a raven, doe and fawn took off behind the cabin.

A flock of ravens, like Solo and fawn, knew something was up.

Might they have been following the wolves?

The large black birds, near rulers of winter's sky, had circled and glided and circled on the northwest wind sweeping up the face of Rainbow Ridge. One raven had landed in a dead red pine as other ravens, swerving and dipping, settled in adjacent pines above the trail on which the wolves had passed.

Ravens, I knew, liked to feed on wolf-kills.

They scavenged carrion.

Hadn't they eaten a full third of the yearling I shot?

With the deer suddenly gone, the air was charged with predator presence. It was a tightening of energy, an up-rush of heightened sensitivity, a sure and certain knowledge that something dangerous that can no longer be seen isn't necessarily harmless.

Hunger for meat was on the move.

It sought satisfaction, needed to kill for it, and was willing to.

All life seemed charged with this ancient tension, this true, keen vibrancy, and although the tension eased this day it did not pass.

The deer were scattered for the rest of the day, and all the next, although one of the fawns, alone, showed up several times. Ruff, who had been hanging around in the moonlight, was gone . . . gone to wherever it was he hung out, bedded down, roamed, got away from the commotion that made him edgy: bigger bucks, wolves, people who carried rifles.

Soon: wolf tracks on the driveway.

Hunting conditions had to be hard with the deep snow. The lake, with slush between snow and ice, was essentially impassable. For the wolf, winter conditions sucked, and they'd take every road, trail and path they could to find what they needed to find.

Surely they were due mealtime.

It was, after all, the season of feast or famine for the wolf.

Although a wolf can go three to four days without eating, when a wolf gets a choice it will gorge up to eighteen pounds at a kill. Sometimes they'll eat a full fifth of their body weight at one time. There are aerial photos of the wolves of Isle Royale, same species as the Quetico-Superior's, spread out and lying flat on their sides, stuffed with moose meat. Looks like an American family wasted on couches after dinner on Thanksgiving Day.

On average, wolves eat a lot of food: five to ten pounds a day. They'll eat the muscle meat of deer, any fatty tissue, and crush bones with their powerful jaws to get at the marrow, swallowing bits of bone in the process. The same for wolves eating moose, beaver, and, as I saw one time, snowshoe hare.

I was out on the deck one evening (scoping the moon's Tycho rays with a telescope and looking for the crater Copernicus) when I heard an animal down on the crunchy snow at the tip of the cove. Soon I heard another approach on the lake and spotted a wolf through an opening in the trees. It, too, was on cove ice and heading for the cove tip's ravine. Then I heard a *third* wolf and saw it through the trees, the wolf just loping along, following the first two.

Snow was crusty loud as they headed into the woods. I stood very still.

In moments I heard the distinct crunching of bone and remembered a flock of crows had congregated in the ravine a few days earlier. Was a wolf-kill down there?

Bandit was missing.

When I checked the following morning, after a night

of northern lights, I saw immediately it wasn't a deer. Instead I found a string of entrail pellets from a snowshoe hare. The hare had apparently been bedded down beneath a small balsam fir when it was surprised or flushed by one of the three wolves. Not much left: scattered gray-brown fur, the strip of entrail, possibly the stomach, and part of the skull which was chewed to hard bone.

The hare, beneath moonlight, became wolf.

So will mice, which supplement a wolf's diet, along with grouse, squirrels, and bird remains.

"Wolves fish, too," Barry Lopez, speaking generally about wolves, says in *Of Wolves and Men*. They'll "wade-herd" salmon, arctic grayling, or whitefish "into shallow pools where they're trapped. They also mouth-spear them in swift water from the bank with well-timed lunges. They eat carrion and occasionally insects, especially when they encounter them in epidemic populations. And they feed on domestic stock. They hunt by intent but are opportunists, too."[1]

Occasionally, as I saw with Bojo back on Burntside Lake, wolves will kill and eat dogs.[2]

Wolves even eat vegetable matter, including grass, which can make up as much as 6 percent of their diet, albeit eaten as roughage, not for nutrition.

Where whitetails are abundant, however, as in the Quetico-Superior, as at Hocoka, forget the grass and fish. Scat studies indicate whitetails comprise up to 80 percent or more of a wolf's diet. Biologist Mech, arguably the world's foremost wolf expert, cites a study years ago by Milt Stenlund of Ely, Minnesota, showing that a group of three wolves will kill a deer about every four days.[3] Using this ratio, Stenlund/Mech postulated a large pack of wolves, say of fifteen, would need to kill .8 deer a day. That's over 140 deer during a six-month winter. That's a lot of life and meat.

If a deer population can't withstand such wolf pressure, compounded perhaps by severe winters and human hunting tolls, wolves are going to go hungry.

Which, of course, they often do.

Wolves are more or less *always* hungry, Lopez says.

Rare is the deer population that doesn't occasionally fall. Rare is the winter that doesn't bring slushy lakes or, as on Rainbow, deep snow. For the wolf, it's one thing after another getting in the way of a steady, dependable diet as they make their rounds, testing this trail or that ridge, sniffing bedding areas or catching scents, spending a third of their life on the hunt.

Hunting as the two wolves were in the falling snow of Rainbow.

I had seen that wolf-threat flick of Solo's tail before, that little wave side to side, that she and the other does used, even the bucks, among their repertoire of group signals.

It is the tail of the whitetail, in fact, that helps set the species apart. Longer than a mule deer's and blacktail's, it can, at approximately a foot long from rump to hair tip, communicate everything from mild nervousness to full-fledged bolt. Tail coloring helps. Brown on the outside, or dorsal side, with camouflaging gradations of black, the tail can be held down when the deer hides or, completely white underneath, the tail can be flared out and up, brandished like a flag (hence the nickname flagtail) when a deer is fully alarmed.

White hairs on the edges of the tail add to the com-

plicated language. They can be fluffed outward, framing
the tail, giving outline, or turned inward so no white hair
shows. Variations in use and possible meaning thus seem
to range from whisper to shout, from "Something's up" to
"Scram" with an occasional "No threat, all's cool": just a
simple flick like the wave of a hand as if a possible concern was really nothing at all.

It's the full flag, though, that most people know: that
upright splash of white bounding through woods as a
deer, skittish, commits to full flight. No one is certain
why whitetails, does more than bucks, do this. It's an
alarm signal, true, but it often seems to mean more.

Why, after all, would a deer want a predator to see
where it goes?

Perhaps a doe is giving her fawn a sight-picture to follow, a visual hint which way is safest. Or, as Leonard Lee
Rue III suggests, maybe a deer, tail up, is sending a message to a predator that it's been discovered.[4]

Predators, thinking they're sneaky, will often abandon
a hunt, a stalk, when their stealth has been detected.
This saves them energy in a dance where focus and effi-
ciency count.

The tail, of course, and how it's moved, is only part of a
much larger repertoire of whitetail communications.

There's also stamping, a spectrum of vocalizations,
posture, and mere presence or absence.

When Solo's fawn, seeing the wolves, stamped her
hoof, she did so carefully, choosing a smooth raising and
lowering of the leg, gently tapping the ground, rather
than stomping hard. The motion, like use of the tail,
could have had any manner of gradations of nuance. It

could have been the beginning of an alarmed, jerky, stiff-legged walk, when the hooves are brought down harder than during a silent walk, or it could have been a full pounding of a hoof down on the ground: sending sound and vibration out like a shot to warn bystanding deer of danger.

Other deer pay attention in proportion to the alarm.

Often, while feeding together, they'll stand back-to-back, facing opposite directions, covering their flanks. As one or more deer dips to eat, another deer, having eaten, or simply chewing cud, will stand erect and look around. They seem to take turns. Two dipping, one on guard. One dipping, two on guard. Always a guard deer. If one of the guards picks up on something, alerts, and stamps lightly, the other deer will ignore the light taps or gracefully pause from feeding to look around themselves. If, while feeding off each other's senses and body language, they find something they don't like, things will escalate. The stamping gets harder, the body more rigid.

All the deer take serious notice.

Perhaps the stamping is softest when a deer doesn't want to betray its presence. It sees trouble, wants to relay the message to kin, but doesn't want to attract the trouble in the process. Sight, as subtle as a branch moving in wind, is involved at this stage, as is touch, but not sound. Deer, keen to movement, catch the motion of kin, or they feel the ground tremors rippling beneath their feet. But the arena of sound, that vast void of all else beyond the ken of vision, is sometimes left undisturbed.

Wolves passing—missing by sight what they might still hear—are best left silently passing.

When stamping softly, or steadily in place, a deer will

sometimes use the same leg several times in a row, or it will switch back and forth from leg to leg. Its head, meanwhile, is held erect as eyes attempt to find, or fixate on, threat.

I tried speaking to the deer one day, using their leg language, just to see what might happen.

I was walking along the trail between cabin and road when I passed beneath a rock slope with pockets of sumac and a beautiful, lone cedar. Solo, standing on top of the slope and looking down at me, caught my eye. She stood boldly out in the open against the sky. Behind her, partially hidden by the slope, was the ever-present fawn. Solo raised one leg stiffly then tapped it back on the ground. She did it again. And again. Here was a doe that knew me, that had seen me, heard me, and smelled me for years, and yet she was warning her fawn of danger.

It seemed strange so I talked back.

When Solo raised and lowered her right leg, I did the same with mine. When she used her left leg, I switched over. At a pause, I went first, using my right leg.

Solo matched me.

I switched to my left leg.

She went left.

And just when I thought we had something going, she mismatched me, disappeared with her fawn, and my impromptu body language test was done.

What was innately complicated for me was made even more difficult to understand by another consideration.

When whitetails stamp hooves with force, scent from their forelegs' interdigital glands is spattered to the ground or, at least, released in the air. This might be an olfactory warning, adding to stamping's motion, sound, and feel. It is also a way to leave scent, not for the predator, but for related deer, particularly the young, to follow.

The interdigital glands of a whitetail are located in the forelegs right above the hooves. Waxy hairs in these earlike openings conduct sudoriferous or pheromonal chemicals to a surface point where they can be shed as scent. The function is usually sexual, capable of making a rutting buck's head spin, yet with the interdigital gland deer also simply keep track of one another.[5] Each deer has a unique scent. As it moves, walking across the ground, slipping through brush, trotting or bounding, it leaves a touch of its own smell on snow, stone, sand, and branch.

Even in the air.

Does will locate missing fawns by following their scent, just as fawns will find absent does: one step, one sniff, at a time.

Could it be, I wondered, that when a doe stamps a foreleg in alarm it sets loose a stream of scent up which a fawn, like a salmon, can swim?

Could it be that just as an upright tail is something to follow when all hell breaks loose, jettisoned scents—one bound, one touch-and-go, after another—are olfactory jolts cuing startled, frightened followers to possible safety?

Whitetail paths to safety are certainly signaled by vocalizations.

Deer talk. They communicate orally.

They especially break their silence when they know

the chase is on: trouble has arrived: it's unavoidable: it's coming down hard, fast, and right now: SCRAM!

They snort. They blow air through the nose with force, fluttering nostrils. The explosive sound startles everything like a loud, muffled hand clap. Or deer, mouth open, use a higher pitched snort, almost a squeal or whistle, that's one step up from the nose-snort. They're more excited, feverish, hyped-up.

Anything more subtle might be missed, perhaps, and there's no time to leave threatening sign in doubt.

Carlos Castaneda, in *Journey to Ixtlan: The Lessons of Don Juan,* tells of how don Juan heard a deer whistling but not as warning.

"Once I was in a forest of thick trees," don Juan explained, "in the mountains of central Mexico when suddenly I heard a sweet whistle. It was unknown to me; never in all my years of roaming in the wilderness had I heard such a sound. I could not place it in the terrain; it seemed to come from different places. I thought that perhaps I was surrounded by a herd or a pack of some unknown animals.

"I heard the tantalizing whistle once more; it seemed to come from everywhere. I realized then my good fortune. I knew it was a magical being, a deer. I also knew that a magical deer is aware of the routines of ordinary men and the routines of hunters."

Don Juan, laughing at his own storytelling mischief, goes on to explain that the deer communicated with him, encouraging him not to be sad. When Castaneda balked, refusing to believe such a wild tale, don Juan assuaged him.

"I don't blame you," he said. "It's one of the darndest things."[6]

Regardless of whether don Juan's magical deer existed, it is well known that whitetails use softer sounds than snorts and whistles during normal daily behavior among kin.[7]

Does apparently have a soft mew when calling their fawns. The young can reply with bleats like a young calf without the lamby stutter, the soft bleat merely a call in the brush: a little squeak of presence like two trees rubbing in wind.

The bleat can be louder, too, almost like a whining bear cub when the fawn is anxious in its loneliness, missing mom, feeling the wind and space and that crashing vulnerability. I've stopped on my trails and listened to this sound, once a tree-squeak getting louder, closer, coming toward me as I stood on the trail with a backpack of firewood, curious about the sound until I saw the fawn, spotless and tawny brown, calling, I knew, for Solo, whom I'd seen moments earlier: the bleat unmistakable, then shut-down silent, me spotted, smelled, the fawn veering off toward cover of brush.

The bleat was very different than another sound I'd heard coming from young deer: a little grunt while they were underway, often trotting after their dam: a drawnout, gravelly, low rumbling little grunt. It reminded me of a burp or soft belch.

Was this just the bleat surfacing in juvenile voice?

A little growling of "Wait for me"?

There's no question about the sound of an injured deer.

When the wolf attacked the yearling by the cabin,

the deer I later shot, she had bawled out, quite simply, in terror. Fear and trauma were in that plaintive cry as the wolf chewed neck and haunch. The deer was quite sure of herself and I knew what she was saying.

She was hurtin' and she was afraid.

Surely her mother, standing in snow nearby, heard the wail of her young. Mothers do this. Yes, the doe was probably in the shadows somewhere, ears erect, breath streaming out of her nose or mouth, eyes scanning, every muscle tight and ready for flight, she—like me—wondering if she should respond to the bawl, try to drive the wolf away, or stand her ground as the blood of attachment, the instinct to protect, strained in every cell at the most critical of moments for certainty about the right thing to do.

Then the bawling stopped, died away into the winter day, and there was a terrible, telling silence.

Just as deer use sound and stamping to get a point across, they also use various postures as effective body language.

Tense, they'll hold their heads straight up, ears focused or swiveling, trying to aim every sense they have at what is curious, mildly bothersome, or blatantly menacing. They'll stand poised. Often still. Other deer notice this and tune in. Deer won't chew cud when they're thus alarmed. Others will sniff the air more, seining the scene for stray scent, gingerly nosing the gathering data with which to make decision.

Otherwise, are the deer walking? trotting? hell-bent bounding?

Bedded?

Every posture and motion, even the calm of rest, seems a ripple of response to movements elsewhere.

Calms are times of resting and cud-chewing, grooming and nuzzling.

Alarms, when they come again, are times of disturbance, as if a tide of possibility passes through the landscape. Nerves draw taut.

Such extremes create a rhythm, an ebbing and fluxing of nonchalance and agitation, moving one way then the other, occasionally switching in as little time as a whitetail needs to catch its breath.

When whitetails run, they suck air, breathing it deeply: big gulps of air sucked down into lungs kept healthy by, in part, practice runs and play. Young deer are particularly conspicuous at this. Many times I watched at least one young deer pause from his feeding, dart one way, spring off to the side, then run full throttle off into the woods, circle around the cabin, or just come running back down the trail, kick up his heels or buck around among the other deer in the feeding area, then take off again.

The deer would run the circuit several times, sometimes trying to rouse other deer to join the ruckus or, finished, the deer would just stop.

With his energy spent, the deer would simply stop his run, stand by the feeding area and, lips grimacing, breathe hard through his mouth a few moments until everything was cool again.

Then he would act as if nothing, no nothing at all, had happened.

Beyond behavior and posture, deer communicate by their mere presence or absence.

It was normal for Solo and her fawns, along with one or two other matriarchal groups, plus a buck or two, to visit Hocoka early in the morning, randomly throughout the day, then concentrate for feed at sunset. Windy days might hold them back, keep them hidden where they felt less vulnerable, but otherwise their presence was predictable. I could count on their arrival, their being in the yard, as surely as I knew stars would appear after cloudless gloaming.

If the deer were *not* around, something was up.

Wolves, most likely, were in the neighborhood.

I might not be able to see the wolves, or hear them, but I could suspect wolf proximity simply through deer absence. A pattern was disrupted, a routine altered. The change created a new pulse of the land. It radiated outward like ripples: waves of energy rolling, shifting, expanding concentrically, rhythmically, past Hocoka's ravines and ridges, through woods rarely walked, up through hidden groves of red pines and beyond Vulture Ridge, perhaps even through all the other predator-prey dances and pulses, every unseen species interaction in syncopation: an orchestra of advance and response, all rhythms woven together and shifting as one moves, speaks, notices the absence of deer.

Only later, with deer scattered or outright missing, would I find wolf tracks, scat, or the actual bones of the dead.

When the deer were gone, sometimes for days, avoiding Hocoka for whatever wild reason, I nevertheless found their tracks on the perimeter of things and read them, best I could, like braille.

I had become a tracker.

By following tracks, reading sign, I'd learned how a connection could be made, a sacred stitching, between who I was, where I lived, what and whom I shared the land with, and where it is I thought we were going together in our closeness. A primordial synapse, a longtime connection, grown dull by time and technological distraction, seemed gapped when tracking.

Stitch by stitch. Thread by thread. Sign by sign.

Not only did all life touching the earth appear to leave tracks, those tracks seemed a way life kept in touch with itself. Tracks bridged interspecies boundaries. Thus they lured me further and, like a code read and learned over time, led me from one mosaic of fascination to another.

Like Thoreau, I favored tracks in snow.

In snow, on snow, and brushed against snow's fluff, were footnotes of motion.

Footnotes, then, of feet, hooves, paws, wingtips: records and shadows of a heart's intention, direction, outdoor business. Many tracks were fresh: sharp on edges with insides that crumbled when touched, suggesting recent passage. Other tracks were several days old: thawed slightly then refrozen into brittle ice or half-filled with windblown snow: hinting of history. I read them while snowshoeing or skiing. While hauling water, sledding wood, or just walking around. Tracks in the glow of flashlights and headlamps. Tracks seen as I lay belly-on-snow, squinting closely: seeing how sunlight and shadow filled them: how claw marks delineated toeprints.

Tracks touched with the numb fingers of subzero cold.

Tracks everywhere.

Always, like echoes of the past, they fringed the point of contact between the present and what came before.

"The first track is the end of a string," Tom Brown Jr. explains in *The Tracker*. "At the far end, a being is moving; a mystery, dropping a hint about itself every so many feet, telling you more about itself until you can almost see it, even before you come to it. The mystery reveals itself slowly, track by track, giving its genealogy early to coax you in. Further on, it will tell you the intimate details of its life and work, until you know the maker of the track like a lifelong friend."[8]

Brown had good reason to know.

Not only did he grow up in New Jersey's Pine Barrens, a sandy wilderness of pines and dense brush large enough to confuse, if not swallow, any man, and teach him a few good lessons, but as a kid, age seven, Brown had the good fortune of making friends with a young Indian while hunting fossils. Rick, the new pal, introduced Brown to an 83-year-old relative, Stalking Wolf, an Apache medicine man who apprenticed both of them as trackers.

"Apache scouts were superb survivalists," Brown soon learned. "They were mobile, their awareness was second to none, they were legendary trackers, and Grandfather was one of the best."[9]

Stalking Wolf was a "coyote teacher": he'd never answer questions directly but steer the questioner in a new direction, sometimes asking a question himself.

After twelve years Brown was good enough to track deer and rabbits in the dark while crawling on his hands and knees. He and Rick could sneak up on black bears and smack them on the back. After much scouting, Brown killed his first deer while clutching a homemade spear and jumping on the buck's back from a tree.

This, anyhow, Brown claims.

As year led to year, skill to skill, Brown's apprentice-ship deepened until Stalking Wolf died in 1970. Brown spent a summer living naked and surviving off the land in the Pine Barrens, survived several days treed by a pack of wild dogs, fought off—in Billy Jack–karate-fashion—a gang of poachers, confronted a grizzly in the Tetons (during a ten-year, post-apprenticeship, back-to-the-land journey), and rescued a runaway retarded child whom he found after several days of tracking.

"Aw, c'mon now," Eric Lindskog, a friend of mine, once said as we talked about Brown and his tales in *The Tracker*. Eric's voice boomed above a boat motor as we jounced across Burntside Lake's north arm to track deer. "I think-!-you have to take that book-!-with a grain of salt! Maybe Brown exaggerated-!-a little bit."

Hyped or not, I figured, *The Tracker* was a story by someone who knew tracks.

All you had to do was try tracking, read the book, do more tracking, and think about it all to realize Brown, or whatever imaginative man wrote *The Tracker*, was some-one who tried to interpret almost every track he could.

For Brown, diligence paid off.

Rescue agencies and law enforcement personnel hired him to help track the lost, missing, and overdue. Before Brown was thirty years old, he'd helped locate forty peo-ple. By the time he was forty-one, in 1992, that number had risen to 160: dead or alive.

"Each trail is one of a kind," his keen eye had

observed.[10] "The same combination of weather, land, temperature, and creature are probably duplicated no more often than snowflakes. The same interactions between so many variables probably never recur. Even within the easily identified, habitual gait of a person there are nuances made by the changing flux of emotions as he or she moved."

Although Brown found the variety of tracks astounding, and what they taught irresistible, they had to be read quickly.

Tracks were temporary:

"They fade, and as they dry the wind sweeps them relentlessly level to ease its way across the ground. Tracks exist at the interface where the sky drags along the surface of the earth. They exist for a relatively brief time in a narrow level near the surface of the ground where the wind and the weather move across, changing the temperature and building information into the track . . . Nature conspires to steal even the traces of passage. Most tracks in the world go under unseen."

Inevitably, whether a track is raised and icy or blown away pronto by wind, each track is part of a unique language spoken by an animal: usually with its feet. The land, sun, and wind reciprocate by holding the message or allowing it to wear away.

A giving and taking occur.

Except on bare rock, like the granite of the Precambrian Shield, or on glare ice, it's almost impossible for a deer not to leave a hoof track. Whitetail hooves are hard, sharply pointed, and designed for walking, trotting, jumping, galloping, and bounding.

Whitetails need to dig in.

They require traction.

Hooves are approximately three inches long and two inches wide with front hooves slightly larger than rear hooves. They are made of keratin, a kind of hardened hair, like human fingernails. At one time deer had five toes but, as the earth's ecosystems changed from predominate forest to emergent grasslands, the need for speed nudged an evolutionary edge until the whitetail's "thumb" toe disappeared, the two side toes pulled back into dewclaws, and the two remaining center toes hardened into cloven, ground-purchasing, shapes. When there's no snow, hooves have a central spongy undersurface, slightly convex, that makes ground contact; otherwise the heart-shaped hooves, concave and hardest on the edges, do the work for run or bolt.

Dewclaws—in muddy, swampy, generally wet areas, also on snow—are used and splayed, doubling a deer's bearing surface.

Regardless of how the hoof is used, and its seasonally conditional shape, it grows continuously. Like a beaver's teeth worn by wood, only by being abraded on rock, sand, and soil does a deer's hoof keep trimmed.

Growth and abrasion, hence, work in tandem to ensure a whitetail's best grip on the world.

Shape of tracks depends on what a whitetail is doing. Was it walking . . . browsing as it moved along? Did it accelerate the walking pace to three to four miles per hour? Trot at ten to twelve miles per hour? Break into a full run at thirty-five to forty miles per hour? Or was it standing still, ghostlike, blending into its surroundings, motionless in secret, exercising its preferred evasion tactic: just standing, looking, and sizing things up like a sentient shadow of gray on a winter day?

If the deer was moving, there's a chance to tell if it was buck or doe.

According to Rue III who studied, photographed, and lived among deer for over thirty-five years, the average difference between a buck and doe track is only 5 percent; however, because bucks don't lift their hooves any higher than they have to, they leave drag marks with the tips of their hooves as they sweep their legs forward. Although all deer leave drag marks if there's more than an inch of snow, bucks will drag hooves in *less* than an inch, especially during rutting season as they conserve energy or spread scent.

This drag mark in snow (or sand), Rue claims, is the only reliable way to tell a whitetail's sex from a track.

Snow, meanwhile, reveals many other things about a deer's tracked passage. Tracks are "fresh" if they aren't filled with windblown snow or snow from a recent snowfall, and can be dated this way. If daytimes bring melting temperatures, as they do in early and late winter, are the tracks glazed from thawing and freezing? Do the insides have bits of ice crust from a hoof punched through old glaze? Or are the tracks simply too large to believe, made by the buck of a hunter's dream?

This can happen when a track in snow simply melts away, expanding into the slush of a bright, warm day.

The reverse, too, can happen.

As Thoreau—a tracker if there ever was one—noticed, thaws not only destroy tracks but occasionally help them endure.

"The snow," he journaled on February 18, 1855,

"which was originally compressed and hardened beneath the feet,—also, perhaps, by the influence of the sun and maybe rain,—being the last to melt, becomes protuberant, the highest part and most lasting. That part of the snow compressed and solidified under the feet remains nearly at the same level. The track becomes a raised almost icy type. How enduring these trails! How nature clings to these types. The track even of small animals like a skunk will outlast a considerable thaw."[11]

Yes, tracks everywhere: fresh, old, freezing, thawing.

Tracks, when it came to deer, through alder swamps. Tracks across ridges riven with cracks angling through sumac. Tracks and buck rubs in jackpine stands. Tracks in willows, hollows, over rock knobs and meandering through cedar thickets. Tracks trailside, or the found bedding areas where warm bodies of deer left impressions of calm moments chewing cud beneath sun, moon, or star.

Eventually, of course, tracks end.

The end of Brown's string of mystery is reached.

There's the animal, its carcass, or whatever it is one was stalking. Just beauty, perhaps. If an animal, perhaps there's nothing left but a smattering of confused and panicky tracks, a few tufts of fur, or a skull.

Brown was into skulls.

"A skull is the ultimate track a creature leaves," he concluded.[12] "When everything else has been unshaped by time, when every scratch and print is gone, the skull remains . . . skulls simply mark the point of departure and the direction of flight, like the brush of a bird's wing in the snow."

Here, despite Brown's beautiful prose, I had to disagree, maybe even side with Lindskog in that jouncing Burntside boat.

If there was an ultimate track in my *mainganikan* (place where there are wolves), it was a wolf track or deer track. Sometimes you could see both at once. There would be a deer track pressed in fresh, white snow, brilliant in morning sun, while next to the cloven print, sprinkled, startling with contrast: a few flecks of bright red blood.

That kind of deer track—the way things were heading at Hocoka—about summed things up.

You read the deer track directly, the wolf by inference.

And the track's makers?

They were still moving, marking, very much alive.

Not surprisingly, with sign of so many deer around, there came a March day when the wolves reappeared: hunting, perhaps, a lame buck I'd seen on Kapsch's Island.

Hard to say.

The buck had a red, bulbous wound on the inside of the left rear leg. I thought it might be a broken bone, the femur, as I watched the buck hobble around but, four days later, when he showed up at Hocoka, the wound seemed more likely a total dislocation of the hip . . . angling the femur out in a grotesque bulge.

Had the buck slipped on glare ice, ripping muscles, tendons, and cartilage, as whitetails sometimes do?

The buck appeared to be in pain, could only hobble around, and the wolves would likely find it.

On the same day the lame buck arrived at Hocoka, I found remains of another deer on Rainbow Ridge: scattered fur and chunky, dry intestinal food.

Nights, meanwhile, brought northern lights: flashes of horizon red mixing with faint green, silhouetting the forest beneath stars or, other times, wind swept the trees of Rainbow: distant wind in trees as moonlight shone on snow.

One night a fox barked in darkness.

The darkness was barking.

Yet it was wolves, not a fox, that arrived the next morning.

It was sunny and unseasonably warm at 49° F when I caught a glimpse of fur coming up the cove trail . . . past balsam fir . . . a wolf, gray, coming all the way to the deer-feeding area in front of the cabin. The wolf looked around as its tongue hung loosely from exertion. Soon it came up near the cabin deck to stand among small firs and oaks where I hung suet feeders for the birds. The wolf—average size, average gray—had a scratch behind its right eye. Restless, it turned and trotted back down below the cabin to lie on a snowbank on the edge of a granite ledge slanting into the lake.

The wolf gulped snow as it glanced around, panting, panting, thirsty, breathing heavily between gulps of snow.

In moments a second wolf arrived from down the cove trail. It joined the first wolf but, although also tired and breathing heavily, it was too restless to lie down. Hyped on scent? It came up toward the cabin, checked the feed areas out, then trotted downslope to the cove and out onto the lake where the other wolf joined it.

Both wolves crossed the cove.

There, the exhausted wolf again lay down: this time in shade on a snowdrift sweeping up from the lake onto the bank of Rainbow. As the lead wolf continued eastward along the shoreline, pausing, waiting, the other wolf would get up, walk a ways, then flop back down. The lead wolf eventually cut up Rainbow Ridge and disappeared.

The second wolf followed, slowly but surely, pausing again in a sunny spot among red pines.

Its fur glowed gray-gold.

I thought of Bandit and Ruff, then, whom I'd seen earlier in the day. Ruff had looked lanky, strong and swift. As for Solo, she'd been gone for days, as had Princess, Shy, and a new doe with small fawn: hadn't seen them since migratory crows arrived on the 13th and rain fell on the 20th: first day, that winter, of spring.

The prism herd, it seemed, was pretty well scattered as the wolves passed through.

The first deer back was the lame buck.

He returned to Hocoka the day after the wolves. He still hobbled . . . could not run, as far as I could tell. Perhaps he was looking for food, or just plain peace, or—beyond hope now—the painless joy-of-being he had once known: snorting and stamping and raising that fine flag with a running catch-me-if-you-can attitude.

All gone now.

So perhaps the lame buck was even looking for the wolves themselves: tracking his predator. Get it done with. Fuel the necessary violence. Strum the ancient tension.

Who knows?

I never saw the lame buck, or its tracks, again.

Rip

Full Moon in Clear Sky/Stars: 38° F: Barometer Falling

*Staring at a photo of a ring nebula tonight: was
struck with lingering wonder at the stars, the known
universe of light, stars appearing in globules, clus-
ters, some exploding, their stellar dust flung out and
giving birth to other stars, on and on, a great exha-
lation of sparkling light: an endless sea of it as we
go about our little business.*
—journal, Hocoka, Winter

When I found Rip, Chris's and my black cat, dead in the cabin on a cold winter night as the deer mingled out-side, I knew part of my life, my close life with Chris and Rip, was over.

It was, some might say, just a cat's death, but it was more than that. Rip's death was real yet symbolic. It was a wide-ranging ending.

A bridge was burning and some of its wreckage lay before my eyes.

As countless couples in the North American outback know well, the hinterlands are afloat with marital flot-sam. Half-built cabins are scattered throughout the lake country, woods, and mountains. First came the mutual dream of living together beyond the concrete grip of metropolitan conclaves, *getting back to the land* some called it, or *coming into the country*, then there was the purchase of land, cabin building, the seemingly endless chores and tasks, and even more insidiously, the grim reality of economics. There was rural loneliness, lack of meaningful professional jobs to test talents and skills, lack of household conveniences easing the load of self-maintenance, and scant social support: people bound by a common scheme of going against the grain, living an independent life, toeing a lifestyle line, all in order to live closer to nature: to touch earth and sun.

The Ely area, with its fringe counterculture and millions of acres of beautiful backcountry, didn't have all of the outback's most dire deprivations when Chris and I settled at Hocoka. Still, good jobs were scarce and making a living was tough. Chris commuted forty to fifty miles a day in an aging Saab to manage Voyageur Outward Bound's food program, being laid off winters. I was a writer, earning erratic checks, and dreaming soon of rangering. Chris loved to sing, for music was in her family, yet Ely's community choir was not sufficiently fulfilling. I had a worklist of cabin projects promising years of manual labor.

The discontent, the tension, began to fester.

Sometimes, on long winter evenings, as restlessness rode winds, wolves howling, the season a long subarctic freeze beyond the glow of kerosene lamps, accounts juggled tight, emotions perplexed, both Chris and I sensed trouble scratching at the door.

And the day came.

The day came when we answered that scratched door and Chris walked right through it.

She needed to go away, she said. Try something dif-

ferent. Return south. Like Thoreau leaving Walden
Pond, there were other lives to live. Whether this was
self-affirmation for Chris, as some might call it, or libera-
tion, it became clear through heartfelt talks that it was
time for Chris to move on.

Leave Hocoka. Leave me.

Certainly it was something I did, said, didn't do but
should have, or did do but shouldn't have. Or I had created the situation by something I didn't give or gave too
much. Or the mouth that should have kept its lips
sealed, the passion that should have been smothered,
didn't and wasn't.

The edge coming: the edge.

It was anybody's guess, after Chris left, as to who was
right, wrong, or when the rift truly began, at what precise instant, lack of touch, or dream run wild on the rope
of risk.

Anybody's guess.

"Irreconcilable differences," the divorce papers eventually stated.

It was a nice, broad category like *irregular snow crystals*:
encompassing about every reason, angle, urge, damned-
if-I-won't excuse under the winter sun.

The heart knew, though. The heart couldn't be
fooled.

Trouble was, my heart cared way too much.

Now it had to love enough, in its own bumbling way,
to let a relationship rest in peace.

Chris had left Rip with me, for which I was thankful.

Rip adapted well to Hocoka over the years. By the
time Chris left, Rip and I had known each other

through six winters. She had slept countless times at the foot of the bed or next to my shoulder. She had sat next to me, purring, as I read my books and penned my hopes on the coldest of days. During summers, she would alert me to bears or any approaching visitor. Come winter, she'd keep the cabin clear of mice or just sit somewhere in a loft, on a chair, on an old treadle sewing machine, or anywhere pleasing her and giving perch to keep watch.

To ease her way, I had built cat ladders throughout the cabin: two by fours with little steps connecting the main floor with the sleeping loft, rafters, and storage loft. Rip could go anywhere in the cabin and, with Hocoka's surrounding open spaces, its animals and wildness, the great silences and starry midnight glows, she had the world by the tail.

In the end, with Chris gone, Rip took the edge off stark solitude. I would make other friends, but there was a black hole no one could fill, a depth to a loss which nothing could assuage, a break I did not want but could not stop. My bills doubled. Income dropped. I began borrowing money from friends, using canoes and guns as collateral. Each land payment became a battle. And the time came, sure as economic cancer, that I faced the loss of Hocoka.

If I couldn't make my payments, all that I'd invested— the money, energy, dream—would slip through my fingers and come to an end.

And there would be Rip: her gold eyes looking at me from some corner, ladder, or when snuggled next to me in a chair.

She had done well trotting across the snowy lake to Hocoka that first day. She had come to a home that, I suspected, we both now wanted to keep.

Where else was there to go?

Looking at Rip, petting her, feeding her, she was a friend who wouldn't surrender. Chris, I knew, would eventually take her, bring her south for a new journey, yet for the time being she was a black, living thread holding me, Chris, and Hocoka tenuously together.

I did not want anything to happen to her.

The night came, though, when I found myself sitting in kerosene lamplight beneath a bright moon as Rip stiffened from rigor mortis.

She was wrapped, near my feet, in an old quilt made by Lea, my grandmother, its presence that night a convoluted story blending into my weariness and confusion.

Two days earlier, I'd left Hocoka to go to Blackduck, Minnesota, to help a brother-in-law and sister move my mother to a new apartment. I had left adequate food and water for Rip, yet I drove home fast. When I reached the cabin, I put a box of old letters I carried on the deck and went around to the back of the cabin to turn on the propane gas. Moonlight lit my movements yet I wore a headlamp, the kind mushers and skiers use, and as I entered the cabin door my beam of light flashed off walls then down to the floor.

Rip was sprawled on the floor by the sink.

I picked her up, shocked, and looked at her in the glow of my headlamp.

"Rip?" I said.

Nothing. Eyes glazed. Body limp. I opened her mouth and put a finger inside. Still warm.

"Rip?"

I laid her on a counter.

I looked around. Someone break in? Nothing seemed broken, moved, or missing.

Crumbs in the food dish. Ice on the water dish.

And Rip dead.

She grew colder and stiffer on the counter, her eyes more glazed as an orange moon rose to wax white, the moon's silvery light dancing on the cove water and new shoreline ice below the cabin.

"You know I loved you," I said to Rip. "You know that."

Tears. *Jeez.* A grown man shedding tears for a black cat he sometimes called Swivel Ears. A man might be understood when he grieves for a dog lost to wolves, a car, or one's own gun, but a black cat?

The edge—moonlight—coming closer.

A grown man. Respect. Just a black cat. Chris's cat. Our cat.

Just Ripper, man, she's gone.

I was glad no one was around.

I petted Rip's body then picked her up and took her out onto the deck overlooking the lake. I held her against my stomach this one last time, then raised her up in my hands toward the moon and stars to let her spirit go: return to the timeless, endless sea from which she'd washed upon my shore. Soon, when the time was right, I brought her body back inside the cabin where I wrapped her in the quilt.

Grandma Lea's quilt.

As the cabin clock ticked.

The quilt had come a long way.

While rummaging through old stuff in storage at my mother's, I had found the quilt which I kept with other belongings. Much time had passed since I was given that quilt as a boy. Grandma Lea, the healer whose hands had made the quilt, had died. Grandpa Joseph, her husband, had died. And the quilt had once inexplicably disappeared from beneath a bed in my St. John's University dormitory room, only to be found two months later under the same bed by Japanese students after I'd moved elsewhere. So the quilt had history and psychic resonance. When it surfaced in Blackduck, however, it had become musty, ragged, and tore easily.

I decided to throw the quilt away.

What would I do with it anyhow? Throw it in the loft? Who would ever repair it?

I brought the quilt down to a trash bin and threw it in along with old paintings, football spikes, and wall hangings.

The next day, troubled, I had second thoughts.

I started feeling guilty about the impersonality of the disposal. Hadn't I decided to bring old love letters home? Didn't the quilt mean as much to me as someone's fading script? Wasn't the quilt a kind of love letter to a grandson?

I didn't say a word to my mother as I hustled back

down to the trash bin and retrieved the quilt. I'd decided to bury it at Hocoka: make it part of the land: let its fibres, and the work of my grandmother's fingers, fuse with the soil.

Throw down another anchor.

Little did I know I would be wrapping Rip in the quilt's fragile threads.

I had two options.

I could bury Rip with the quilt or, possibly, cremate both. There was a large pile of brush behind the cabin. I could burn the brush, Rip, and quilt at the same time beneath stars. But, no, this bothered me. *Flame*—Couldn't say why—*Flesh.* So the next day, as the lake froze solid beneath sunny sky, I shoveled a hole in the ground back in the woods. I put the quilt and Rip in the hole, slipped Rip's food dish and water dish inside the quilt, and covered it all with dirt and leaves.

Soon fresh snow would come.

Perhaps Rip had died of a heart attack.

Maybe she had heard me come up the trail in the dark, set the box of old cards and letters down, then go around back to turn on the gas. Excited, she had skittered down her cat ladder and across the cabin floor as she had done many times, and died right on the spot.

Near the sink. By the door.

The next time she went out that door she was dead in my arms.

When I opened the box of cards and letters, to take a quick look, the top card caught my eye.

An illustrated cat lay on a table. Near the cat's head was a vase of flowers. The cat's tail, curving so gently, dangled over the edge of the cat's tabled world.

Rip visited me one more time, in a dream, with a wolf.

I was standing in a cabin and looking out the window toward a narrow bay with grassy banks.

It was a summer day of open water.

I noticed a wolf down the shore. It was frolicking, looking around, twisting and turning then coming my way. It loped in the grass along the shore until it was next to the cabin. I looked down at it through the cabin window, the wolf's fur thick and brown, its back to me as it sat. A woman was with me, perhaps my sister; she moved around and I whispered to her to stand still so she didn't scare the wolf, which might see her through a window.

Suddenly the wolf was chasing Rip . . . a great blur of motion circling around and around the cabin.

A wolf chasing Rip: Rip running from the wolf.

I was excited and afraid. Excited to have the wolf so close. Afraid it might catch Rip and kill her.

They came into the cabin: a mass of black and brown fur whirling around me, knocking over chairs, tipping lamps: and suddenly the wolf was gone.

Rip, with the nonchalant way of independent cats, walked straight toward me, the tip of her tail red with blood. I fetched a bowl of water for her. She ignored it. I cupped her shoulders with my right hand and slid her toward the dish. She resisted. Firmly, but gently, I pushed her head down toward the water. As her mouth touched water I stirred in my sleep, awaking, floating in the warmth of blankets, surfacing from sharp images of dream up . . . up . . . through a fog of realignment to Hocoka's winter world.

Rip, I realized, was dead.

She was buried and frozen, along with more of my life, in the needled shade of a fir.

Omens

Cloudy: 42° F: Barometer Unknown

Feeling down today, frustrated by events.

 Walked the driveway à crépuscule *[at twi-light] and—following a snow bunting flitting and flying and hopping in front of me—found a blue-jay standing in the road.*

 It had its head turned backwards and its beak tucked in shoulder feathers.

 I squatted down and, with a finger, petted the bluejay's head.

 The jay awoke, flew off, and landed on a branch of a nearby spruce.

—journal, Hocoka, Winter

Rip's death: the wolves in dream and along Rainbow Ridge: the wolf attack of the yearling: the lame buck: a bluejay that let me touch it: a doe on the deck: it was hard to tell what were normal events, luckily noticed, or what—drawing me in, there partly for me—was a sign or omen.

If some of the incidents were omens, what did they mean?

To whom were they addressed? And from whom—or what—did they come?

Were omens hocus-pocus, as many people believe, or was there some underlying phenomenon occurring that could be explained, albeit incompletely, in enduring spiritual and psychiatric terms?

Was the land speaking to me through its animals, life forms, swirling vortices of energy?

Or was it all nothing at all? Just me, some resident deer, and a few wild predators passing through looking for meat?

Tough questions, these.

Tougher—and riskier—answers.

Perhaps, then, I could be pardoned some dark winter nights for sidestepping questions about omens when they arose or, like any wary naturalist, keeping the alleged explanations to myself. Any fool could see the topic needed to be broached with great caution. Not only did I suspect the subtlest of realities couldn't be articulated, that what sometimes happened was rooted beyond the ken of words, but I was fully aware that any understanding of an event in my culture was scoffed at if not "reasonable" or corroborated by science. Contemplating the possibility of omens was very tricky ground, best kept private, proffered publicly at great risk, yet when a doe appeared on my cabin deck—during a moment of heavy decision—I had to admit the visit was strange, coming as it did at that hour.

Or any time, for that matter.

The doe came near the end of a short winter day which had begun with hoarfrost. Winds were calm: sky overcast. I had gone into town to run errands, had returned home to haul water from the lake, and as I rounded the cabin corner, lugging my water buckets, there was the doe.

We stood face to face.

Who is this? I wondered. *Where'd* she *come from?*

Now it must be understood that all day long, and for weeks previous, I had questioned whether I should leave Hocoka and go to Alaska for a few months. A friend wanted to live there. I was willing to take a look around, weighing possibilities, but my heart was at Hocoka. Could I inhabit the best of both worlds? keep one foot at the center of the circle while exploring wild country to the far northwest with the other?

What should I do?

It was one of those questions that nag you, that go around and around and around, that seem to bear critical importance as if the answer or decision you reach will alter the course of your future. Such moments are intense, often riddled with confusion and angst, for it's vital in the long run the decision is right. That it's soulful. Otherwise one slips into a stream of dissonance as the mind, heart, and soul get torn in irreconcilable directions.

Some people flip a coin.

Others, apparently, sometimes need a deer.

The doe stood patiently by the deck as I put my buckets of water next to the cabin door, stepped into the adjacent shed, and got a sack of corn. Perhaps it was time, this early winter of 1993, to begin feeding the deer. Maybe the hour had arrived to resume the connection. As I stepped out of the shed, the doe walked right up to me. She was closer than any deer had come before. No sign of illness, foaming mouth, halo. I opened the corn sack, grabbed a handful of corn, and she came closer, licked my fingers, then ate out of my hand.

I gave her another handful, and another, maybe five altogether. She'd walk away between handfuls then come back. At one point she raised her muzzle about six inches from my face, sniffing me, and I stroked—fleetingly—the side of her cheek.

Dusk. And a deer eating out of my hand.

What was *this* all about?

I put some corn out for Solo and the other deer, but the tame newcomer stayed by the deck.

Later, in darkness, I stepped back outside and stood in lamplight shining out cabin windows. From out of the darkness came the tame doe. She stepped up on the deck and walked up to me. Her hooves slipped a little on the icy wood.

Again she craned her head close to me. I could have reached out and touched her.

"Tomorrow," I said.

But there was no tomorrow, at least not for us.

Just as that doe had stepped out of deck darkness into the limited light of my intense world, she returned to that darkness from which she never emerged again.

A sign?

Omen?

Was I being told to anchor myself more firmly at Hocoka and pay closer attention? Or that I would go to Alaska, as I did, but that I'd return to Hocoka after a hard lesson?

Or was I just being showered with deer affection at a time of personal confusion?

Don't leave us, don't leave us, don't leave us.

I didn't know what to think although I sensed somehow, some way, I was spoken to.

Let me say now I had an inbred, enduring respect for the unusual long before my trail reached Hocoka, where a deer shocked me with tame behavior. I was baptized a Catholic and reared a Catholic which, with its belief in miracles, meant a desert bush could burst in flames on a rainy day in front of my eyes and I wouldn't lack an explanation.

If nothing else, God did it.

Here was an opinion I could count on.

And here, I suspect, was a position associated with my French-Canadian ancestry, its attendant religious education, and, when I was twenty, a story my mother told me.

"Listen to me," she said when we were alone at a dinner table. "I've waited to tell you this until you were old enough."

My mother did not take things lightly, so, staring across the kitchen table, I was all ears.

The story was about Lea, my maternal grandmother, wife of Joseph: a woman known as a healer; people traveled miles to see her. On the night she died, she complained of a headache, went upstairs in the family farmhouse, and, in bed, passed away of a brain hemorrhage. She also appeared at the white clapboard home of her parents ten miles away in Red Lake Falls.

She knocked on the door in the middle of the night.

"Your greatgrandfather," my mother said, "answered the door. 'Lea,' he said, 'what are *you* doing here? I'll get mother.'"

I glanced at my hands, trying to betray nothing.

"The next day," my mother continued, "when one of my brothers—your uncle—went to Red Lake Falls to tell your great-grandparents Lea died, they said 'Yes, we know. She was here last night.'"

Her body, however, had never left the farmhouse.

"Do you *understand*," my mother asked, "what I'm trying to tell you?"

And I sat nodding to my mother's words like the theological numbskull, the spiritual child, I was.

My own mother chancing me with news of a miracle.

I feigned calm—*cool, man*—as if she'd just asked me to shovel March snow off the sidewalk on a Saturday afternoon.

What was I to say?

Call my mother a liar?

That she was not.

For once, like the intelligent young man I allegedly was, I kept my mouth shut. If people ever heard this story, I figured, and they scoffed, that was their problem.

A soulful story was told, and same as any oral tradition, this is the way the story came down.

Obviously there was a tolerance for the inexplicable among my mother's people: an openness: an ipso facto, there-without-saying, granting of the possibility there was more to life, or death, than what met the scientific eye or could in some other way be reasoned, explained, understood, or dismissed.

This a mere twenty-five years ago.

What amazes me now, after many winters have come and gone, is that it didn't dawn on me when I heard my mother's story (sitting at that table as I, home from St. John's University, no doubt sipped oh-so-grown-up coffee and eyeballed mom's smokes on the counter) that no one, least of all my mother and blood, was questioning the relationship of miracle and mystery to the general tenets of Catholicism, let alone science. Miracle and mystery were just accepted. If you were a believer, God or Jesus simply worked miracles through his children and there wasn't much more to say about it.

Didn't Catholics throughout the world confess to a belief in a virgin birth?

Didn't they profess a savior, Jesus of Nazareth, who taught unconditional love, was crucified, then rose from the dead: an event celebrated at Easter each spring when sunlight saved life from crystalline annihilation?

Was not Saul, no, St. Paul, struck from his horse with the lightning power of conversion?

It took a while for me to get it.

My mother's people, through their innate French-Canadian piety and local take on Catholicism, did indeed embrace a belief in miracles: physical events, according to the *Random House Dictionary of the English Language*, that surpass "all known human or natural powers and [are] ascribed to a divine or supernatural cause."

Huh.

Seems to me I should have thought about that a little more at the time.

Either I was too engaged in my private life of music (Jimi Hendrix, Jefferson Airplane), books (Herman Hesse, Alan Watts), mind-expansion (long pause), those days being what they were, or the weird event, the spontaneous miracle, was so much a part of my heritage that a young man of my stripe, sailing through college, wouldn't bat an eyelash if seas parted and tablets of commandments fell from the sky.

Then again, maybe I wasn't going to touch this business about miracles, signs, and omens with a ten-foot pole.

What a man wants isn't necessarily what he's going to get.

I might have pushed the whole idea of omens, signs, and inexplicable happenings away, in part by ignoring the question of their possibility, yet important things have a tendency to circle around to leave a second impression. This was true of omens and signs when I found mention of them while tracking the work of Tom Brown Jr.

Brown of *The Tracker* fame.

Brown, the student of Stalking Wolf.

"There is a world beyond that of our everyday physical, mental and emotional experiences," he begins *The Vision*.[1] "It is a world beyond the five senses, and different than the realm of the imagination. It is the world of the unseen and the eternal, the world of spirit and vision."

Of all the essays that followed, however, whether "The Trail," "The Veils," or "Crystal Vision" (engaging stories of Brown's spiritual probings, his quests), it was chapter 13, "The Omen," that most caught my attention. In it, Stalking Wolf is teaching young Tom and Rick about omens, how they can be misconstrued or read too easily in everything, leading to an insanity paralyzing with fear. It was imperative the boys knew more than they did. Stalking Wolf's inevitable explanation, albeit via Brown in a Berkley paperback, was at least an attempt by *someone* to address what most formal spiritual literature essentially ignores.

It helped, initially, to suspend judgment.

According to Stalking Wolf, if an omen or sign is associated with an animal, as they often are, it is vital to remember natural entities like animals live, like people, dual lives: physical and spiritual. An animal's routine life—its moving, eating, resting—is its physical existence, which we can observe, and learn from, but nothing more. When the animal appears in "spiritual consciousness," sent by the Creator, he becomes an omen or sign.

Stalking Wolf was very clear about a difference between the two.

"A sign," he said, "is something asked for. It is a beckoned response from the Creator or Creation. It answers a question, gives you a direction, or comes in time of need. As with all things sent from the outer world, its meaning is very clear and vivid to the individual. For it is he who asked for the sign, and the sign will be his alone."[2]

Because signs are inherently personal, only people receiving them should attempt interpretation. A sign's significance, its impact, is purely subjective.

"An omen," Stalking Wolf explained, "is something not asked for that comes as a powerful warning or answer. As with a sign, an omen's meaning is immediately apparent. If, for instance, you are walking in the woods and see an owl, this is not a warning of death, but simply an owl. If, however, you are speaking about a friend who is dying, and an owl appears out of context, then it is an omen. By out of context I mean that the owl would be doing something that he would not normally do, like appearing very close to you, gesturing, as if to get your attention. This then is an omen."

Omens often happen, he said, during times of great personal confusion, interior questioning, and doubt: as if the Spirit disturbs the trapped flow of possibility, or allows enlarged clarity to surface.[3] The inward movement, or exterior event, comes when one is too troubled or blocked to be sensitive to things around us or the subtle interior resonances, the intuitive glimpses, that often guide our way.[4]

Omens, then, are gifts. So are signs. They are the Creator-Great Spirit-Universe communicating with us, *to* us, in ways changing us forever.

"It is the Great Spirit's way of telling you to slow down," Stalking Wolf said, "to pay attention, and to take the time to search your heart. A man, living through his heart and spirit, will never need an omen or sign, except in times of dire need."[5]

Can a person, Brown asked Stalking Wolf, ask for a sign anytime he wants one?

Stalking Wolf had two warnings:

First, a person must be worthy.

Second, asking for signs too often shows a lack of faith.

Brown, really, wasn't onto something new.

Long before he was relaying Stalking Wolf's wisdom about signs and omens to a spiritually hungry American public, ethnologist Frances Densmore (1867–1957) was exploring the customs, beliefs, and spirituality of Great

Lakes Ojibwe/Chippewa. In the fruition of that work, *Chippewa Customs*, she never mentions omens or signs but they are very much implicit in the content of Ojibwe dreams and the respect given them.

"In the old days," an old Ojibwe told Densmore, "our people had no education. They could not learn from books nor from teachers. All their wisdom and knowledge came to them in dreams. They tested their dreams, and in that way learned their own strength."[6]

As Densmore explains, dreams were essential to Ojibwe life. Not only was a child feasted and named several months after birth by a dreamer, usually a member of the Grand Medicine Society who had dreamt about the child, but the *ability* to dream was encouraged from the earliest days of childhood. Kids were told to try to remember their dreams. The Spirit spoke through these visions.

Dreams and visions, apparently, were interchangeable. They could come at night or be evoked through awake, daytime duress.

The most important dream was usually sought at puberty. Usually a young man or woman would be isolated from the village, or sent off alone into the woods, where he or she would fast for up to ten days in order to cleanse the mind. Only in this way, together with general purity of life and, occasionally, through mediation, could one *secure* the right dream: beckon it: lure one's guardian spirit or tutelary to manifest itself. The guardian could be an object but often took the form of an animal. Its power was obvious and immediate to the dreamer who, for the rest of his or her life, would call upon it at critical times.

The Ojibwe told Densmore that in dreams they often returned to previous states of existence or, conversely, what a person dreamed about could later surface— appear—in everyday life.

There was a fluid, albeit baffling, connection.

"Thus it was said," Densmore adds, "that a warrior who had dreamed of a certain animal would call on it in time of danger, and if he were wounded, his comrades would hear the cry of that animal and see it run away. On searching they would be unable to find the body of the warrior, and believed he had returned to his previous existence and escaped in the form of an animal."[7]

Other Ojibwe dreamers had premonitions of things to come. Some saw things none of the people had seen at the time but, years later, were recognized by the dreamer when he or she saw them.

Ships under sail, for example. And frame houses.

Inevitably, the Ojibwe honored the potency of their dreams with articles and artwork that reminded them of their dreams. They believed spiritual essence could dwell in its representation. Such articles were kept and carried on journeys as a hedge against bad luck. As the basis of artwork, dream subjects were painted on wigwam doors and clothing, sometimes outlined with beads or, more commonly, woven into beadwork itself.

Headbands and neckbands were often decorated with images making no sense to anyone but the designer and dreamer.

Johann Georg Kohl, living like Densmore as an ethnologist among Ojibwe of Lake Superior in the 1850s, once met a man who painted his life's main dream symbol on his blanket. In the center of the blanket, in which the man wrapped himself for warmth, was a star symbol: a circle with a point at the center while eight lines radiated out from the circle's circumference.

The star was painted purple.

The man's name, as Kohl discovered walking with him, was *Makwa* (Bear). The star symbolized the early morning star, which had appeared to him in a dream.

"It glistened and shone continually on my path," Makwa said, "now rising, now sinking."[8]

It spoke to him, saying it would be his guide. Makwa, like the star, would "glisten and shine" yet, also like the star, he would someday set: die. Until that time the star would be Makwa's guide and protector.

Since the dream, Makwa—as was the custom of other natives[9]—had held the morning star in remembrance by painting it on the backs of his blankets.

Ethnologist Kohl got a charge out of Makwa but it was Kagagengs, the old dreamer and snowshoer, that really gave Kohl a kick.

Kohl had urged Kagagengs to tell a story, bringing him tobacco and a few yards of flowered calico for a new shirt. But not just any story. Kohl wanted Kagagengs's puberty dream, his life dream, the dream that had brought him guidance for most of his hundred-year life. When Kagagengs heard this, he sat still and silent. He was afraid if he told the story, he'd possibly commit spiritual treason.

"These dreams," Kohl's interpreter told Kohl, "are always kept very secret by the Indians. They think about them their whole life through, as a mighty mystery.

Only on their dying bed would they speak about them, and describe the dream to their relations."[10]

Kohl continued to coax Kagagengs, promising not to tell anyone in the village and that it wouldn't matter what he, Kohl, told his own people "across the big water."

Kagagengs kind of coughed, not sure of himself, and told Kohl he was the first man to ask about his dreams. The old man then filled his pipe and smoked it all the way down to propitiate any vengeful spirits.

Then he was ready.

When he was very young, Kagagengs said, he had gone out in the autumn to gather wild rice. He heard gunshots coming from his village. Then he heard shots from another village. It was the traditional way to relay news of someone's death.

Kagagengs instantly—and inexplicably—knew his mother had died.

Sure enough. People were sent to tell him.

"We buried her with many sighs," Kagagengs said. "I wished, however, to weep out my heavy grief alone, and I longed to go out in the forest."[11]

His family, however, seeing Kagagengs act strange, wouldn't let him go. He had to escape. Once far from the village, he started weeping and calling for his mother, running, running, until he climbed a tree where, exhausted and emotionally drained, he passed out. Soon a black figure, a woman, appeared to him, and together they stepped from one tree top to another, covering large distances between trees, until they reached a mountain. They had journeyed three days. The mountain split open revealing a ravine with a bright light at the other end. In the light there was a house which Kagagengs was told to enter. He did. Inside was another light which he approached with fear and trembling, covering his eyes with his robe.

It was the Lamp of the Sun. It invited him closer.

Kagagengs stepped closer and was told to look down. He did, seeing all the earth with its forests and water. He was told to look up. The sky was filled with brilliant stars. Then he was instructed to look straight ahead.

Kagagengs did and saw himself.

The Lamp of the Sun told Kagagengs that he was always in its sight. Happy. Sick. Whatever. The Light was there. As a gift, it would give Kagagengs four sons and a long life . . . until his hair was white.

And Kagagengs felt joyous.

"In remembrance of thy visit to me," the Lamp of the Sun said, "and for a good omen, I give thee this bird, which soars high above us, and this white bear with the brass collar."

He was then told to go back home with the woman guide he'd come with. The white bear and eagle would remain his protectors. Fine by Kagagengs. Eventually he arrived back in the tree where he had started, although too weak to do anything but let his sisters find him, carry him down and bring him home. He was so weak he couldn't eat any food for three days.

But he surfaced.

In time he had four sons, lived a hundred years, and had white hair.

The most powerful dream of Kagagengs's life came true.

Kohl, who liked to call Kagagengs *Petit Corbeau,*

French for Little Raven, asked him if he'd really brought back an eagle and bear from his vision.

"Not so," he said.

Then Kohl's interpreter once again jumped in.

"In Indian dreams," he said, "it is not necessary that the presents which spirits make them should be really led away. The gift is rather a spiritual present. The idea or image of the thing is given them, and they then have permission afterwards to make the best use of it they can."

Apparently Kagagengs, in his later years, caught some young eagles, raised them, and let them go free in memory of his dream. He also carved a white bear with brass collar onto his pipes and made a symbol of the bear out of wood which he carried in his medicine bag.

Kohl had to ask one more question before he let the old man go.

Had Kagagengs dreamt of his mother again?

Every year, he said, but only in autumn during the rice season: same time he'd first heard those relayed gunshots. When the wild rice was ripe he would walk the path of the dead, see his mother, and talk with her.

The rest of the time?

Never.

The Ojibwe were just one of many Native American peoples who believed in the power of dreams and visions, good or bad.

Just to the west of the Ojibwe, for example, and among their traditional enemies, the Lakota (Sioux), lived a man of extraordinary power. His own people called him a *Wichasha Wakan*: a prophet.

His name was *Tatanka-Iyotanka*: Sitting Bull.

Born, probably, in 1831 at Many Caches on a tributary of the Missouri River, Sitting Bull (also known as Jumping Badger and *Hunkesni*: "Slow") grew up among a horse-and-bison people, the Hunkpapa ("Campers at the Opening of the Circle") tribe, who believed in *Wakantanka*, or the Great Mystery. Bravery was a cardinal virtue, as was fortitude: the ability to endure discomfort and pain. Equally esteemed was generosity. Most important among personal traits, however, and growing out of the others, was wisdom: the gift of insight rooted in a rich spiritual life.

"A man who possessed wisdom," Sitting Bull biographer Robert M. Utley wrote of the Hunkpapa, "displayed superior judgment in matters of war and the hunt, of human and group relationships, of band or tribal policy, and of harmonious interaction with the natural and spiritual world."[12]

This interaction was subtle and, in daily life or night dreams, all-encompassing. Religion was not compartmentalized by the Lakota. There wasn't a word for it. There was simply a strong sense of the sacred, *wakan*, an incomprehensible power permeating all things. A young man was expected to learn this, along with riding and shooting, for without it he would not grow whole.

Everything living, Utley explained, "especially the buffalo and the eagle; every tree, plant, bush, and blade of grass; the streams and lakes, even the rocks and the very soil itself; the sky and all its contents of sun, moon, stars, clouds, and the winds from the four directions—the form, cycle, and habits of all were studied and observed in detail. Since all were *wakan*, the particular powers of each for good or evil were absorbed, together with the ways of eliciting the good and warding off the evil."

Men who were particularly adept at this connection, especially through dreams or induced visions, sometimes developed an ability to see the future. If so, they became *Wichasha Wakan*, holy men. Some sat on every council, their say influencing decision.

Only occasionally was a holy man also a war chief, as in the case of Tatanka-Iyotanka.

As legend and history have it, Sitting Bull astounded everyone as a relatively young man when, after a purifying *inipi* (sweat bath) and with no physical clues, he announced the location of a missing pony he'd given to his nephew, One Bull. The pony was found exactly where Sitting Bull said it would be, although dying.

Sitting Bull, saddened by his nephew's grief, gave One Bull another pony.

Sometime later, in 1870, Sitting Bull foresaw during a vision song a battle with Flatheads two days away. In the battle, he predicted, many enemy would die as well as some Lakota. He'd also seen a ball of fire come at him although it vanished right before contact. Two days later, in the battle Bull had foreseen, he was shot by a Flathead while trying to steal the man's horse.

The rifle bullet, like a ball of fire, hit Sitting Bull's left forearm.

Perhaps Sitting Bull's most remarkable premonition, however, involved General George Armstrong Custer and the 7th United States Cavalry. It came to Sitting Bull during a sun dance. All his life, at least since the age of twenty-five in 1856, Sitting Bull had joined his people in

honoring and celebrating the sun, *Wi*, the source and
sustainer of all good things. The sun dance combined
festivity and, for the men, self-inflicted pain. Whether
the pain was from fasting, or from hanging off the
ground by skewered muscles until one tore loose, the
focus was on a man's fortitude and relationship with the
spirit world. For some men it was an individual experience, going one-on-one with *Wi* and its power, while
among the greatest of men the suffering was a communal
obeisance, a proffering of one's being to the mercy of
Wakantanka.

Anything, during the intensity of a sun dance, might
happen.

It was in early June of 1876 that Sitting Bull dreamed
of Custer's military command and advance. The sun
dance occurred in Montana's Rosebud Valley near
Muddy Creek and Yellowstone River. Sitting Bull, in
keeping a vow he made to *Wakantanka*, had Jumping Bull
cut fifty little pieces of flesh off each arm. Bleeding,
dancing, squinting at the sun, Sitting Bull saw soldiers
and horses advancing on a Lakota village:

*Many, many soldiers . . . upside down, their hats falling, their
feet to the sky.*

Some Lakota, too, were inverted, and a voice was
heard.

"These soldiers do not possess ears," it said. "They are
to die, but you are not to take their spoils."

Sitting Bull told his vision to Black Moon, a holy man.

Black Moon, in turn, told it to the people.

A few weeks later, while Sitting Bull was camped
among a large gathering of his people and other tribes in

the Little Bighorn Valley, Custer advanced with his cavalry of 750 men. Bound for flamboyant glory, perhaps even a United States presidency, Custer intended to attack. Trouble was, eighteen hundred warriors awaited him. They were Hunkpapa, Blackfeet, Miniconjou, Oglala, Brule, Cheyenne: men with a mean attitude: dedicated, unto death, to protect their women, children, and a life they loved enough to kill for.

When the clash with the 7th Cavalry was over, June 26, 1876, Custer lay dead among all the 210 troopers under his direct command at time of battle. Another 113 soldiers were killed or wounded in surrounding bluffs and ravines. About forty Lakota, Cheyenne and fellow warriors were dead.

Many men—on slopes, in hearts—fell upside down.

It was called the Battle of the Little Bighorn.

Who can say whether Sitting Bull always asked for his signs and visions?

Certainly skewering his muscles in hope of contact with the Great Spirit was earnest prayer, a most sincere beseeching; and certainly when Sitting Bull went roaming alone among the grassy or snowy hills, his heart sometimes yearned for answer or release like a taut bowstring. But these are secrets he alone knew on the wild stallion of his privacy.[13] Looking back at him, all we can infer is Sitting Bull seemed to connect with Spirit most fervently at times of transition: those times when, as personal or communal touchstones, he most needed to.

Intense times.

Either the lives of his people were at stake or his own

life—complicated and often endangered—needed fresh understanding and direction.

This Sitting Bull business of signs and omens, especially as they apply at times of imminent crisis, would possibly have faded like bleached bones beneath prairie sun as meaningless, a cultural quirk, if not for the work, in part, of Carl Gustav Jung.

Jung (1875–1961) was the Swiss psychiatrist who studied under Sigmund Freud but broke free to study the human mind in what can only be termed a more soulfully sensitive context. Like Sitting Bull, a man he never knew, Jung believed in souls, not so much as distinct spiritual entities but as force fields—individuating energies—that constellate in a person's life. All souls, Jung said, albeit apparently separate on the surface, are rooted in a collective unconscious shared by all sentience: human, animal, and plant. This infinite well of experience and knowledge, through which we move like whales in the deep, is passed on from one generation to the next as assuredly as biological flesh and bone.

"Our souls as well as our bodies," he affirmed late in life, "are composed of individual elements which were all already present in the ranks of our ancestors."[14]

It was this theory of the collective unconscious, and its transmigration of soulfulness, that set psychiatry on edge. Not only did it postulate a unifying continuum of nonmaterial being, one manifested in dreams, art, and mythology, but it forced the youthful science of psychiatry to re-examine its theses about personality development, the growth of the self, and how it is we're grounded in—and relate to—an infinitely large, un-boundaried whole. (Dream interpretation, for example, gravitated from the sexual id-ego-superego mechanical determinism of Freudism to possible reflections of mythic, soulful journeys reappearing microcosmically in the individual just as they've fueled the evolution of human culture.) It was Jung's fascination with the whole, the interconnected oneness of mind, body, and spirit, the Self, that inevitably led him to speculation on telepathy, clairvoyance, and precognition which he circumscribed in his theory of synchronicity.

Here, in relatively modern vernacular, was a possible home for omens and signs.

Synchronicity, in its most distilled sense, is simply the principle that there is an acausal dynamic in consciousness that links a person's psyche with an event in a *meaningful* coincidence. The experience is innately subjective, intuitive in registration, and cannot be explained by cause and effect (hence *acausal*). For example, you start thinking about an old friend you loved very much but haven't communicated with for years, and the phone rings, you answer, and it's him or her. Or you dream of a house that burns to the ground and, next day, your lake cabin goes up in flames. It's the subjective linkage that counts. An event resonates with a thought, feeling, idea, insight, or dream, and a connection is made, a meaning seen, that a person intuitively links together.

The personal tie, the vibrant juxtaposition, is everything.

Jung specified three types of synchronicity in two major essays.[15] The first type of synchronicity is the "coincidence" between mental content (feeling or thought) and an outer event. The outer event, like the friend's phone call, reflects what is happening psychologically the moment it occurs. In the second type, a person has a vision or dream—coinciding with something happening at a distance—that is later verified and was totally undetectable by the five senses. The third kind of synchronicity is when a person has an idea or image of something that will happen in the future, which then occurs. Such premonitions can come with a subtle but certain intuition, in a vision (like Sitting Bull?), or in the labyrinths of a dream as happened to Kagagengs.

Animals (deer? wolves?), and even inanimate objects, can play a role in events, images, or dreams.

Jung knew he was onto something and he followed this trail as far as he could. The spiritual ramifications of synchronicity alone were intriguing. The phenomenon seemed to underscore a dual stream of existence: the cause-and-effect world (don Juan's *tonal*?) we all think we know well, and an acausal parallel (the *nagual*? spiritual?) of incomprehensible depth, infinite time, and total universality we all share. The personality has a foot in both waters, it seems, while psychic growth—ever so delicately—hangs in the balance.

Could it be, Jung inevitably wondered, that the goal of psychic growth is the self and all it can be aware of? And could it be, furthermore, that such growth, albeit linear at first, evolves into a perpetual "circumambulation" (circling) and enlargement of one's own center?

And what should the totality of the center be called anyway?

Soul? God? God-image? Absolute Self? Tao?

Here the great psychiatrist—perhaps smoking his

pipe and paging through his latest midnight manuscript—didn't know what to say. He knew what he was referring to, had even been touched and guided by it, yet the exact word, the precise linguistic pictograph, would forever escape his amazingly prolific pen.

Leave it to Jean Shinoda Bolen, then, to carry Jung's principle of synchronicity one step forward where, in the context of Taoism, she suggests synchronicity is *communicative*: that we can get signals (signs? omens?) from the full context of our life as to whether we're on the right or wrong path.

Here was a fresh track for me and I looked at it closely.

In Bolen's small but intriguing book, *The Tao of Psychology: Synchronicity and the Self*, she summarizes her Jungian studies under Joseph Wheelright at San Francisco's Langley Porter Neuropsychiatric Institute, thus establishing her credibility. She follows with a description of Jung's principle of synchronicity, how it relates to the collective unconscious, and how it implicates the presence of Tao: the unifying reality, or spirit, underlying the perpetual motion and changes we experience as our conscious and unconscious lives. (The word *Tao* cannot be fully interpreted; equivalent terms include God, the Greek *logos*, the Primal Unity, Great Spirit, and the One.) What I found original about Bolen's work, however, was her emphasis on how synchronistic events heighten the feeling of connection between psyche (mind) and event, between inner and outer worlds: a sense that what is outside of us is, simul-

taneously, within us, and that we are deeply and mysteriously joined to all life.

When this goes beyond idea to intuitive, immediate
registration, such as during a strong, synchronistic experience, the world and its patterns of association are
transformed.

We feel, as Bolen says, "part of a divine, dynamic, in-
terrelated universe."[16]

By paying attention to these moments, we can detect
the presence of the divine more vividly and, through
close perception, be led along a path of psychological
and spiritual growth.

The signal moments themselves, Bolen explains, are
invariably subjective, for they presume—as Jung insisted—a personal response. (Without personal meaning
attributed to a coincidence, there is no synchronicity.
Only coincidence.) Often there are spontaneous emotional reactions: feelings of flooding warmth, awe, chills
up the spine, outflowing and encircling love, or a *knowing*
that cannot be explained. An intuitive resonance is sensed
so strongly, so viscerally, that the reefs and questions of
cause and effect surrender to a felt influx of tidal grace.

"Sensing the existence of a divine energy *is* the experience," Bolen says. "What does it matter if we think of the
Tao or of the Self—when the crucial similarity is the experience of grace in the moment, the source being beyond our comprehension and ineffable[?]"[17]

Synchronisitic experiences, Bolen adds, can be either in-
stantaneously charged with significance or require time
for clarification.

Although they likely happen most days, they seem more noticeable during periods of emotional intensity: when we fall in love, for example, wrestle with creative struggle, suffer grievous loss of a loved one, or simply rise to meet critical states of emotional conflict. Tension, stress, and inner turmoil sometimes open people up. Dreams are stirred. Logical understandings (shields) are shattered. We are less sure of ourselves and the heart aches for new levels of orientation and confirmation.

Might some of the natural events I witnessed at Hocoka, I wondered, be a reflection of—even a response to—my inner journey?

The doe on the deck.

The bluejay I touched.

A bull and cow moose, first time ever, that circled Hocoka's cabin where I questioned spending another winter. Then, later that day as I sat at supper with a friend, how I glanced outside where I'd seen the cow moose in the morning, and there, in the exact spot, *in the fading light of twilight between cabin and lake, and as I thought about the powerful passage of moose corralling me at Hocoka: the cow moose passed again.*

What can one do in the face of such synchronicity, such mystery, except look and listen with more humility, openness, and respect?

Bolen's spin on Jung suggests there's positive and negative synchronicity at work in our lives.

Positive synchronicity shows us the path we're on is good. Negative synchronicity thwarts us, nudges us, tricks us, or worse.

This all presumes, of course, that whether we call the sum of everything the Tao, God, or Great Spirit, whether we look at it through the eyes of a Chinese sage, the eyes of Jung, or the eyes of an Ojibwe, the totality has a higher order, an essential harmony, in which we are called to destiny. We each are given a path to walk, a fate to fulfill and, as all major spiritual systems attempt to convey, it's in the best interest of everything and everyone that we discern this soulful journey and follow it faithfully.

Here, Bolen underscores, is our path with heart.

Here, among a myriad of other possible paths (people to meet, places to go, jobs to get, mountains to climb, fantasies to fulfill), is the way that intuitively feels good, right, and joyful. It is our highest calling: what most fully and soulfully engages us. It is what we are uniquely designed to do, *want* to do at the deepest level, and is the most alluring direction to go despite, sometimes, great risk.

Our path with heart, moreover, makes us strong.[18]

When we are on track, Bolen says, the Tao, the Spirit, lets us know in many ways.

"Dreams," she explains, "are usually nourishing; they seem interesting and pleasant, often imparting a sense of well-being. Synchronistically, opportunities seem to open fortuitously, the people we should meet accidentally cross our path, a flow or ease accompanies our work.[19] Each facilitating, unsought event then begins to confer a feeling of being blessed, each serving as a lantern along the way, illuminating the path with heart."[20]

Negative synchronicity, on the other hand, concatenates when we go against our inner feelings and values. Dreams get negative. Things seem hostile. Coincidental events and circumstances pile up, block, and altogether frustrate what we're trying to do. Whether we call this *extreme dissonance,* as psychiatrists might, or—like Stalking Wolf—simply bad signs and omens, there's a pervasive sense we're being warned:

Shift direction, change focus: Stop right now.

This is all conjecture, of course, a kind of talking in tongues about mystery, yet it was something to consider on cold winter nights as deer meandered outside on crusty snow, as I recalled boyhood stories, mulled my life as a single man, or when I weighed the future's writing and rangering opportunities. It is through this glass I looked—a pane of many possibilities—when I found Rip dead and a wolf's approaching trajectory included a yearling, bloodshed, and the .357 in my desk drawer.

I was not prepared, however, for what happened next.

The Dark Night

Cloudy: 42° F: Barometer Rising

Went walking about three o'clock. Met Russell Niskala. He told me a "beautiful" wolf had visited his cabin on Cedar Lake.

One of the wolf's feet was caught in a mink trap which the wolf dragged around.

The wolf came by several times. Niskala finally called the Department of Natural Resources. A guy came out to trap the wolf, in order to remove the other trap, but the wolf was trapwise and couldn't be caught. The DNR gave up.

Niskala heard later the wolf was found dead of starvation.

Reminded me of Cormac McCarthy's book, The Crossing,[1] *in which an old man is explaining the wolf to young Billy. The old man says the wolf is "a being of great order and that it knows what men do not: that there is no order in the world save that which death has put there."*
—journal, Hocoka, Winter

Another winter was coming. I could feel it in the east wind whipping across the length of Lake Superior a hundred miles south of Hocoka. As large gray waves heaved into whitecaps beneath a gray sky, spray was tossed forward, snakes of foam writhed waves, and wind ripped at my jacket.

A chill swept through me.

Carefully, I walked the shoreline's boulders. Sand filled hollows among gray rock ledges. Gulls wheeled in the wind. Another gull stood among the rocks and sand near my feet.

The gull tried to move forward but toppled headfirst into the sand.

Its neck was broken.

Cold wind. Gray sky. Foaming waves.

The gull stood, stepped once or twice, then fell forward again.

I received the bad news a week later.

I was stationed as a park ranger at South Twin Island of Lake Superior where, surrounded by the archipelago of Apostle Islands National Lakeshore off the northern coast of Wisconsin, I was wrapping up the season as gale force winds gusted out of the north. Possible snow was in the forecast. For most of the day I had busied myself with chores: cleaning the *NPS Gull*, my twenty-one-foot Boston Whaler patrol boat, scrubbing firehoses, sweeping the boardwalk and dock, writing year-end reports, inventorying the medical kit, and cleaning the cabin. Packing boxes. Defrosting the refrigerator. Caching firewood. It was my last scheduled day on the island and I felt the impulse to migrate, leave the great lake to its winter power, and get on home.

Even the island's lone goose, which visited me at South Twin every year as autumn's gold leaves flashed against blue sky, had continued its journey south.

Restless yearnings now. Stirrings. Imminent transition.

I would, as usual, head north to Hocoka for winter.

The radio call came at twilight.

"Two-three-three? Two-three-one."

I answered promptly and listened carefully as District Ranger Tom Bredow explained how one of my sisters, and a lady-friend, had called wanting me to know my mother was hospitalized. I was also advised to call my sister as soon as I reached Little Sand Bay on the mainland. Urgent.

How handle?

It was getting dark. Little Sand Bay was twelve miles to the west: past Rocky Island, Bear, Raspberry, Point Detour, and York Island. The *NPS Gull*, soon to be replaced by a new boat, had no radar for night travel. And I was only half-packed to leave.

I knew, once I left the island, I would not be coming back.

There was little doubt what Tom's call meant. My mother had been battling cancer. She had suffered through misdiagnosis, then, once her cancer was identified, the severe discomforts of chemotherapy. Now her condition had worsened and she was in a hospital's oxygen tent. Only later would I learn she'd suddenly had a convulsion.

"The doctors," Tom said, "make no promises. They're doing a CAT scan tomorrow."

"Tell my sister," I said, "I'll boat to the mainland and call first thing in the morning."

I felt helpless that last night on South Twin as faint moonlight spread among the islands. My mother lay in pain, dying, four hundred miles away. Should not a son be there? And how strange, earlier that day between chores, that I'd gone on my last boat patrol to Devils Island. I'd seen a pair of eagles along the island's east shore and, as I rounded the sea caves, my boat bobbing on the lake's great swells, I spotted a self-loading freighter: almost a thousand feet long, about five miles out to sea. The freighter was heading for Duluth.

I gave chase.

Just for the hell of it, I turned the *Gull* seaward and tried to catch the freighter as its distant bow sliced water into white plumes of rolling wake. I had no reason for my impulse: did not know why I suddenly headed further out to sea than I'd ever gone before. I felt free, reckless, daring. It was just me, the boats, and the rolling blue lake.

Or so I thought.

I got halfway to the freighter, turned around, cruised down the west shore of Devils, and, as air grew cold and a gold sun set, returned to South Twin where Tom's call found me.

It didn't make sense.

Joy and grief had collided like two fronts into explosive storm.

I was too tired after leaving South Twin the next morning, boating twelve miles, making my call, and driving 350 miles to northwestern Minnesota to think much about myself, and what was going on, by the time I reached the hospital.

I was numb.

I'd been told on the phone my mother was going to die but was waiting until she saw me.

I took the elevator: walked the marbled hall: passed a

nursing station to a room at the end of the hall where my mother, breathing oxygen through tubes, was . . .

"We need to talk to you for a minute."

It was my oldest sister, Joan, intercepting me on the way to bedside.

"Come in this room."

She guided me into a waiting room where my younger sisters, Josita and Jennifer, stood watch. Couches: good: I'd need them. Coffee table with magazines. Old styrofoam cups with stale coffee. A TV that would go unused.

"Mom wants you to act as power of attorney," Joan said to me. "Also executor."

"Why me?"

No one knew for sure.

"Is this true?" I asked Josita and Jennifer.

They agreed it was . . . had heard my mother make the request in front of them and the doctor.

I needed a cigarette.

"What does this mean?" I asked.

"It means," Joan explained, "that while Mom's alive you'll have authority to act as her representative. Get into her checking account. Savings. If she gets too sick to make her own decisions, in the life or death matters, that'll be up to you."

I let that sink in.

"As executor," Joan added, "you'll be handling her estate. Bills. Household goods. Various personal and legal dispositions."

"We're getting ahead of ourselves," I said.

Joan looked out the door and across the hall.

"Mom," she said, "wants to talk to you now."

I went in, kissed her hello, held her hand, and asked her the normal, dumb hospital question about how she felt. I could see things were going to get tough.

Someone came in the room and I turned to face the window. An orange sun was setting over the flat, prairie horizon: a prairie Ella Mae Huot had known all her life: at birth, through sixty-two winters and, now, most likely her end.

"Kind of pretty, isn't it?" I asked her.

She moaned, seemed to nod.

She was beyond enjoying a sunset.

Leave that to her damn boy.

I had tears in my eyes and turned back to face the window.

"Oh, James," she said, "you've always been so sentimental."

As if I don't, I thought, *have a good reason.*

"Just a cold, Mom," I said, fooling no one.

She asked me, as her only son and executor, to make three promises:

No flowers at the funeral.

Cremate her: "Don't put me in the cold ground."

And she asked that her ashes be buried near the graves of her mother and father, Lea and Joseph, in the small country cemetery on the edge of the village of Dorothy a mile from the family farm.

"Will you do this for me?" she asked.

"Yes."

I felt like I was suffocating. I didn't want to hear the words I was hearing. *No, no, no.* But I said *yes,* and meant it, and would brook no compromise from anyone if they stood in the way of these deathbed promises. My mother was asking me to do three last tasks. I would follow through with them if it killed me.

A wise lady, she began to quiz me aloud when other people were in the room.

"What'd I make you promise?" she'd ask.

I'd then recite her requests.

Once, while my aunt Marion stood near, I saw what my mother was doing. She wanted other people, especially her sisters and brothers, to hear her final wishes. That way, when it came time to carry them out, they wouldn't think they were more of Jim dale's lingering hippie ideas.

No one in the Catholic clan, as far as I knew, had been cremated before.

Her condition grew worse.

Morphine dosages were increased.

She would wake up, pass out, then wake up.

One night, as my nephew, Jacques, and I rested on cots next to her bed, she suddenly said she wanted to go home. The wish was barely coherent. Did she mean home in Thief River Falls where she had an apartment as manager of a senior citizens complex? Did home mean heaven? that vast vault of the unknown, locus of mystery, from where she'd come and to where she was going? She lunged out of bed in her nightgown. Jacques and I caught her, eased her back to bed, and tried to decipher what she meant.

"Home," I told the doctor out in the hall. "She wants

to go home. What will happen if I take her out of here, leave the hospital, stop the morphine and oxygen and other medication?"

"She'll probably go into convulsions," he said, "or into a coma."

"Is there anything we can do that we're not doing?" I asked. "Is there any hope at all?"

"No," he said, little knowing his own mother would die within months. "Everything that can be done is being done."

I went back into the room.

What time is it? I wondered. *What day is it?*

"Mother?"

She was unconscious.

And I knew, there in that hospital at that dark hour, if anyone was doing this to her besides life and the shadow of death, any man or woman, any person causing such harm, I'd stop them or kill them on the spot.

Home.

Hadn't this woman, my mother, always wanted a home she could call her own?

How could I forget the time we were ousted from a house, the rent money unavailable, my father in prison? Grandpa Huot had picked us up in his Nash and drove to an abandoned farmhouse near Red Lake Falls, grass on me waist-high, linoleum flooring wrinkled, windows broken. *Live* here? There was a creek nearby, which was a good sign, but where—I asked Ma—would I go to school?

She indicated the countryside's one-room schoolhouse. Not the one she'd gone to school in, but a homely one I'd spotted along the way, my boy nose pressed to the car's backseat window as I peered out, my imagination flying an open cockpit biplane, again wondering where, really, we were going.

I felt sad.

The school wasn't St. Joseph's. It wasn't near my friends.

Fortunately, Grandpa wasn't going to have his Ella Mae and her kids live in a house wind howled through. He turned the Nash around, gingerly crossed back over a stream's log bridge, and we never went back to a house that haunted me more in that hospital hour than it did that day as Grandpa led the way.

How forlorn *ma mère*, with four kids in her care, must have been. Single parent. Late twenties. No income. Disappointment and humiliation among people who believed in place, loyalty, and family values.

The problem wasn't my father being in prison. My mother put him there. She no longer wanted anything to do with him. At wit and heart's end, she'd nailed him—with help from priest and county—for lack of child support.

"Of course," he later told me when I'd tracked him down, "the county also had other reasons to put me away."

He, too, was from a broken home.

His father, for a $650 legal sum, surrendered rights to him to my German grandmother before disappearing from us all.

My father came out fighting, drinking, and pushing

his luck. In the end, as I lived to know, he lost the best thing he ever had.

Ken came.

Ken MacDonald, who had navigated our canoe down the Little Missouri River in North Dakota's Badlands years before, came unasked and unannounced to see how I was doing. We met in the waiting room, then went down to the entryway of the hospital for a smoke. We stood in silence as he checked my eyes, my energy, how things fared in the stern on this new, dangerous river.

He knew, from his own father's grim passing, the bomb that was going off in my life for all time.

Everything that had seemed important prior to this ordeal was now on the edge of things. Little bits of life's flotsam, once stage center, were now eggshell shards barely holding light on the rim of a vast and expanding crater amidst glass, stainless steel, and a door opening to what was and would be.

"James?"

My mother was asking a question. I'd said something about God, the Great Spirit, whatever the word was meaning the full power permeating the world.

"Yes?"

"I didn't know you believed in God."

You gotta be kidding.

Here was a woman who had been Catholic all her life, who attended Mass in full faith and soul, who believed in heaven and hell, the saints and angels and Virgin Mary, who said her prayers behind closed doors, whose fingers had polished beads of said rosaries, who had ushered her kids through Catholic elementary schools, Catholic high school, and me through a Catholic college, hoping—if the call came—I'd devote myself to priesthood, then watched me as I changed my ways, veered this way and that, and stopped going to communion. Then Sunday Mass. And because of this twisting trail, this alteration of ritual devotion, she thought I'd fallen away from the spiritual path and no longer believed in a higher power.

Without saying a word to me. Without a scolding. Without a righteous threat of what was, by god, bound to happen.

She had simply anchored herself in her quiet faith, her love and, I suppose, a deep trust that there lived in me, like a candle flame in wind, hope I'd reacquaint myself on some fine day—when the light was gold and meadowlarks sang—with my soul.

How had we gone so wrong?

How had I so misrepresented myself?

How she must have suffered fearing her only son, who had so much hope, was a goner.

"Not true, Mom."

She looked at me with those dark brown eyes challenging all inkling of deceit.

"Just because I rarely go to church these days," I said, "nor take communion, doesn't mean I don't believe in God. A Great Spirit."

She seemed to relax as I, thankful for this moment to set the record straight, leaned into and out of a sadness, a panic, over what had almost happened.

In the end, my sisters and I gathered around our mother and told her, as we held her hands, we loved her.

She had been the one person in the world who, when push came to shove, when fun or opportunity rubbed against responsibility, had stuck with us. She had fed us, clothed us, and given us hope.

We were thankful and it was important she know this.

Another day went by as we came and went from the hospital, always one of us with Mother, us getting little rest: living on cookies, coffee, tobacco, and, pure gift, chicken soup made by a friend who, with the wisdom of woman and caregiver, knew we needed nourishment.

It helped give us strength to pray that final night.

"Our father, who art in heaven . . ."

How many times, countless, had we said that prayer as kids in her presence? Now we stood at the foot of *her* bed.

". . . hallowed be thy name."

Of any woman alive, she had connected with that prayer, meant it when she said it, and was now being called to the spirit she had faithfully addressed.

". . . thy kingdom come, thy will be done . . ."

Her feet slowly turned blue. Her fingers turned blue.

". . . on earth as it is in heaven."

And her skin became cold.

She was gone. Oh god, she was gone.

I stepped alongside the bed and kissed her on the forehead.

"I want my mother!"

Josita was crying, pounding on my chest.

"I want my mother!"

I put my arms around Josita and hugged her. Let her

cry. I wanted to cry. Let her cry. Something wanted to rip loose with a howl. A great vacuum was forming. A void. I wanted to cry. I couldn't. Everything was crashing, imploding, shifting. *The gull with broken neck.* Outside was night. Inside was night. *Winter in the wind, gray waves,* cry, *the gull flopping forward,* too exhausted, *into a pool of* what? *promises.*

I had to keep the promises.

Far from Hocoka, far from beautiful Solo, her fawns, and the glory of night sky, far from anything but the heaviness of cold darkness, I went to the home of my youngest sister. I was given a niece's single bed to sleep in. Numb. Wasted. I took off my clothes in the small, strange room with dolls and girl things, and crawled into bed without turning off the light. I was leery of the dark with its swirling possibilities and the manner it might evoke vivid last images.

Was I a boy afraid of the dark or a death-shocked man?

I didn't know, didn't care.

I wanted to see *things* when I opened my eyes. I wanted visual ground I could set an anchor in, where it might lodge, where it might keep me from spinning further into a yawning black hole that sucked now at my own life.

Grandma Lea.

Might my mother, like *her* mother, appear to me now?

I doubted my heart could stand it.

Too much feeling. Too much ache. Too much wrenching of the cord, the connection, the sure and certain line of flesh to flesh, love to love, severed now by the inevitable way of the world.

Death's order.

She wanted cremation and so I made arrangements.

There was a wake, the condolences of family friends, yet the dawn came gray and cold when I sat in a car heading for a crematorium in Fargo. Marlin Brule, a brother-in-law, and Dan Duquette, another, rode in the car with me on our journey of solemn purpose. My mother's body had already been shipped ahead to the crematorium. I was to sign papers approving the cremation then, later in the day, after the task was done, we would bring the cremains to the cemetery where my mother wanted to be buried.

A Catholic priest would meet us for a brief burial ceremony.

That, anyhow, was the plan.

We found the crematorium among tall trees off to the side of a large cemetery. There were two buildings, one with furnace and storage area, where the hearses backed up, the other a maintenance building where a man younger than myself had me sign legal papers in a messy office. We immediately walked over to the crematorium where I was shown where and how bodies were cremated. There were two bodies in coffin-shaped cardboard boxes ready to be burned.

Was one my mother?

I had promised her this grim morning.

I told the man who operated the crematorium I wanted to look in my mother's box. I had to know she was there, that there could be no mistake, as much for my own peace of mind as keeping a deathbed promise.

"That's not recommended," he said.

"Jim, I'll look," Marlin said.

"No," I insisted. "Let me."

The box was opened. It was my mother. I traced a small cross on her forehead with my thumb, as she would have understood, and bid farewell again.

"Three hours," the man said. "Come back in three hours."

There was no place to go this cold, windy day, except to a mall where we wandered stores and ended up in a restaurant.

Marlin and Dan managed small talk and food.

I could handle neither.

Burning.

Right this very moment: the one person in life who had always been there, who had spared me the physical and emotional beatings of her own frustrations, who had lived for elders and young ones: burning this instant in a strange city whipped with cold wind.

It made me nauseous but I had to make a phone call.

The grave needed digging.

So many decisions and now one more.

Marlin had been kind enough to build a small pine box for the cremains, yet I still needed to decide exactly who was going to dig the grave. The cemetery was on the edge of a small village where the locals took care of themselves. I could either have a local man, likely a distant relative, dig the grave, or I could do it myself.

Who was it going to be?

There was a pay phone in the doorway of the restaurant.

Where was I going to draw the line? When and how was I going to let go? In my desperation to do what I was asked, must I dig my own mother's grave?

Enough, I thought. *You've gone far enough.*

I walked to the phone, fed a quarter in the slot, and called for help.

Three days later, with my mother's ashes in the ground where she wanted them, it was time for me to go home, return to Hocoka, lay my tired body and heart down where they could get some needed rest.

See Solo.

A snowstorm, however, had just passed through the Quetico-Superior leaving a foot of heavy wet snow snapping branches and toppling trees. Roads were icy. It would be prudent to wait just a short while.

Then I'd go.

I had just enough time for a quick trip to Huot Park, what the state calls Old Crossing Treaty Memorial Park, a few miles away from my mother's grave and her girlhood farm of innocent days. I'd known the park, while growing up, more as a beautiful place to go than a historic site where *métis* ox cart trains once forded Red Lake River between Winnipeg and St. Paul. More, even, than the site of an 1863 treaty where Ojibwe ceded the Red River Valley to an expanding and won't-take-no-as-an-answer America. My dad had taken me fishing there at

least once as a lad or, more like it, I'd tagged along with
him and a buddy. During high school, I'd partied hardy
at the park only to rev it up later during journeys home
from St. John's University: getting high as an old peyote
medicine man in the night shroud of the park's cottonwoods. I'd slept next to campfires on the river's grassy
banks.

There was a timelessness there, rich with the shadows
of passing peoples.

I needed them now.

Sioux warrior. Ojibwe hunter. Prairie-blackened ox
cart driver. Raven-haired women in doeskin skirts washing their riverside feet: *Bon jour, ma'am.* Cavalry officers
barking orders, polishing buttons and sabers. Tents and
tepees, baying mules, letter carriers with sled dog teams.
Tired French-Canadian settlers pausing to talk plow,
heifers, crop disease.

And the big cottonwoods themselves, their leaves
rippling in summer breeze or bare branches moaning in
bitter January wind: all a collage calling me—short of
Hocoka—to anchorage, singing:

Come sit by the river: lay it all down here boy.
Don't wait.

Serena Duquette, my seven-year-old niece, Josita's
daughter, came with me, riding shotgun to an uncle's
grief.

We rode in silence in my mother's car, us staring
through glass at dirt fields, the car dipping down then
into the river valley where farms gave way to cottonwood groves and the slick, brown sheen of the inces-
santly flowing Red.

I parked near the bronze statue of an erect Ojibwe

elder holding a peace pipe in his arms: a Red River Valley shrine: a symbol, I figured, rich in gesture by a culture that came to call the shots.

"Serena," I called, "come here."

I was standing by the riverbank, she around the bend. She came.

"Let's see if we can throw a rock across the river. Hit the other side."

We tried.

Plop: nope, my stone fell short.

Plip: hers did too.

We threw again and again, my shoulder getting sore, my eyes drawn to clamshells and shards of shoreline stones. I squatted, picked up a stone, and glanced to my right. Gold sunshine gleamed on straw-colored grass. I looked closer. The cold day had been cloudy, heavy with gray, yet light at last rayed through sky past cottonwood to nip the tips of breeze-swayed grass. The grass rustled. It swished a cold-season song while beyond— bathed for an instant in rich, gold, light—the river banked to the left as it curved out of sight.

She's here, I thought. *She's here in the beauty of gold-lit grass.*
She's here in my love for Serena and kin. She's here evermore in what I embrace, whether earth and sky or river and snow.

Again the grass rustled, swishing with wind, as I took Serena's hand for the infinite way home.

There were flies, countless flies, on the cabin windows when I finally reached Hocoka.

I killed them and more kept coming.

There had been flies in the cabin before but rarely more than a few at a time. They would snap into the shade of my lamp, whacking it in crazy orbits, spiraling around faster than a right-handed catch: likely lured to heat and light. Now they seemed to hatch out of nowhere. Maybe they came from inside the bark of firewood, or from a dead mouse in some unseen cranny of the cabin walls. Regardless, they did nothing good for my mood.

Which was worse, after all?

The flies or the self-image of a man whack-whack-whacking flies with a swatter in a large window of a remote cabin in a crack between long nights of winter grief?

If a person stepped back far enough from the scene, he or she might not even see the flies. Just a tormented man swatting at his reflection on glass.

I became impossible: short on patience with dissonance.

Any trouble people gave me, all unnecessary demand, was deflected. There simply was no energy left except to meet the basic needs of self-maintenance. Food. Water. Rest. Letters and calls to siblings as they needed attention, questions answered, assurances. It was pure conservation of resources protecting life force. No different, really, than a starving deer on its last leg at the end of a severe, malnourished winter.

Every step, each movement, counted.

My feet were heavy . . . darkness a force to fear. My chest ached with an abiding, physical pressure.

Boxes of my mother's legal papers, journals, and checks were piled in corners of the cabin. A freak rainstorm leaked in walls from neglected caulking.

More flies.

Flies in the storm-tossed ship as seas, building, battered hull, cabin walls, rails, deckings.

Emptiness a hollow hole with water gushing in, gushing out: the hole a two-way flow, a wound for the blood of all seas to wash through on the edge of everywhere.

Visibility: zilch. Electricity: gone.

Communication systems: all but shut down.

More night wind yet.

One evening I drove to Ely and called a lady-friend from a restaurant's pay phone to postpone a visit because of sleet and icy roads. Neglected, she was angry, hollering into my ear. I held the phone away from my face and knew, that instant, I'd had enough.

"There'll be no more phone calls like this," I said, "at my expense."

I returned home, wrote her, and tried to explain but drew boundaries clear and certain. Sorry: other priorities. She couldn't, of course, understand. She'd never lost someone she loved, let alone a blood mother, in front of her eyes.

She wrote back soon.

I had gone over the edge, she said.

We were done.

Six weeks and two of the most important people in my life were gone.

And so the great loneliness deepened, a kind of natural stain coming with departures and isolation, as if tannin leached from the roots of life, of social connections, of man's natural gregariousness, into the clear waters of a remote reach.

I could feel the sense of isolation sharpest at night when driving home from Ely after errands. The two-lane tar road became a gravel road, which turned onto a half-mile single lane driveway, where, at lane's end, I parked then walked, snowshoed, or skied to the cabin with its cool, dark rooms. Often, as I stepped up to the cabin, I would flash my headlamp toward the deer-feeding areas. Solo? Princess? There were times when the wild eyes of deer reflected my light as the glowing eyes, bobbing, looked up. Many times no eyes shone in the dark.

Still, even then, I knew the deer were somewhere nearby in that bottomless darkness. I could sense their presence as I lit lamps, fired-up stoves, and called upon what courage might be mine one more long-lasting night.

I lay in bed one night by the main stove and looked out the window, then up at the cabin's ceiling beam.

A man, I thought, *could hang himself from that.*

But, no. It would take too much from them. Josita. Serena. Jennifer. Their energies, like mine, were barely at a sustainable point. Didn't I have responsibility to help everyone through the hardest time of our lives? I *couldn't* surrender. Never. To the contrary, from now on I had to carry more weight: help stabilize a large vacuum swirling in vortex like black water down a drain: threatening to pull everything, me included, with it.

What energy remained had to be more than nurtured. It had to surface enough not only to sustain myself but those of my blood and in my love.

You must go on.

For the first time in my life I felt old.

I looked back out the window.

The stars Castor, Pollux, and Procyon shone in the east as they tracked over the heights of Rainbow Ridge. To their right, sparkling even higher in the clear sky, were the stars of Orion or, as some Ojibwe called him,[2] *Gaabiboonoke*: Wintermaker.

The stars somehow seemed more eternal and, in their incomprehensible distance and isolation, more beautiful than ever.

The best I could do, of course, given events, was to trudge onward: keep looking, listening and, like Dylan sings, keep knocking on heaven's door.

Hard questions nevertheless surfaced to deepen the darkness.

What in the hell, after all, *was* I learning on my paths in the woods? from my alleged simple cabin life? or while looking at stars in the full sweep of winter isolation?

What was I learning saying farewell to a spouse and mother?

Everything and everyone was coming and going: living, leaving, or dying: the whole gamut with me entwined and lacking the sense to just get up and go.

Instead I stayed, always stayed, asking my questions, looking for sign, and hoping the mystery would shift more clearly into view and I'd find some of the bliss I bargained for.

Hadn't I given my life, all that I had and was, for a little godforsaken insight?

Where was the enlightenment striven for in youth?

the wholeness and peace I'd envisioned a cabin in the woods might bring?

Where was the happiness we all want when we awaken each morning, having prayed for a break right around the bend?

It came down to this sometimes:

I had to ask the questions and stand ready for the answers whether I liked them or not. And I had to risk Sri Nisargadatta, an Indian spiritual master,[3] being right.

"The mind creates the abyss," he once said, "and the heart crosses it."

But crosses into what?

A twilight came, then, like a soft, surprising snow, and it was time to fetch water.

I grabbed the scoop and water buckets and walked down Hocoka's slippery slope toward the lake. I eased my way down, angled between young pines, then switchbacked to the cove's shore. Soon I was kneeling and scooping water. Only eight gallons this time. There was a good supply of water up at the cabin and I would just top it off.

Still, at least forty pounds to carry.

How long can I do this?

On the way uphill back to the cabin I decided to check on the canoe barge. Pulled ashore, it was fine. I looked out over the lake. Distant shorelines were dusted with snow. The eagle of two days earlier, which I watched soar in falling snowflakes high above the lake, was nowhere to be seen.

I returned to my task, began walking toward the cabin, and stopped.

There was company.

Renard, the fox with missing paw, was sitting near the trail in front of me. He watched me closely as I also spotted Solo beyond him. They were lined up. She was framed by pine trunk and bough as, in dusk's last light, she chewed cud and looked off to the side.

Renard. White pine. Solo and cabin.

I knelt down in such dream-life, remembering the way, the long way, and Renard limped toward me in the gathering darkness.

The Haunting
Moon

Clear Moonlit Sky: 19° F: Barometer Steady

*At dusk, while I chopped kindling and did last day-
light chores, the clouds seemed to thin then suddenly
grew thick and began to snow.*

*Snowflakes drifted down from the sky, angling
slightly south: wads of flakes falling . . . silently
falling . . . thickening. First Hub's Cove disappeared from view, then the lake, all of it.*

Whiteout.

*Nothing could be seen toward the lake except
all-encompassing whiteness silhouetting nearby
trees. The deck, birdfeeders, everything was coated
with powdery snow.*

*Soon the snowing clouds passed and gave way
to tonight's moonlight.*

—journal, Hocoka, Winter

A nd just like that, every moon
began to haunt me.

They had risen full, cratered, orange-paling-to-white:
silhouetting pine branches on cold ridgetops in winter
or rising full and swollen over the restless waters of Lake
Superior. There had been moons over the prairie of the
Red River Valley, shining over countless lakes of the
Quetico-Superior canoe country, sparkling on night waters of remote, serpentine rivers, glowing on snow of

subarctic taiga, or shining winter after winter through Hocoka's cabin windows.

Many moons for me, at least 540, each with its own story.

Now, however, with the passing of Hocoka's darkest night, the moon had a new edge to it and I was beginning to understand why.

Emotional tides.

Although everyone is affected by the moon, which marks our months with light, biorhythms, and moods, I began to see there are those among us, including myself, who experience great swings of lunar resonance. They can come as softly as a strange sense of something amiss or askew, or they might surface with full fear and trembling as they ride restless night wind. Anything might be evoked: the peck of owl, stealth of wolf, moose's fearless stare, unseen watch of cougar, even a scary gritching of psychos on the loose.

Yes, we might even feel, in a moment of bravado, *rise oh moon, rise: swing across our night: make the midnight shadows dance with surprise and coup.*

Or, tide falling, we might go down.

We fret. Worry. Feel the wrongness of things. We obsess about our loves as the old ship of abandonment sails night waters. We remember the look and taste of someone we loved as our mouths—hot and wet: tongues probing—pressed against moonlit flesh. Some of us gnaw our nails, sense strange and distant longings, look at scabs or twirl a lock of hair in nervous fingers, and we know the ice we walk, the life we talk, is thin.

Everyone else better walk over there. Not here.

There are cracks everywhere, the roof is coming

down, we're gonna be found out, and there's no one to call.

The night is kissed with peril on a blind date with doom.

Such a moonlit tide, then, we might feel, as if some sea within us heaves parallel to, if not beyond, gravitational pull.

Should this surprise us?

Are we not more than microcosmic Atlantics and Pacifics pressing against the molten earth or swelling away?

Are we, who are mostly water, still not more than H_2O in the cup that so gently tilts with measurable tide?

And what of the dewdrop on wild rose? The drops of water from muzzle of streamside doe? Or rain wet on a jay's feather, beading on blue as clouds part, revealing the moon, what then?

Are we one with all the droplets and seas of the world, and the energy binding them, in a subtle leaning toward night light?

Who can speak, really, of such mystery?

It's an intuitive flow, a waxing and ebbing of powerful tide, something primordial going back through all the lives, psychic dimensions, karmic chains, and easy drink-side tales of what's what.

Who—or what—can swim this sea except the unfathomable soul?

Some people, of course, think they know what the moon is up to.

They say one's reaction to the moon might be based,

in part, on when we are born. Someone born during a new moon, for example, when it's lined up with the sun and lost in solar radiance, might respond differently to the power of moon than someone who comes into this world on a night of pull and shine.

But what, then, of those among us who, like myself, were born three or four days after a full moon? And what if, ditto, that full moon was eclipsed to the tune, say, of .629 in shadow?

It was in such waning March moonlight I came into the world of Thief River Falls in windswept northwestern Minnesota. Now, at Hocoka, it was in waxing moonlight, a moon of any name, that I felt another emergent presence.

This, in part, is what haunted.

The emergence was the unknown coming into being.

It was heaven and hell, bliss and terror: all the polarities, opposites and extremes on the loose.

It was chaos birthing harmony.

This, anyhow, I hoped.

Moons are known by many names.

Among the Quetico-Superior's native Ojibwe, those names have always referred to the seasons and the spirit world.

January, for example, has the moon of the Great Spirit. February has the moon of suckers, which begin swimming upriver. March comes with the moon of snow-crust, as hot sun helps make the month a good time to travel. April's moon refers to cracked and broken snowshoes: snow has melted revealing rock, log, ledge, all abrasive to wood and sinew; what's not damaged is destroyed by their owners as snowshoes are no longer needed.

May has the flower moon, June the strawberry moon, July the raspberry moon, August the whortleberry moon, and September the moon of wild rice.

October's moon, reflecting the season, is that of the falling leaf. The freezing moon hails November.

And December? the month of darkness, cold, and limited mobility?

Its moon, not surprisingly, is that of little spirits.

The Ojibwe—just to keep right with the sun's cycle—occasionally added a thirteenth, nameless moon.

This is the moon, some months, I grew leery of.

This is the moon that might sneak up behind me some night, shine me on the shoulder, and deliver bad news.

Black Elk, the Oglala Lakota holy man, viewed moons differently than the Ojibwe.

"The moon lives twenty-eight days and this is our month," he once explained.[1] "Each of these days represents something sacred to us: two of the days represent the Great Spirit; two are for Mother Earth; four are for the four winds; one is for the Spotted Eagle; one for the sun; and one for the moon; one is for the Morning Star; and four are for the four ages; seven for our seven great rites; one is for the buffalo; one for the fire; one for the water; one for the rock; and finally, one is for the two-legged peoples. If you add all these days up you will see that they come to twenty-eight. You should know also that the buffalo has twenty-eight ribs, and that in our war bonnets we usually wear twenty-eight feathers.

"You see, there is a significance for everything, and

these are things that are good for men to know and to remember."

There was a time, before Hocoka's dark night, when I would plan my backcountry trips around full moons. I wasn't intimidated by them. I used them.

Moons were friends, allies, guardians.

They blessed my nights with sparkling beauty and lit the way across calm waters.

It was more than romance.

On many of my long canoe journeys I would come across large lakes impassable by day's wind and waves. As day waned, however, winds would calm and waves subside. Calm waters often coincided precisely with sunset. If my companions and I were going to cross a predictably restless lake, we had to do it at night. And so it was we found ourselves paddling *à la belle étoiles*, under the beautiful stars, in the open air, often in the glow of moonlight:

Liquid silver flashing, sharding, zigging, flashing, and splintering on undulating swells of silvery waves.

Sometimes a moonbeam would be a path for the paddle, or it would angle toward us from the side, bathe us with light, and cast a ghostly glow on a nearby shoreline.

We scanned maps by moonlight, found tent sites by moonlight or, already hunkered down, we'd sit on a moonlit shore and gawk at it all.

That was before I shot the yearling, buried Rip's stiff body beneath stars, or lay in my cabin bed looking through a picture window at the full moon rising so pure, clear, fine: yet seeing a hospital room, feeling a cold wind in Fargo, and sensing fully the shock of mortality.

Couldn't help it. Came the tide.

The power of personal passage had struck home.

I was reminded, perhaps, that just as moonlight dances on the waters of my days it also strikes a sheen on a prairie gravestone.

But what, I inevitably asked, of the *general* turbulence?

Why do so many people—in the light of bright moons—feel strange, uncertain stirrings?

Crime rises. Hospital beds fill. Cars careen crazily on highways as we oddly pace, ponder, or leave the house altogether with pack, canoe, car, or skis for god-knows-where.

Perhaps, as lunar pundits allege, it's all just a matter of energy and the force of attraction.

During a new moon, which we can't see, the moon is lined up with the sun. Their combined gravitational pulls give us a steady, assuring charge. As the moon drops back, however, rising an hour later each day, its gravity and reflected light split us.

We get pulled in two directions in a kind of celestial schizophrenia.

We step on the cat, drop dishes, break straps, trip with snowshoes, fall skiing, or swing an axe, miss the wood, and nearly drive cold steel clear to shin bone. We feel and say things that we can't, later, believe.

We are, in short, haunted.

It is time to get bravely moving and cross the water: whatever that, in body, spirit, or wintertime, might mean.

Life Ascending

Clear Sky: 32° F: Barometer Rising

No, nature is not God, but nature is an expression of God, and it is largely a beautiful, awesome expression, causing the heart to open in wonder, and this opening—like true prayer—is a way of letting God's force in: from it we learn, see, and make our way in the world.
—journal, Hocoka, Winter

As the haunting moons bore down, and as the ship which was my life careened among winter reefs, I had a hunch what crossing moonlit water might mean.

It meant passing through darkness.

It meant facing one's fear.

It meant following what little light there sometimes was, moving from sign to sign and—blessed or shocked, strengthened or weakened—trusting one was on a trail of evolving, ascendant life.

It was a journey, essentially, of soul.

Come deeper, now, come deeper the wolf had seemed to say when it left the yearling alive for me to kill. *There's no turning back. Come as far as you can see.*

And I had.

Yet right where the trail led—where my navigational lines of latitude and longitude now crossed on the chart—was the course of a man I wasn't sure I wanted to know.

I needed to get across the water.

Here was a hard look at myself and it chilled me to the bone.

I needed my path affirmed at least one more time, preferably over and over, by the natural beauty and wildness I had embraced as a young man at Big Elbow Lake, Burntside Lake, then even more wholeheartedly at Hocoka.

Natural beauty, and the wild force from which it upwells, was what I'd lived for. How else would I understand it? How else bridge the wild with modern culture except by stepping as deeply into the wild as I could? How else see what we are losing, what we've cut ourselves off from: what we take for granted but experientially know increasingly less about? It was a path leading away from steady paychecks, pension plans, and the technological cushions that take the edge off hard living. Not surprisingly, especially under the circumstances, I could be a man hungry for the feedback of wild contact.

Without it, clearly, I was a spiritual dead man.

It was more than a matter of sunsets or splashes of pretty scenery.

It was the way nature speaks to you: touches you, reveals itself, thwarts your way and shakes you deep or affirms your path and blesses you.

Barry Lopez, for example, tells of sitting among hunters in a remote village of Alaska's Brooks Range when one of the men, a Nunamiut, told a story about a wolverine.

The man spoke matter-of-factly without embellishing events.

Apparently a hunter on a snowmobile was following a wolverine, which he hoped to kill. The man followed tracks over the rolling tundra until he spotted the wolverine, just a distant speck on the crest of a hill where the wolverine stopped to look back. The hunter continued the chase with the wolverine always over the next rise.

"The hunter," Lopez recalled, "topped one more rise and met the wolverine bounding toward him. Before he could pull his rifle from its scabbard the wolverine flew across the engine cowl and the windshield, hitting him square in the chest. The hunter scrambled his arms wildly, trying to get the wolverine out of his lap, and fell over as he did so. The wolverine jumped clear as the snow machine rolled over, and fixed the man with a stare. He had not bitten, not even scratched the man. Then the wolverine walked away. The man thought of reaching for the gun, but no, he did not."[1]

The other stories, Lopez said, were much like this: not making a point but "evoking something about contact with wild animals that would never be completely understood."

I didn't completely understand it either, yet there seemed something in the wild mosaic flowing around me that could touch me, hitting me in the chest, when least expected and, often, most necessary. I simply couldn't deny the uncanny juxtapositions, nor the timely occurrence, of powerful events.

They nurtured and sustained.

They kept me going and led me forward.

It made me think of a remark Loren Eiseley once made in *The Unexpected Universe*,[2] similar to an Apache belief, that a legend had come down to linger among native people "that he who gained gratitude of animals gained help in need from the dark wood."

With all that was going on, had I inadvertently gained gratitude from animals by paying attention to them, respecting them, and appreciating their beauty?

When I, in turn, needed soulful life—when troubled hours scratched at the cabin door—were the deer, wolves, fox, and all the wild beauty of the Quetico-Superior my help?

Of course.

I sensed this deeply when Solo and Renard appeared to me as I hauled water in the gathering gloaming. They might simply have wanted food, yes, yet I couldn't shake the possibility they came, in part, because they sensed my spirit. They, or the force they manifest, knew I was sometimes lost on the edge of fucking nowhere and I needed sign. Touch. Contact. Didn't many natives believe whitetails gave themselves to hungry, worthy hunters? Might not deer, and all their relations, give themselves in a similar way to soulful situations?

Who can say?

Who can say why a wild fox and essentially wild deer would stand twenty feet apart, look at someone, and practically line his path to a cabin that once housed, and still did, infinite hope?

It's one man's data summary against another's.

Or it's her footnote against mine.

For me, it became an arrogance to think some kind of soulful connection wasn't possible. It was rude to the possibilities of life and indirectly called men like the historical Kagagengs—with their spiritual sense of life's oneness, its guardians, and powerful dreams—liars: perhaps spouting off quaint, spiritual oddities for the amusement of ethnologists. This attitude is the ultimate indignity shown a people. Moving natives onto boundaried reservations is nothing compared to dismissing the insights they hold close to their hearts.

Cultural arrogance, I could see, ran very deep.

The hard questions, of course, stayed with me.

The mind took care of that.

You surface from direct, living experience, and there they are, the questions, laughing like hyenas in your face or flying ahead like mocking snowshoes.

What *was* I learning on my paths in the woods, and by living the way I was?

How *had* the wolf and deer spoken to me during that killing winter?

Had they spoken since?

If so, what were they saying?

If I couldn't fully understand death ripping through space in front of me, whether in a hospital or with a crude hollow-point bullet from a stainless steel .357 in my own hand, how could I possibly decipher the more subtle rocks, fire, water and, one supposes, snow?

How read this sea?

How understand with soul immutable life?

How convey it?

It seemed a task words could not reach: an awareness unfolding layer by layer, revealing itself, yet increasingly more difficult to comprehend or articulate. And the mystery was mine, unique in aspect and mysterious in design. No guidebook on a bookstore's bookshelf was going to touch this stuff.

At a certain point, I realized, we are all on our own.

We go into a place of danger where there are no paths, no trails, no self-help New Age paradigms: because no one, in quite one's own way, one's own manner, has been there before.

Lessen your wants, the great Po Chu-i once advised for the journey, *husband your powers*:

> And you will have no need to
> Buy provisions along your way.
> You will cross many rivers and come at last to
>   a sea
> So wide you cannot see the further shore.
> Yet you will go on, without knowing whether
> it will ever end.
> Here all that come with you will turn back.
> But you will still have far to go . . .[3]

There was a question of an intellectual nature that I couldn't shake as I contemplated my winter life among deer and wolves.

I'd noticed something deep flowing through all things, an infinite array of energy alignments and realignments, the comings and goings, the manifestations and dissolutions, and I'd sensed in it a sometimes harsh but innate balance. Nothing new in this. From death, of course, came other forms of life, the wolf's life from the deer's life, my life from a stream of ancestors, all of it a regeneration allegedly evolving in aeonian striving.

But toward what?

Here is the question all great naturalists, like all philosophers and theologians, nay, all people, must inevitably answer. Or try to. This is no small feat. To bring one's ideas into a comprehensive explanation of what is going on in the universe is the culmination of a profound thinker's life: the gold at the end of intellectuality's rainbow.

Most of us never get there.

I knew all about this dance: its subtle sidesteps and dodges.

We wallow in all the possibilities. We flounder in the deep snow of relativities. And we are reminded again and again, by intuition, dream, or experience, that so much lies beyond the reach of words. So we race on, turn to this channel or that, check the E-mail, take a peek at the stock market, spin our wheels, and let everyone else do the talking as we continue to weave what we hope someday gets woven.

A rare exception to such evasiveness (or is it, sometimes, moral cowardice?) came to my winter attention with Alexander F. Skutch's *Life Ascending*. Although the book was essentially ignored by the environmental press, *Life Ascending* revealed the work of a consummate naturalist. After sixty years of studying animal, vegetable, and bird life in tropical America, Skutch assembled what he called a "highly personalized attempt at a philosophic synthesis of what is known and currently theorized about the universe."[4]

What might have been a ponderously dry, overextended theme for stove-side study, however, ended up a stimulating look at what a world-class naturalist believes.

Skutch's vision, in essence, was—and remains—a defense of conservation and the preservation of nature important to our time.

He began by calling attention to the uniqueness of Earth and its fitness to support life. He describes Earth's location in relation to the sun and other solar systems, and how life such as ours couldn't have evolved elsewhere. He explores the intricacies of inorganic and organic life: how both have fueled the development of plants, insects, animals, and people.

Even the intricacy of fact is intriguing.

We learn, for example, that the total mass of animal life in the oceans is estimated at six times that of vegetable life. That terrestrial flora weighs about a hundred times as much as all terrestrial animals. And that insects comprise about three-quarters of the estimated one million known species of the animal kingdom. Skutch focuses on how the chain of plant-insect-animal led to humans and the ascent of unique consciousness. Here, apparently, is where Skutch's vision breaks loose from other evolutionary theory as he attributes the rise in human consciousness to the development of four correlated faculties: upright posture, manual dexterity, intelligence, and speech.

All have kept pace with each other in the evolution of hominid reason and, inevitably, a most rich psychic awareness.

"A world without beings that feel and enjoy," he says,

"would appear to lack significance. No matter how fair its skies, how balmy its air, how green its landscapes, without sentient inhabitants, it would appear as desolate as the Sun-scorched, lifeless spheres of Mercury and the Moon. All the value in the Universe—everything that, as far as we can tell, gives it meaning and worth— depends upon its psychic aspect . . ."

Brave words.

At the heart of psychic development, Skutch says, is our quest for—and contemplation of—natural beauty. Beauty delights our awareness. It has been an alluring light in our evolution all along the way, cheering us, and fortifying our will to live. In this way beauty has been the "spiritual cement of the cosmos" encouraging people, if not all life, to adapt aesthetically to their wider world.

Can it be, he asks, we have become—above all—instruments or organs for the perception of beauty? That this is our most significant contribution to the whole to which we belong?

"When we enjoy beauty," he adds, "as when we know and understand, we are the Universe appreciating and understanding itself by means of organs which, by means of aeonian striving, it has created for this purpose."

Conservation, like compassion, Skutch says, is born of beauty. Conservation is "where ecology and ethics meet." It is nature's indirect attempt to compensate for the excessive reproductive powers of humans, our greed, and a means to express grateful appreciation of Earth's beauty.

"Only the thoughtless person," he explains, "can fail to recognize that the ultimate foundation of everything he cherishes is the natural world, and, if capable of gratitude, he will stubbornly defend it."

To do so, people must work from a center of specific attributes and attitudes. We need to know love, which grows from gratitude. And we need to be frugal, foresighted, and approach decisions with humility and reverence. From reverence (and related attitudes traditionally considered religious) comes fervor to protect the environment, without which efforts to preserve nature will ultimately fail.

What is a convincing presentation of human capacity to appreciate beauty erupts at book's end into an analysis of expansive spirit, appreciative minds, and human organs of appreciation. Skutch explores love, individuality, and cosmic loyalty defined as devotion to "harmonization," sentience, and "advancement of cosmic striving."

Perhaps optimisim is the greatest value of *Life Ascending.*

In our age of microchips and superconductivity, and at the tail end of religious movements that have ideologically separated humans from nature, one finds in Skutch's worldview a coherent vision of human significance. We're not just glorified cancer cells, as some critics say. We are to the Earth what Earth is to the solar system: the chief expression point, as far as we know, of what the creative energy can accomplish when it finds favorable natural conditions.

The best among us, moreover, are currently the psychic carriers of an appreciation fueling an evolutionary spiral of cosmic importance.

Life ascending.

Life generating life generating consciousness.

Consciousness blooming from the planet's abundant verdure and animality to appreciate life's infinite beauty.

I liked this.

It was good to see a naturalist go this far.

Skutch's purpose, of course, wasn't to answer all questions nor explain all mysteries. His intention was to explore values. He wanted to suggest ways of viewing our relationship to life that would elevate our respect, strengthen our loyalty to Earth and its natural forces, and help us all feel less alien.

Even wild man don Juan, brought to us by enigmatic Castaneda, might have given Skutch—had they ever met in the cold shadow of a high country snowstorm— a nod.

Don Juan subscribed to the idea of psychic development and sentient evolution. Enhancement of awareness, he argued, was why all sentient beings existed. It was an old discovery among seers, yet one of great magnitude.

Carlos, when asked by don Juan if he knew a better answer, a more refined reason, for existence, got defensive. Carlos said the question was ridiculous because it couldn't be addressed logically. Any discussion was reducible to religious beliefs: faith.

No way, don Juan said.

He agreed rationality alone couldn't comprehend reasons for being, but added the old seers, by pushing themselves, "risking untold dangers," had actually *seen* the indescribable force they were alluding to: the Spirit-that-moves-through-all-things.

"They called it the Eagle," he said, "because in the few

glimpses that they could sustain, they *saw* it as something that resembled a black-and-white eagle of infinite size."[5]

The Eagle bestowed awareness. It created life so it would enhance the awareness given it. The seers also *saw* that the Eagle devoured that awareness, inevitably relinquished, at death.

"For the old seers," he said, "to say that the reason for existence is to enhance awareness is not a matter of faith or deduction. They *saw* it."

Skutch. Don Juan.

It was more opinion, of course, albeit from some good minds, and I didn't need to be Einstein to realize I would need many more winters, if ever, before I'd hone my beliefs into such creative or imaginary form.

I was stuck, for the time being, with a much simpler approach.

Hauling water. Chopping wood.

Cleaving the present moment.

I'd noticed, years earlier at Big Elbow Lake, that when I left the immediate experience of a task, or the purity of an observation, I could expect trouble. Questions: questions: questions. Some, like those Skutch raised, were good to ask and deserved answers: from them paradigms bloomed. Other questions led to doubt, confusion, sometimes dissonance: the forest of the mind. Salt on old wounds. New fears. Memories of evil in the world: smells of betrayal. That forest. What was true at Big Elbow and along Solid Bottom Creek, however, remained true at Hocoka almost a quarter-century later.

True through 240 full moons.

Peace lay in the vibrant beauty of the present moment.

How, though, stem the mind and heart's wildfire?

How shift perception from the mind's multifaceted concerns, obsessions, and fragile probings to be fully present in the blossoming instant: the miracle of the moment?

What, in other words, and as a Zen apprentice once asked his spiritual master, *is the secret of spiritual awakening?*

Hauling water, the sage said, *chopping wood.*

The rabble of analysis, psychological spin, and reduction of situations to rational interpretation sometimes simply slides to a standstill when you become one with motion and task. When the answers are so hidden in the infinite dimensions of the present you embrace the silence that flung the questions forward. And there, surrendering the struggle for conscious understanding, and by paying attention to what is panned across the senses, the pure suchness of things, one finds the gifts of vibrant beauty.

When the wolf's fur glowed gold in setting sunlight near a pine of Rainbow Ridge: there was a slice of raw, wild beauty.

When the rising sun shone a golden glow on sparkling snow the morning I shot the yearling: there was beauty.

When snow whipped icy bright in hissing waves of gold around my snowshoes: there, again, was breathtaking beauty.

Beauty, then, in the heart of a wild land whose creatures—the wolf, the deer, the sleek red fox—live their lives in a world where, as Cormac McCarthy noted of all wild worlds, storms blow and trees twist in the wind "and all the animals that God has made go to and fro yet this world men do not see."[6]

Yet some of the time we *do* see.

The wild world out on the edge, when we engage it with respect and humility, grants us glimpses of its doings.

We also *hear* it.

The sound of deer hooves—*tung . . . tung*—on thin November ice as I fetched water. Dry oak leaves rattling in late March wind. The crunch of wolves biting a snow-shoe hare beneath moon. Squirrels skittering in branches as I split wood. Screech of eagle. The bawling of the yearling. Deer snorts, stomps, or *thud* of flail. A gray jay's whistling song. Fox barks. The *whump . . . whump* of thick-ening ice held by granite and drummed by infinite space.

It all colors the senses and fills the spirit with the power of its being.

This force can be dramatic, surface explosively, and remind us that wild beauty includes harshness and terror. Or it flows smoothly, subtly, simply slides across the senses with an intricate, infinite sweep.

Here, it seems, is a syncopating harmony, caught in flashing shards, and the moments come as graces.

Graces like walking beneath winter's northern lights: pulses of flashing, transparent lightwaves—flash, disap-pear, flash—the same silent wings of white, milky green, and faint red shooting toward night sky's zenith I'd seen for twenty years or more: flash, flash: as precious as any-thing, any event, any sighting: a fusion of winter night and light, solar-born.

Graces like pausing alone on a cold, moonlit trail on a

January night and hearing a clitter of branches as deer approach. Squeak of hooves on cold snow. Trees, silhouetted, with rimed, snowy branches. Stars. The Big Dipper standing on its handle. Chimney smoke wafting upwards from the cabin, straight up toward the stars, as the smoke's moonshadow skitters away across moonlit snow.

Subzero silence.

Cold air in lungs.

Frost on beard.

And a clean, clear essence spanning all time as the silhouettes and shadows of deer draw near in crystalline, ghostly passage.

Or the grace of having the deer come around after a night of howling wolves. Ruff. Bandit. Solo and fawns. Precious. Princess. The whole family accounted for as the ancient tension ebbs. Then, at dusk, and while standing among the deer, reaching out and touching a doe's left flank.

The graces of Hocoka.

Such moments—caught amidst the swirl of things, embedded in the present moment—were small moments of happiness: movements of clear connection that were perfect.[7]

Over time they added up, kept the balance, buoyed the soul.

Thus the challenge, as don Juan drummed into Castaneda, of an impeccable warrior: to balance the terror of being a man with the wonder of being a man.

This, perhaps, is the journey.

This, perhaps, and here I hoped, is how the heart

crosses the mind's abyss into a deeper, more compassion-
ate love for a world that nurtures until death, and perhaps beyond, its every creature.

No matter the twisted angles.

No matter the pain, the sadness, the loss and hard
dark nights: all the *witchery*, as Leslie Marmon Silko
calls it.

If the path leads to bitterness and stays in darkness,
stopping there, settling for less than light, never ascending, the journey is doomed and must begin again.

Another track, another trail.

Closing the Circle

Stars: 15° F: Barometer Steady

*Had a dream of a bunch of eagle feathers under
water. They were attached to each other, and had
red ribbons.*

*Other feathers—smaller ones—fringed the
eagle feathers, all running parallel, like a blanket or
shield of feathers.*

The feathers were in a flowing river.
—journal, Hocoka, Winter

The circle of Hocoka tight-
ened and closed, I suppose,
on a starry winter night when I howled with the wolves.

Inevitably the snows had come, again and again,
deepening, astounding even old men and women of
many winters. By March the snow-depth approached
the all-time record of 122 inches, almost double the winter average, almost three feet more snow than what deer,
wolf, and people were used to.

It was winter 1995–96.

It was my thirteenth winter at Hocoka.

There'd be days of ten inches of snow, then a few
inches, then a blizzard dumping two more feet. Or just a
foot, then another foot a week later. Tree branches
broke. Roofs in Ely collapsed. Sheds at remote cabins
crumbled. Bitter cold followed snowfall after snowfall.
All life cringed when the thermometer bottomed-out at
-60° F: 92° F colder than ice on puddles.

The effect of so much snow and cold intensified over time.

Slowly, yet inexorably, the wolves stopped ranging except on roads. Never had I seen the wolf patterns so disrupted. Usually a pack would pass through Hocoka about every three weeks: often along Rainbow Ridge and the smaller ridge behind the cabin. They seemed to drive deer through the woods of these ridges out onto the lake where, with a wolf coming from two directions, a deer might make a fatal mistake. This changed as the snow became too deep for the wolves to travel in without bounding. It cost too much to jump. Hence the wolves shrank back to what avenues were open: the plowed corridors of people and their packed trails.

There was a trail into my place, granting entry, but the deep snow beyond Hocoka made for a dead end.

The deer, meanwhile, began to starve.

I saw it in their ribs, their flanks, their growing lethargy.

While out walking a road one afternoon, for example, I came across a fawn that ran away from me and disappeared around a bend in the road. When I rounded the bend moments later, the fawn was curled up, exhausted, on the plowed edge of the road. At first I didn't realize what it was until, getting closer, the skinny fawn stood, ran another thirty feet, then plopped down on the roadside. The snowbanks on the side of the road were five feet high, or more, and although deer tracks led over the top into the woods the small fawn no longer had the strength to leap up and over the barrier.

Just as I thought of turning around, the fawn scrambled up the snowbank. I could see, as I walked by, it didn't go far but merely collapsed on the other side of the bank.

Head up, ears swiveling, it marked my passage.

The fawn was likely going to die.

Deer biologist John J. Ozoga put it this way in *Whitetail Winter*:

"Death from malnutrition is an insidious, pathetically slow process. Fat depletion and physical weakening progress with nearly undetectable signs, until it's too late for recovery. In the final stages, however, a deer's coat roughens, its hip bones show, and hollows appear in its flanks. The starving animal spends most of its time bedded down, in a curled head-to-tail position to minimize body surface exposure. It adopts a lethargic, uncaring attitude, no longer bounding away, flag waving, as danger nears. Small deer, especially, stand hump-backed, their front legs spread slightly, back legs close together, and hold their head up at a 45 degree angle. Deer so weakened become easy prey for predators—a sudden and merciful fate compared to a lingering death from starvation."[1]

Maybe so.

Maybe not.

I soon saw another deer, though, who might have agreed with Ozoga. I was down on the lake near a rock point, fetching water, when a buck walked around the corner. He stopped broadside twenty feet in front of me. The buck was not a regular visitor to Hocoka nor did I know who he was. It was clear, however, he was exhausted. His hip bones and ribs showed. His head hung low. Each step was heavy and slow. Most significantly, perhaps, when the buck saw me he did not run. Did not move or flinch.

Just stood there.

Spare energy, at this point for anything but standing, simply wasn't available anymore.

For me, living as I did, chores multiplied as the severity of winter progressed.

There was twice as much snow to shovel off roofs, deck, and paths as during a normal winter. There was more sledding and handling of firewood. Getting water required snowshoes instead of mukluks on a packed trail. I needed a shovel more often to get at the wooden waterhole cover, and there was more-than-average chiseling of ice followed by a delicate slog with buckets uphill to the cabin.

Mornings were colder to awaken to (with, sometimes, ice in water and slop buckets . . . getting thicker during the coldest spells). The cabin took longer to heat and, some nights, I'd need to rise to an alarm clock to feed the stove, meaning less deep sleep. Even trails had to be packed with snowshoes more often and sometimes that didn't do much good.

I'd slip off the packed snowshoe trail, either stumbling on my snowshoes or, risking mere boots, hitting the trail's unseen edge, losing balance, and falling sideways or forwards. My arm couldn't reach through the deep snow all the way down to the ground for support so I'd wallow, flounder, kind of swim in snow until I scrambled upright.

Falling and getting up used a lot of energy.

Once, seven times from car to cabin.

I'd laugh, I'd curse, I'd keep going.

But I could feel the drain.

Losing weight, burning energy to stay warm or do chores, I'd eat all the time—bananas, apples, cheese, fig newtons, pizzas, beef jerky, gorp, granola, crackers, peanut butter: anything edible—eating for energy, eating for heat, yet still losing ground like the deer out my cabin windows.

Bad head trips didn't help:

Winter's seasonal, post-rangering unemployment.

The beautiful young woman of soulful aspiration who stepladdered through me—too old now—and left a trail of bizarrely slammed doors.

Memories of Chris, Rip, my mother's cremation: ghosts all around on long, isolated nights.

It wore on a man.

Even a canoe expedition from northeastern Minnesota's Quetico-Superior to Hudson Bay hounded me. For years I'd wanted to flow like a feather on the waters of my life, the rains and snows of my years, and of Hocoka, downstream to the sea. But I had always put it off. I'd return to rangering: to duty, responsibility, obligations, paycheck, the challenges of Lake Superior, and the potentials of human companionship. There were bills to pay. Money to make. Primary partners to nurture. Alleged security. There were countless excuses for postponing a canoe journey that wouldn't go away, that was preposterous in scope, yet that called for some unknown soulful purpose for five years, ten, forever: most powerfully at critical personal junctures.

But never had I gone.

There were always too many bridges to burn. Too much at risk.

Would I *ever* embrace my quest for the sea or was it all just talk on the deck?

Maybe, as I grew older, I lacked the guts to go.
My soul felt stifled.

The head trips, the physical drain of deep snow and persistent subzero cold, the penetrating presence of a season civilization insulates itself against: it all reminded me
of how the great naturalist Richard Nelson remarked
that the earth's core is winter.

Even the universe is winter.

"Life is only something taken for a moment," he wrote
in *The Island Within*,[2] "rubbed warm and held back from
the chill . . . Winter waits and finds all life. In the end,
each of us stares through the dark eyes of winter."

A March night came when I heard wolves howling so
I stepped out on the cabin deck beneath winter's
stars.

I'd seen no sign of wolves for six weeks and missed
their wild presence. Everything, it seemed, had been
building to a head: all the winters, the cold and darkness,
the starving deer, the inexorable loneliness of living on
the edge: even the wolves were gone. Perhaps now,
however, as winter's snowpack crusted over and provided better footing, the wolves were heading back into
the hinterlands.

It was good to hear the wolves again.

They were howling toward the southwest, toward the
lake the Ojibwe once called Kawasachong from the mist
and foam of its adjacent waterfalls, while other wolves
howled from the east. Likely one split pack.

I howled back.

Silence.

I howled again and the wolves joined in.

Deep, chesty bawls rose into the night through a flurry of high, excited yapping. There were moments of silence then a lone, distant howl, more howls coming from the other direction, my own rising wail, then more howling yet. Deep. Chesty. Songs drawn-out, falling, fading. Barks. Yipping. Then the deep howl again: summoning, announcing: crying out against the wintry night of all time.

Feel it the land speaking *do you hear-feel it?*

And I felt, more than knew, why the land-through-wolves was howling. Felt why. Felt what the deep pool of silent knowledge, the voice of all primordial time, was singing.

It rose through my spirit like a wave passing onward, onward, into the infinite light of stars.

The howling.

Winter warming but the howling here.

Life worn out.

Life, sometimes, worn to death.

I awoke later from a restless sleep in the middle of the night. Very unusual for me to have insomnia. Tossed and turned.

Something happening?

Darkness filled the cabin.

I listened carefully.

Silence.

I refused to get up, as I had two nights earlier, to light lamps at 4:30 in the morning to start my day.

Why, though, the waking? Why the waking?

The first thing I saw the next morning, as I lay in bed looking out the window, was a bald eagle.

I jumped up and looked more closely.

Circling with the eagle, beneath cloudy sky, were ravens: all swooping and gliding above the cove where, *Oh no,* a deer carcass was sprawled on the snow.

Soon I was on snowshoes and, with staff, shuffling toward the deer. The snow was crusty above a layer of slush. Wolf tracks converged from several directions. *They'd come.* Flecks of fur. Deer shit. Then the deer, a yearling, twisted and mangled. Eyes gone. Rib cage red with blood. A rear haunch was ripped open and eaten.

I squatted near the yearling—one of Princess's? Solo's?—and smoked some tobacco, saluting the four directions in honor of the whitetail's short life, its hard winter struggle, and its final terror with wolves.

It was easy to understand the wolves, of course. I'd howled with them, sensed their need, and knew, like people, they had to kill to live. Still, the death, like the yearling that died at my own hand four years earlier, saddened me.

Death seemed the hunter, life-heart the prey, with soul cut by sensitivity to a tragic but necessary violence.

I'm too soft . . . too soft, I thought while snowshoeing back to the cabin. *She was right. Too damn sentimental. Feeling death like a hoof's blow yet loving enough to feel.*

A cursed blessing. A blessed curse.

Two more bald eagles joined the first one—circling 'round, screeching—as I phoned a friend, canceled her visit to Hocoka, and left the cabin for a walk out to the road.

Should not the dead yearling, eagles, and ravens be left alone?

Even as the scavengers celebrated, there was grief in the air.

There would be no gawkers this hour.

The eagles were gone when I returned although Renard was walking on crusted snow along the cove's shore.

Ravens spotted the fox, set up a racket of alarmed calls, then a lone raven flew over to Renard to swoop in circles around his head: buzzing him, harassing him: *ka-roke, ka-roke*: then land on white snow. Renard, having found shelter in brush behind a shoreline pine, came back out onto the lake and walked toward the raven, getting close, until both raven and fox knew when close was too much.

The raven leapt and flew.

Renard ran into the woods.

Later, at twilight, the hour of power, Renard crossed the cove to the dead deer and ate.

Snow began to fall.

There was no sign of Princess and her fawns, Pan and Saut, the next day. This began to concern me.

They had been daily visitors to Hocoka and, over the years, I'd become particularly fond of Princess. I named her for her slanted, Oriental eyes, and their almost sovereign expression, yet I could have named her Patience instead. She would often stand patiently by the deck and look at the cabin door or, if I was outside splitting firewood, she'd watch me until she seemed to stare me down.

I'd have to say something endearing to her or, as she likely preferred, get corn.

The last few times I'd seen Princess, shortly before the yearling was killed, she seemed nervous. Different somehow. One day she held up a leg several times and shook it as if it was sprained or annoyed her. Later I noticed her eyelids had begun to twitch which, of course, I assumed was involuntary. Half-wink twitches. She'd look away then back at me as if she knew something I didn't, suspected something, or perhaps sensed the coming presence of a force evoking violent shift.

Maybe, now, it was one of *her* fawns, possibly Saut, that was dead on the ice.

I'd gone back to the carcass after watching an immature eagle circle and soar above it, get driven off by harassing ravens, then fly back to the deer, land, and feed. By the time I got there, all that was left of the yearling was its head, skinny legs, fur, and spine gnawed clean to bone.

But where, meanwhile, was Princess or, for that matter, Solo?

I decided to look for them.

I skied to the far end of the lake, seeing old wolf tracks along the shoreline all the way. In one of the last coves, I found a piece of fur that looked like the foot-long end of a wolf's tail. I could see where bone or cartilage had ripped through and free.

Had a wolf tried to escape another wolf who bit its tail, hung on, or gave it a yank?

The next day, still searching for sign of Princess and
Solo, I skied around the north end of Pine Island where,
at its northern-most point, I noticed tufts of deer fur
along the shore. There was discolored snow and a
stained, well-used trail leading up into the woods.

I took off my skis and followed the trail into a grove,
no, *grave*, of white pines where I found the body of a
large doe. It was spread out, ribs showing, in trampled
snow of wolf tracks, fur, blood, and viscera. Above the
dead whitetail was a large white pine beneath which the
doe had bedded.

Had she been surprised by the wolves? I wondered. *Or had she
chosen to make this spot her last stand—tired of winter, no place to
run, so be it?*

I looked closely at the doe's face.

She might have been Princess but it was hard to tell.
Her face was too disfigured. Ravens and eagles had gone
quickly for the eyes.

Two days later, a Monday, beneath overcast sky and as
temperatures nudged above freezing, I awoke to another
wolf-killed deer.

Saw it first thing, like the other one, straight out the
bedroom window.

Down near the cove's water hole.

Enough, I thought, rolling out of bed to put my mukluks on. *Enough*. I'd slept in socks and sweater so *that*, at
least, was taken care of. *Tired*. I put on pants, a wool
shirt—*Tired of the killing*—and made a cup of coffee.

My next task was loud and clear.

Two immature bald eagles, adult-sized but brown
with flecks of white, and a flock of ravens (black, black,

black) fed on the freshly killed deer *Which one this time?* as I finished my coffee then hiked down to the cove to disturb the congregation. My turn. The eagles and ravens flew off. I paid my respects to the deer, a yearling doe, *Pan?*, and decided to move her. She was too visible from the cabin, suggested more than I wanted to bear every time I glanced outside, and her remains—fur, bones, scat, along with raven and eagle shit—would settle into the ice too close to my waterhole.

Maybe contaminate it.

Right or wrong, I grabbed a leg and slid the deer to the nearest shore, scrambled through a knee-deep snowdrift, and left the stiff carcass beneath a small cedar.

Ravens found the deer by afternoon.

An eagle also returned. It perched near the top of a dead red pine along the slope of Rainbow Ridge. There, not dropping to feed, it posted a gold-eye watch on Hocoka's wild world.

"Admit it, Jim dale."

Dirk Hanson, an Ely friend and author, was challenging me after listening to some of my stories about the deer, wolves, and related fallout of the most brutal winter on record.

"Admit it. You're drawn to the dark side."

"Huh," I said, thinking:

Not so much drawn as found *there.*

Renard came by again the evening I found the last yearling. He hadn't located the new carcass yet so worked on my attention until I tossed him a chunk of suet.

Such eyes on that fox: golden, quizzical, finding mine

in what seemed intelligent recognition: a pooling in those eyes of wildness, some glint of acknowledgment I couldn't quite grasp.

Could he see clear through me?

How little or much, really, did Renard know?

Were there reasons deeper than suet for why he was at my door? And why, as day ended and darkness settled, he curled up nearby to sleep?

How could I ever know this except to catch some winter sign of certainty?

Two bad dreams came back-to-back as the fuzzy light of comet Hyakutaki, visible only once every ten thousand years, passed the stars of Ursa Major with its Big Dipper.

In the first dream I was walking a grassy field with a friend and saw a lion coming toward us at an angle. It had a thick, shaggy mane that rippled and shone as the lion approached over the rolling hills. Yet as the lion got closer I saw it was a cougar. My friend and I lay down in the grass, face to the earth, as the cougar came closer. I glanced up and it was upon us.

The cougar bit into my thigh and started lifting me as I fought back.

Soon I was walking away from the grassy fields and down into a wooded area of red pines and cabin. My friend's dog, Buckwheat, was there; he, too, was scratched, bitten, mangled up. I held him and coaxed him to strength. My own wounds hurt but wouldn't be fatal. People milled around like ghosts.

Three nights later, after wolves had returned to feed on the deer beneath the shoreline cedar, and as snow fell, I dreamt of black bears attacking me. At least three bears coming, charging, across the cabin deck. One large bear stood threateningly at the cabin door.

I shot it with my rifle.

If the gifts brought to people by bears in event or dream are strength, introspection, and self-knowledge, as some people believe they are,[3] then I lost my chance.

If, however, the message was that being unaware of my limits, throwing caution to the wind in certain settings, can be dangerous, then I got the point.

I also sensed—fighting the cougar, shooting the bear—that perhaps I needed to fight back with more force in my life. Somehow resist the hostile forces of death swirling around me and, by now, within me.

Clearly, contact had been made at Hocoka and there was blood on the tracks.

But how fight back?

By embracing life more indomitably? More impeccably? By letting the spiritual warrior surface?

Winter, I could see, doesn't just come after the body. It fully challenges and, for those who survive, strengthens the soul.

By March 24, a little over a week since I'd howled with the wolves and they'd swept through Hocoka, I knew of at least six dead deer within a half-mile of the cabin.

Princess and Solo were still missing.

There was a dead doe and yearling at the far northeastern tip of the lake. There was the dead doe on Pine Island,[4] possibly Princess. There were two dead yearlings on, and along, the cove below the cabin. And there was another yearling—in Lund's Cove to the west—that had partially settled into meltwater where, cold weather returning, it froze in solid ice.

A fox had gnawed exposed bone.

It seemed there were deer carcasses everywhere.

Certainly, I thought, *deer feel pain, shock, and terror when they're killed.*

This wasn't anthropomorphic, some kind of human emotion cast onto the Bambis of the world.

Why else do they bawl out when they're ripped into?

Pain hurts. Life wants more life. And life prefers life joyful.

The terror of losing life, the beautiful terror, so that other life might live, could send a shudder right through me.

Nights came, some with moonlight, and I'd glance out cabin windows looking for the usual silhouettes of winter deer.

There were none.

One more deer carcass surfaced to shock me.

Deer number seven.

It was late winter, bordering on spring, and the snow was melting fast. Trails were high-ridged and treacherous, caving at the sides. A full moon, haunting, had passed. Fresh snow had fallen. Then, as days grew warmer, patches of meltwater formed aquamarine puddles of all sizes on the lake. Four eagles, perhaps those I'd seen circling each other high against a haloed sky, fed off the yearling carcass by the cove cedar. I'd started watching those eagles through binoculars: one eagle gliding through thick snowflakes along the face of Rainbow Ridge, another settling into clear water of a lake puddle where—perfectly reflected—its legs sent ripples toward bordering snow, and yet another eagle that perched atop a rock bluff's white pine.

The pine overlooked a lake landing where I kept stacks of firewood: the exact same landing, I recalled, where Chris and I—thirteen years earlier—had first found the draw leading up to Hocoka.

It was there I found the last deer carcass.

I was fetching a load of firewood when I sensed something strange, looked up, and saw the dead deer. It was hanging upside down in a fallen balsam fir on the steep slope of the bluff. Completely gutted. Rib cage and spine showed. The deer's head and legs were still attached to the skeleton. It spooked me. I felt nauseous, almost as if, with spring coming, the mangled and skeletal deer had emerged from melting snow on top the prone fir to dangle grotesquely in front of my eyes. It was a reminder, perhaps, one final sign, of all the dead deer that had come before, but this time the carcass hung in branches *above* me, could fall on me, as it baked in late-winter sunshine.

That deer could have been in those branches under snow for a month and I'd gathered my firewood nearby oblivious to its fate.

Had the deer died of starvation during a blizzard only to be dragged by wolves over the edge of the bluff?

Had it leapt down the bluff toward safety only to get

caught in deep snow and the fallen fir's branches, where it struggled until exhausted then died before a burying blizzard?

It made me sick to think this might have happened as I lived my little life, well-fed, and stove-side.

Daylight, now, fading fast.

I returned to the carcass the next morning, a Sunday, as warm sunshine softened night's snow crust.

I brought a rope. Surely I had to move the deer.

I climbed the bluff from the back side, thinking I could get at the deer from above, and found tufts of deer fur scattered in needle duff beneath the white pine where the eagle had perched. That angle didn't work so I scrambled down below then slogged through knee-deep snow *up* to the deer. I tied the rope to a leg and slid the deer—hoping it wouldn't come apart—out of the fir branches, down the slope, then along the lakeshore to a thicket of alders beneath a cliff. I positioned the body as respectfully as I could and covered it with sticks and birchbark.

Stepping back out onto the lake, kneeling, resting in sun, I smoked tobacco in honor of another whitetail's spirit.

"The deer spoke to me."

A friend, a neighbor, was soon telling me of her dream.

In it, a starving deer had appeared to her. Part of its side was missing and its ribs showed. The deer asked her to break boughs off cedar trees so it could eat.

"I was so frightened by a talking deer," she said, "that I ran away."

Inevitably, and as I had after I shot the yearling four years earlier, I skied to the far end of the lake, visited its small island, then turned around and headed home.

Circles. Always circles.

The sun was bright on the undulating patterns of wind-packed snow. Otter tracks stitched together the lake's northernmost islands as paw marks and belly slides scrawled a wild script.

Better glide than me, I thought.

Blue sky.

White snow.

More deer.

This time they were alive and standing among pines of a ridge above me. I skied closer. One of the deer, looking down at me, stood erect and alone in the open of a snowy ridgetop. So beautiful. Solo? Princess? I slid to a stop, looked closer at that deer on ancient bedrock, *Nope, neither,* then leaned on my ski poles and—couldn't help it—just bowed my head.

Bowed, after all, to the wild beauty.

Bowed to the weight of passing winter.

Bowed to my life with whitetails and wolves.

I looked back up.

"Belle wâwashkeshi," I called as the deer began to slip away.

The rear doe stopped and turned at the sound of my voice.

"Beautiful deer," I called once more.

And the light again, crystallizing, that blue sky, the shining brightness, the pines, half-moon, and whitetails, all the comings and goings, the deaths and struggles and coming sun. Such a long trail whitetails had walked: the seemingly infinite time: the wolves and winters: the Ojibwe and other peoples hungering for their meat and skin. Countless whitetail generations had come and gone, year after year, flowing with the wolves across the face of the land.

It was the way of the wolf: the way of the deer.

Call it magic and mystery like critter man Denny Olson. Call it the pulse of the Quetico-Superior, or call it Sigurd F. Olson's singing wilderness.

It was all of this and more.

Death in the white crystal light.

Life in the white crystal night.

Such a vision of terrible beauty.

Tears came to my eyes as I turned—recognizing my gift, my witnessed power, my moment of grace—to face sunshine on snow.

Let it sing, I thought skiing home. *Let it all sing.*

Let the snow and ice and darkness, the winds and shadows, the deer bleats and wolf howls, the grunts and snorts and bawls, the fox barks and raven calls, the countless crystals and brilliant moons, the dreams and loves and enduring life: let the winter sign sing—You took me—*let it sing on and on and on* à la belle étoiles, *beneath the beautiful stars.*

Let it sing.

Then they came back.

The day arrived, about a month after the wolves had

killed at least seven of Hocoka's deer, when Princess sashayed up the slope from the lake as if she'd been gone an hour. I'd seen Ruff again, who looked healthy and strong, and Dusty, who had also returned to Hocoka, but Princess's appearance understandably came as a surprise.

With her were Pan and Saut, her two fawns.

And my heart soared like an eagle.

Two days later, precisely thirty-six days since I'd last seen her, Solo showed up. She, too, looked nonchalant. No cuts, no scratches, no broken bones.

The little tramp.

"Belle wâwashkeshi," was all I could say.

She, too, had been missing since the wolves had so visibly passed through. After being at Hocoka every day all winter, nay, most days every winter for ten years, then suddenly disappearing for five weeks in the wake of wolves, who *wouldn't* have assumed she was a goner?

Part wolf by April Fool's day, perhaps, or part eagle and fox.

"Welcome back," I said, restraining my joy. "Make yourself at home."

And suddenly I knew, beyond doubt, what I was going to do.

I looked at Solo, the melting snow, and the rotting lake ice of Otter beyond. It would be another three weeks before that thick ice was gone but I'd already seen crows and, at night, could hear gulls partying it up in open water beneath Kawasachong's falls. Loons flew by daily, checking ice conditions. And that very day, just before Solo appeared, I had heard the song of spring's first robin.

The winter of all winters was ending.

It was time, soon, to get going.

It was time to start packing.

It was time to varnish paddles and prepare the canoe.

Another circle needed closing.

Or was a new circle, ever so delicately, beginning to open and flower?

When the snow finished melting and rivers ran high, sure thing, I would flow with the spirit of winter's living and dead—honoring Solo's kind, the wolf's kind, my kind—all the way to the sea.

Tracks/Notes

Citations that appear with partial publication information here are listed completely in the Bibliography.

A Path with Heart

1. C. G. Jung, "Sigmund Freud," in *Memories, Dreams, Reflections,* ed. Aniela Jaffe (New York: Random House, Inc., 1961), p.166.

2. My references to Ojibwemowin, or Ojibwe language, are rooted in three sources: Frederic Baraga's *A Dictionary of the Ojibway Language* (originally published as *A Dictionary of the Otchipwe Language*), Judith and Thomas Vollom's *Ojibwemowin* (Ojibwe Language Publishing, 1994), and *A Concise Dictionary of Minnesota Ojibwe* by John D. Nichols and Earl Nyholm (Minneapolis: University of Minnesota Press, 1995).

I prefer Baraga's dictionary. Its vocabulary is rooted further back in time than the others, it anchors dialect differences, and the language documented grew out of a people and time regionally associated with my French-Canadian *métissage* ancestors: first in Québec in the 1600s, then along the shores of the Great Lakes.

One of my ancestors, Etienne Huot, signed on as a voyageur with James and Andrew McGill of Québec's North West Company, and was sent by canoe to Michilimakinac in 1806 (twenty-nine years before Baraga began his Ojibwe studies in Michigan). Another Huot, Joseph, was sent even earlier to the Temiscamingue, Abitibi, and Grand Lac area of the Ontario-Québec border, between the Great Lakes and James Bay, in 1799. This was all essentially Ojibwe (or, as they call themselves, *Anishinaabe*) country. Hence it was among Ojibwe (and some Cree) that some of my ancestors canoed, traded, hunted, married, and, likely multi-linguists for which French-Canadians were famed, swapped stories in log cabins and around campfires.

Not until the late 1800s did some Huots, like many other French-Canadians, move out onto the prairies of northwestern Minnesota's Red River Valley, where they were slowly assimilated into English-speaking American culture.

I concede to this personal history, cultural association, and—thanks to Baraga's linguistic legacy—honor it with word choice.

The only exceptions are when I quote direct sources with different Ojibwemowin spellings.

Hocoka

1. For Black Elk and, following, Short Bull, see T. C. McLuhan, comp., *Touch the Earth: A Self-Portrait of Indian Existence* (New York: Simon and Schuster, 1971; Pocket Book edition, 1972), pp. 42–43.

2. Among our canoe journeys was a retracing of the Kaministikwia River–Dog River route connecting Thunder Bay, Ontario, on Lake Superior, with the heart of the Quetico-Superior north of Hocoka. (The first nonnative of American or Canadian descent to explore the route and region, was a French-Canadian, Jacques de Noyon, from my ancestral Québec. When de Noyon wintered near Rainy Lake in 1688–89, the region had been annexed by France. De Noyon was referred to, in early documents, simply as a "voyageur" from Three Rivers.) For more on the Kam-Dog canoe route, the Quetico-Superior's pictographs, and the author's first encounters with wolves, see *Open Spaces*.

3. Les Scher, *Finding and Buying Your Place in the Country* (New York: Collier Books, Macmillan Publishing Company, 1974).

4. George M. Schwartz and George A. Thiel, *Minnesota's Rocks and Waters* (Minneapolis: University of Minnesota Press, 1954), p. 12.

5. Ibid., p. 20.

6. When Dave Olesen helped move Hocoka's woodstoves, he was on the way to becoming an accomplished bush pilot and writer as well as a rumor in his own time. His first book was *A Wonderful Country: The Quetico-Superior Stories of Bill Magie* (Ashland, Wisc.: Sigurd Olson Environmental Institute, Northland College, 1981). Next came *Cold Nights/Fast Trails: Reflections of a Modern Dog Musher* (Minocqua, Wisc.: NorthWord Press, 1989) and *North of Reliance* (Minocqua, Wisc.: NorthWord Press, 1994).

Solo

1. Solo's phenological arrival was as follows.

March 5, 1985: wolves howling

March 27, 1985: three deer in yard/whistles

April 13, 1985: wolf tracks (and fox)

October 16, 1985: deer eyes in night yard

December 2, 1985: deer on lake

December 3, 1985: wolves moving east to north

December 4, 1985: deer by front door

December 5, 1985: same deer in yard

December 6, 1985: Solo in yard/naming

December 15, 1985: wolves

December 16, 1985: Solo in yard

December 21, 1985: wolf tracks on lake

December 31, 1985: wolves howling New Year's Eve at moonrise

February 4, 1986: four deer Wolf Point; sunset: wolves howling

February 12, 1986: fawn in yard

March 15, 1986: doe and two fawns in yard

March 18, 1986: four deer cross cove at dusk

December 10, 1986: deer tracks on lake

December 13, 1986: Solo returns

2. Rollin H. Baker, "Origin, Classification and Distribution," in *White-tailed Deer: Ecology and Management,* ed. Lowell K. Halls (Pennsylvania: Stackpole Books and Wildlife Management Institute, 1984), p. 5.

3. Forty million population estimate: Richard E. and Thomas R. McCabe, "Of Slings and Arrows: An Historical Retrospection," in Ibid., p. 27.

4. Leonard Lee Rue III, *The Deer of North America* (Danbury, Conn.: Outdoor Life Books, Grolier Book Clubs, Inc., 1989), p. 14.

5. For Ojibwe creation myth, see Johann Georg Kohl, ethnologist, in *Kitchi-Gami: Life Among the Lake Superior Ojibway,* p. 199.

6. Among the many native peoples who depended on whitetail deer for food, clothes, and implements (as tabled by McCabe in Halls, *White-tailed Deer,* pp. 41–47) were: Abenaki, Algonquin, Apache, Assiniboine, Blackfoot, Caddo, Catawbas, Cathlamet, Cherokee, Cheyenne, Chickasaws, Chippewa (northern Minnesota/Wisconsin), Choctaw, Crow, Delaware, Fox, Huron, Iguacas, Illinois, Iroquois, Kalispel, Karankawa, Kickotank, Kutenai, Mahican, Mandan, Menominee, Narragansett, Naskapi, Natchez, Nez Perce, Ojibwa (southeastern Ontario), Omaha, Ottawa, Pawnee, Pawtuckett, Penobscott, Potowatomi, Roanoke, Sewee, Timucua, Tuscarora, Wampanoag, Winnebago, Yavapai, and Yuchi.

Even the Dakota/Sioux, a bison-dependent people of the Great Plains after the 1300s, were historically indebted to whitetails. The Dakota word for whitetails, *tahca* or *tahinca,* meant real or true meat, a term some scholars feel is indicative of pre-Plains Dakota origin.

7. Frances Densmore, *Chippewa Customs*, pp. 133, 173.

8. Johann Georg Kohl, *Kitchi-Gami*, pp. 35–36, claims Ojibwe frequently tamed wild animals as pets: gulls, ravens, eagles, magpies, deer, foxes, even bears, which they'd sometimes tote with rope or chain.

"A voyageur told me," Kohl recalled, "he once met an Indian carrying his bear on his back, because the brute was very tired, and its whining had moved his tender heart."

9. Ibid., p. 134.

10. William W. Warren, *History of the Ojibway People*, p. 266.

11. J. Owen Dorsey, "Omaha Sociology . . . Deer-Head Gens," in Walter P. Taylor, ed., *The Deer of North America*, pp. 245–47.

12. Clifford and Isabel Ahlgren, *Lob Trees in the Wilderness*, p. 18.

13. Alex Kosir, 85, of Ely, Minnesota, who grew up hunting and trapping in the Quetico-Superior, told me in November 1996, he'd seen only one wild cat in the woods all his life: a lynx trapped near Stony River. When I asked him if he had ever seen bobcat or lynx sign northeast of Ely, where he hunts, his answer came pronto: "Never."

Paul Kapsch, on the other hand, told me that years ago he watched a lynx (in Kosir's country) stalk a grouse along the Cloquet Line, a gravel road that was once a railroad spur between Winton near Ely and hinterland lakes beyond. The lynx, made nervous by Kapsch in his car, aborted its hunt.

14. See especially L. David Mech, "Predators and Predation," in *White-tailed Deer*, ed. L. K. Halls, p. 193.

15. R. Larry Marchinton and David H. Hirth, "Behavior," in *White-tailed Deer*, ed. L. K. Halls, p. 165.

16. For an example of black bears preying on fawns, see J. J. Ozoga and Louis J. Verme, "Predation by Black Bears on Newborn White-Tailed Deer," pp. 695–96.

Of the three known fawns killed by bears, what surprised the authors was that one of the fawns was twenty-seven days old, an age when fawns are already "extremely agile, swift runners." Other fawn losses confirmed author suspicions that predation by black bears "may impose a considerable drain on the annual fawn crop where both species coexist in appreciable numbers."

17. J. P. Cohn, "Endangered Wolf Population Increases," *Bioscience* 40 (1990): 628–32. Also cited in Miron Heinselman's *The Boundary Waters Wilderness Ecosystem*, p. 166.

18. For these and related wolf-activity statistics, see L. D. Mech and L. D. Frenzel, eds., *Ecological Studies of the Timber Wolf in Northeastern Minnesota.*

Mech and Frenzel documented maximum net weekly wolf movements of five to fifty miles.

19. L. David Mech, *The Way of the Wolf*, pp. 47–49.

20. Meteorological statistics in the *1996 Minnesota Weatherguide/Environment Calendar*, published by the Freshwater Foundation and Science Museum of Minnesota, indicate approximate solstice sunrise/sunset times for the Minneapolis–St. Paul region as follows. Summer solstice, June 20: sunrise at 5:26 A.M., sunset at 9:03 P.M., daylight of fifteen hours, thirty-seven minutes. Winter solstice, December 21: sunrise at 7:48 A.M., sunset at 4:34 P.M., daylight of eight hours and forty-six minutes.

I add a five-to-ten-minute latitude factor for the Quetico-Superior.

Regardless, days in midwinter are only half as long as they are at midsummer. Nights go from one-third of a twenty-four-hour period to two-thirds.

Although amount of daylight bottoms-out at winter solstice, then—after a short lag—begins to increase, average low temperatures (therefore mean temperatures) continue to get colder as the surface of the earth and surrounding air loses ambient heat.

The rock cools.

Ice thickens, deepens: penetrates more.

21. John J. Ozoga, *Whitetail Winter*, p. 59.

22. Chief Dan George, in Rick McIntyre, *A Society of Wolves: National Parks and the Battle over the Wolf* (Stillwater, Minn.: Voyageur Press, 1993), p. 4.

23. Naming animals based on physical or behavioral characteristics is not unusual. Even the eminent wolf biologist, L. David Mech, named wolves during five summers of wolf research in the High Arctic. There was Shaggy, Lone Ranger, Mid-Back, Mom, and Scruffy. Names grew out of external cues, rooted in character or relationship to the pack. For Mech's extraordinary account of his experiences with arctic wolves, see *The Arctic Wolf: Living With the Pack*.

24. The deer mix I used came in fifty-pound bags from Dan's Feed Bin, Superior, Wisconsin. The corn and oats, with a touch of molasses, had a guaranteed analysis of no less than 10 percent crude protein, 2.5 percent crude fat, and no more than 8 percent crude fiber. Although I rationed fifty to sixty pounds a week to the deer midwinters, it was never enough to sustain the deer. It was important they continue to browse, not only for healthy microbial digestion but to maintain their wildness.

Snow Wonder

1. Ruth Kirk, *Snow*, p. 24.

2. See Edward R. LaChapelle, *Field Guide to Snow Crystals*, p. 10.

3. Cullen Murphy, "In Praise of Snow," pp. 45–58.

4. Peter Hoeg, *Smilla's Sense of Snow*, p. 266.

5. W. A. Bentley and W. J. Humphreys, *Snow Crystals*.

6. For Inuit snow words, see Terry Tempest Williams and Ted Major, *The Secret Language of Snow*.

7. And what had I, coming of age in the Red River Valley, to linguistically compare with the Inuit?
   Among adults there was "damn snow," of course, and "fuckin' snow" when it had to be shoveled, plowed, or driven through, what with tight schedules, and there was *snirt*, a

mixture of snow and wind-blown dirt, but other words for snow didn't come readily to valley lips. Snow was something you didn't talk much about.

Guaranteed downer.

Unless it was a *bad* snow. A storm.

Then the old phone lines were clogged with snow chatter: farmer to farmer, farmer to town-dweller, kid to kid: but the snow vernacular was indirect. It had to do with stuck pickups, damn-near tunnels between house and barn, buried wood-piles, drifted chimneys, backyard igloos, together with various annoyances and impossibilities:

Nope, can't make it.

Wouldn't be wise to leave.

Can't see halfway down the driveway.

There was an art, I suppose, to referring to snow by its effects. What snow created, and the ingenuity it evoked from the hardiest of people, along with their mishaps, was always open to conversation. The actual word, *snow*, however, bore a shadow associated with struggle, hardship, darkness, strange fevers. Thus fenced, for whatever real or subliminal reasons, how could snow blossom into intricate and ennobling expressions as it had among people wise enough to embrace, linguistically or otherwise, what was futile to resist?

8. Richard K. Nelson, *The Island Within* (San Francisco: North Point Press, 1989), p. 251f, and, on Koyukon respect for winter, p. 269.

9. Ruth Kirk, *Snow*, p. 30.

10. As delineated by Frederic Baraga, *A Dictionary of the Ojibway Language.*

11. Edward R. LaChapelle, *Field Guide to Snow Crystals*, p. 15.

12. Miron Heinselman, *The Boundary Waters Wilderness Ecosystem*, pp. 4–10.

13. L. David Mech and L. D. Frenzel, eds., "Ecological Studies of the Timber Wolf in Northeastern Minnesota."

14. One of the best examples of wolf wanderlust came to

my attention in the National Park Service's Ranger Activities Division Report for April 27, 1992:

Apparently a wolf known as 321, born in 1986 and radio-collared in Alaska's Gates of the Arctic National Park in April 1987, was shot by a hunter near Fort McPherson, Northwest Territories, Canada. The male wolf, gray in color, weighed one hundred pounds and was in good health before wandering out of its old territory in April or May 1987. It was located by a Canadian scientist a year later. Accompanied by another wolf, 321 was part of a pack until death. The straight-line distance between capture and kill sites was 434 miles, just sixteen miles short of the known North American wolf wandering record.

15. For Wolfe and below, respectively: Thomas Wolfe, *The Web and the Rock* (New York: Perennial Library, Harper & Row, 1973), p. 134; John Muir, "The Mountains of California" in *John Muir's Wilderness Essays* (Salt Lake City: Peregrine Smith Books, 1980), p. 96; Farley Mowat, *The Snow Walker*, p. 2; Loren Eiseley, *The Immense Journey* (New York: Vintage Books/Random House, 1959), pp. 26–27.

Singing Snowshoes

1. Johann Georg Kohl, *Kitchi-Gami: Life Among the Lake Superior Ojibway*, pp. 192–209.

2. K. Birket-Smith, "The Caribou Eskimo, Report of the Fifth Thule Expedition 1921–1924," in Davidson, p. 157.

3. The Micmacs ("Allies") of Nova Scotia and New Brunswick, who intermarried freely with the French and sided with them in the wars of the seventeenth and eighteenth centuries, sometimes painted clan symbols on their snowshoes. They'd also put the symbols on their canoes, clothes (using beads and porcupine quills), and bodies (tattooed).

See Diamond Jennes, *The Indians of Canada*, p. 268.

4. Kohl, *Kitchi-Gami*, p. 123.

5. Richard K. Nelson, *Hunters of the Northern Ice*, p. 24.

6. Daniel Sutherland Davidson, *Snowshoes*, pp. 6–7.

This 207-page monograph is, to the best of my knowledge, the definitive anthropological study of snowshoes used by native North Americans. It covers snowshoe traits, distribution, frames, netting techniques, crossbars, etc., comparing and correlating as it goes along. Includes maps and bibliography.

7. Ojibwe also used a "bear-paw" snowshoe: oval with no point or tail: efficient in very brushy country. The French-Canadians, or *Wemitigoji*, of the Lake Superior region called bearpaw snowshoes *raquettes pattes d'ours.*

8. Bill Copeley, Assistant Librarian for the New Hampshire Historical Society: letter to author, July 17, 1979.

9. Maria R. Audubon, ed., *Audubon and His Journals*, 2 vols. (New York: Dover Publications, Inc., 1960), pp. 313–14.

The Challenge

1. Leonard Lee Rue III, *The Deer of North America*, p. 318.

2. John J. Ozoga, "Aggressive Behavior of White-Tailed Deer at Winter Cuttings," pp. 861–68.

3. John J. Ozoga, *Whitetail Winter*, p. 153.

4. See John Madson, *The White-tailed Deer* (East Alton, Ill.: Olin Mathieson Chemical Corporation, 1961); or Rue III, *The Deer of North America*, pp. 316–17.

5. Michael E. Nelson and L. David Mech, "Observation of a Wolf Killed by Deer," *Journal of Mammalogy* 66, no. 1 (1985): 187–88.

An Ancient Tension

1. Barry Lopez, *Of Wolves and Men* (New York: Charles Scribner's Sons, 1978), p. 54.

2. See author's "The Land is Alive with Wolves," *Open Spaces* (Minocqua, Wisc.: NorthWord Press, 1991); also *Audubon* (January 1987): 52–61.

3. L. David Mech, *The Wolves of Isle Royale*, p. 73f.

4. Leonard Lee Rue III, *The Deer of North America*, pp. 53–54.

5. Richard Howe, a logger working out of Ely, Minnesota, once told me he thought the interdigital glands above a deer's front hooves also function as ears. Membranous and waxy, they help a deer detect ground tremors. Not only are the glands/organs close to the ground when a deer stands, but deer lie on the front legs—glands touching earth—when they rest. Thus, Howe suspects, interdigital glands pick up the subtlest of vibrations and give deer, in effect, four ears.

6. Carlos Castaneda, *Journey to Ixtland: The Lessons of Don Juan* (New York: Simon and Schuster, 1972), pp. 102, 104. Don Juan's amusing but esoterically relevant tale of a whistling deer appears in an overall context of hunting instruction. Don Juan is explaining that whether a person hunts physically or, as in Castaneda's case, spiritually, a hunter must not be locked into routines but be free, unpredictable, and fluid. The hunter, through fixed notions and consistent quirks, is himself prey. A spiritual warrior's life without routines, however, is a magical life: open to energy alignments otherwise untapped, and in control rather than being predictable and vulnerable to forces one step ahead of him.

Many people take Castaneda's books with a wink of skepticism. Castaneda, in *The Teachings of Don Juan* (Berkeley: University of California Press, 1968), began as a young anthropologist tracking down a Yaqui shaman/sorceror in Mexico only to become don Juan Matus's apprentice. Over time, and a series of eight books, Castaneda delved more deeply and multi-dimensionally into what don Juan taught him. The literary results are so strange to the average reader that Castaneda has sometimes been accused of being a spiritual huckster. I see elaborate parallels in what don Juan says with the esoterica of other spiritual disciplines, and tend to agree with Peter Matthiessen in *The Snow Leopard* (New York:

Viking Press, 1978, p. 284): If don Juan is imaginary, "then spurious ethnology becomes a great work of the imagination; whether borrowed or not, the teaching rings true."

7. Larry W. Richardson, et al., "Acoustics of White-Tailed Deer," pp. 245–52, identified eight stereotypic sounds: bleat, distress call, nursing whine, grunt, alert-snort, footstomp, snort-wheeze, and aggressive snort. Most are made by yearling or older deer, and most are *cohesive*: group welfare communication.

Of special interest among the study's discoveries was that a fawn's bleat can elicit care (nourishment, security, grooming) from adult does *other than the fawn's mother.* The same is true for distress calls: does other than the distressed fawn's mother will often respond. Dams (doe mothers) are nevertheless most attentive to their fawn's distress and will, if people are involved, occasionally charge.

Richardson cites how crews tagging fawns in Texas were charged by does on ten occasions. A year after Richardson's study, a mature doe charged and *flailed* someone ear-tagging her fawn.

Other data, including sonagrams, indicate "unique phonetic qualities" among individual whitetails. Once those qualities are determined, specific deer can be identified solely by voice.

8. Tom Brown Jr., *The Tracker: The Story of Tom Brown, Jr.,* p. 9.

9. Larry Rice "Secrets of Survival," *Backpacker* (Oct. 1992): 42–50.

Tracking the tracker: Rice caught up with Brown in New Jersey where, while living with family in a comfortable farmhouse, Brown taught wilderness survival in a school he established. Nine basic courses ranged from standard training through advanced skills to philosophy workshops. Contradictory and intense, Brown had begun teaching Navy Seals evasion and escape tactics, had been interviewed by Tom

Brokaw, featured in *People,* and had begun to bemoan his life change.

"The Tom Brown in *The Tracker* is dead," Brown, who hadn't been in the wilderness alone for years, told a student. Then, lighting a Marlboro, breaking his own no-smoking rule: "I don't want to be here. I want to be in the mountains more than anything. I can taste it. But I can't live my dream, I have to live my vision. The only thing I can do now is teach and write. I am a very, very desperate man."

10. This and following: Tom Brown Jr., *The Tracker,* p. 13.

11. Henry David Thoreau, *The Journal of Henry D. Thoreau,* ed. Bradford Torrey and Francis H. Allen, vol. 7, bk. 1 (New York: Dover Publications, Inc., 1962), p. 843.

12. Tom Brown Jr., *The Tracker,* p. 14.

Omens

1. Tom Brown Jr., *The Vision,* p. 1.

2. Ibid., for this and following, pp. 163–67.

3. In Brown's *The Tracker,* pp. 89–90, Stalking Wolf claims an omen is not a mere prediction of an event: "An omen is an experience that interprets all events that follow it and reinterprets everything that went before. Good medicine, bad medicine, and omens change our understanding of our relationship to the world. Nothing is ever exactly the same . . ."

4. Carlos Castaneda and don Juan Matus discussed this very thing when Castaneda asked don Juan whether sorcerers could *misinterpret* omens. Don Juan said no. They know the exact meaning, he explained, because of their connecting link with *intent* (spirit). Their certainty depends on how strongly and clearly they are connected.

Intuition, he added, and as Castaneda remembered it, "is the activation of our link with *intent* [spirit]. And since sorcerers deliberately pursue the understanding and strengthening of that link, it could be said that they intuit everything unerringly and accurately. Reading omens is commonplace for sorcerers—mistakes happen only when personal feelings intervene and cloud the sorcerer's connecting link with *intent.* Otherwise their direct knowledge is totally accurate and functional."

When a person is ready, don Juan said, the spirit manifests itself frequently, but such "knocks" or "gestures of the spirit" are not the exclusive domain of people engaged on spiritual paths:

"The entire truth is that the spirit reveals itself to everyone with the same intensity and consistency, but only sorcerers, and naguals in particular, are attuned to such revelations." See Carlos Castaneda, *The Power of Silence* (New York: Pocket Books/Simon & Schuster, 1987), p. 14.

5. Brown, *The Vision*, p. 164.

6. Frances Densmore, *Chippewa Customs*, pp. 78–86.

7. Ibid., p. 79. In an accompanying footnote, Densmore cites a Sioux/Lakota story, documented in a Bureau of American Ethnology bulletin, of a man who, having dreamt of an elk, allegedly left hoofprints of an elk behind him while enacting the events of his dream.

8. Johann Georg Kohl, *Kitchi-Gami: Life among the Lake Superior Ojibway*, pp. 399–400.

9. Some of the other native peoples who applied images of their dreams and visions to their belongings, namely the Montagnais and Naskapi, were members of the Abenaki ("Eastern") Confederacy whose blood, through marriage, flowed into the French north of the St. Lawrence River. The Montagnais and Naskapi believed in animal souls and trusted the guardian spirits of their dreams. So deep-rooted and sincere was their faith that early Jesuit missionaries thought them the most superstitious of all natives. Dreams and visions were the soul's bread and butter. Montagnais and Naskapi, while hunting, went so far as to carry pack-straps decorated with vision symbols in hopes of good luck.

Far to the northwest, Chipewyan painted symbols of their visions on shields before fighting an enemy. See Diamond Jennes, *Indians of Canada*, pp. 273–74 and 387, for more on these and other references.

10. Kohl, *Kitchi-Gami*, p. 203.

11. Ibid., pp. 204–9.

12. Robert M. Utley, *The Lance and the Shield: The Life and Times of Sitting Bull* (New York: Henry Holt & Co., 1993), pp. 12, 27f.

For information about Sitting Bull and his visions, I am indebted almost exclusively to Utley, whose thorough biographical research incorporates the seminal work of Walter Stanley Campbell (also known as Stanley Vestal) along with many other sources.

13. Sitting Bull was shot to death in an arrest melee at his cabin on Grand River, South Dakota, on December 15, 1890. The bullets that killed him were fired by Lieutenant Bull Head (in the chest) and Red Tomahawk (in the back of the head): both men were *ceska maza*, literally "metal breasts" but functionally reservation police commanded by the U.S. military.

More significantly, the assassins were Lakota.

Sitting Bull, in a moment of gloom soon after settling at the Standing Rock reservation, had gone out among the hills where he came across one of his favorite birds, a meadowlark.

"Lakotas," the bird seemed to say, "will kill you."

According to records left by One Bull, Sitting Bull was haunted from that day onward. He couldn't shake the thought he'd be killed by his own people as, in fact, he was. See Ibid., pp. 289–90.

14. Carl G. Jung, *Memories, Dreams, Reflections* (New York: Vintage Books/Random House, 1989), p. 235.

15. See C. G. Jung, "On Synchronicity" (1951) and "Synchronicity: An Acausal Connecting Principle" (1952) Sir Herbert Read, Michael Fordham, Gerhard Adler, and William

McGuire, ed., *Collected Works of C. G. Jung*, vol. 8 (New Jersey: Princeton University Press), pp. 520–31 and pp. 417– 519, respectively.

16. Jean Shinoda Bolen, *The Tao of Psychology: Synchronicity and the Self*, p. 7.

17. Ibid., p. 23.

18. "Does this path have heart?" don Juan advises Carlos Castaneda to ask himself when evaluating an inner or outer journey. "If it does, the path is good; if it doesn't, it is of no use . . . one has a heart, the other doesn't. One makes for a joyful journey; as long as you follow it, you are one with it. The other will make you curse your life. One makes you strong; the other weakens you." See Carlos Castaneda, *The Teachings of Don Juan: A Yaqui Way of Knowledge* (New York: Simon & Schuster, 1974), p. 107.

19. This idea of synchronistically meeting people we need to meet, when the time in our life is right, is a theme— we need to ricochet off this rock—central to the series of Insights found in James Redfield's popular *The Celestine Prophecy* (Warner Books, 1993). Although the book is fiction, and branded New Age literature with its reflections on relationships and power struggles, its take on the significance of co-incidences dovetails nicely into Bolen's study with which, my guess, Redfield was familiar. His insights into proper living and evolutionary direction, surfacing in a rare South American manuscript, included advice to accelerate our spiritual life until its "energy" brings on coincidences that "make us feel there is something more, something spiritual, operating underneath everything we do." En route, we need to identify our life's direction, its spiritual path, and ask the right questions as to what to do or where to go next. Intuition begins to guide the way and, if we're alert and watchful, "coincidences," like meeting the right people, occur to help us move forward.

20. Bolen, *The Tao of Psychology*, p. 94.

The Dark Night

1. Cormac McCarthy, *The Crossing* (New York: Vintage Books/Random House, 1994), p. 45.

2. For more on Wintermaker and his possible representation in the Quetico-Superior's Hegman Lake pictographs, see Susan Stanich, "Ojibway Calendar in Pictures? Artist Sees Wintermaker in Rock Drawings," *Minneapolis Star Tribune*, Sunday, 19 April 1992, p. 2B.

3. Sri Nisargadatta, as quoted by Jack Kornfield, *A Path With Heart* (New York: Bantam Books, 1993), p. 50.

The Haunting Moon

1. Black Elk, in Joseph Epes Brown, ed., *The Sacred Pipe: Black Elk's Account of the Seven Rites of the Oglala Sioux* (Norman, Okla.: University of Oklahoma Press, 1953), pp. 3–4, 80.

Life Ascending

1. Barry Lopez, *Crossing Open Ground*, pp. 62–63.

2. Loren Eiseley, *The Unexpected Universe* (New York: Harcourt, Brace & World, Inc., 1964; reprint 1969), p. 90.

3. Po Chu-i, in Thomas Fleming, *Time and Tide* (New York: Simon & Schuster, 1987), p. 648.

4. For this and following, Alexander Skutch, *Life Ascending.*

5. Carlos Castaneda, *The Fire from Within* (New York: Simon & Schuster, 1984), p. 38.

6. McCarthy, *The Crossing*, pp. 45–46.

7. Mythologist Joseph Campbell, as presented by Diane K. Osbon in *A Joseph Campbell Companion: Reflections on the Art of Living* (New York: HarperCollins, 1991), pp. 251 and 244, respectively, describes such moments of clear connection as *esthetic arrest*: when "the clear radiance of the esthetic image is apprehended by the mind, which has been arrested by its wholeness and fascinated by its harmony." It is a psychological stasis where the polarities of joy and fear, good and evil, drop away as a "rapture in sheer experience supervenes."

Exterior nature harmonizes with interior nature.

Esthetic arrest, furthermore, becomes revelatory when, empty of desire, we recognize the "radiant Form of forms that shines through all things."

Can this possibly be anything other than what's variously called the divine or Great Spirit?

Closing the Circle

1. John J. Ozoga, *Whitetail Winter: Seasons of the Whitetail*, p. 136.

2. Richard Nelson, *The Island Within* (San Francisco: North Point Press, 1989), pp. 27–28.

3. See Gary Buffalo Horn Man and Sherry Firedancer, *Animal Energies* (Sadieville, Ky.: Dancing Otter Publishing 1992).

This booklet attempts to condense traditional and current Native American insights into the spiritual significance of fifty-eight "beings"/species: from alligator through deer (gifts: gentleness and sensitivity) and wolf (balance of dependence and independence) to wolverine. I enjoyed the ideas and possibilities in small doses. Overall, there were just too many animals at Hocoka—an entire mosaic of species in dynamic, daily interaction—for me to attempt, let alone understand, constant specific interpretation.

4. The largest white pine by this dead doe was struck by lightning the following summer. The tree shattered so forcefully that, halfway up, the trunk burst apart and the tree's great crown fell to the ground near what remained of the doe.

Bibliography

Ahlgren, Clifford, and Isabel Ahlgren. *Lob Trees in the Wilderness.* Minneapolis: University of Minnesota Press, 1984.

Allen, D. L. *The Wolves of Minong: Their Vital Role in a Wild Community.* Boston: Houghton Mifflin Co., 1979.

Baraga, Frederic. *A Dictionary of the Ojibway Language.* First published as *A Dictionary of the Otchipwe Language.* Montreal: Beauchemin and Valois, 1878, 1880; reprint, St. Paul: Minnesota Historical Society Press, 1992.

Bauer, Erwin A. *Erwin A. Bauer's Predators of North America.* New York: Outdoor Life Books, Grolier, 1988.

Bell, Corydon. *The Wonder of Snow.* New York: Hill & Wang, 1957.

Bentley, W. A., and W. J. Humphreys. *Snow Crystals.* Originally published McGraw-Hill Book Co., 1931; reprint, New York: Dover Publications, 1962.

Berry, Thomas. *The Dream of the Earth.* San Francisco: Sierra Club Books, 1988.

Bolen, Jean Shinoda. *The Tao of Psychology: Synchronicity and the Self.* San Francisco: Harper & Row, 1979.

Brandenburg, Jim. *Brother Wolf: A Forgotten Promise.* Minocqua, Wisc.: NorthWord Press, 1993.

———. *White Wolf: Living with an Arctic Legend.* Minocqua, Wisc.: NorthWord Press, 1988.

Brown, Tom, Jr., as told to William Jon Watkins. *The Tracker:*

The Story of Tom Brown Jr. Englewood Cliffs, New Jersey: Prentice-Hall, 1978.

Brown, Tom Jr. *The Vision.* New York: Berkley Books, 1988.

Brueton, Diana. *Many Moons.* New York: Prentice Hall Press, 1991.

Buffalo Horn Man, Gary, and Sherry Firedancer. *Animal Energies.* Sadieville, Ky: Dancing Otter Publishing, 1994.

Burgesse, J. A. "Snow Shoes," *The Beaver* (March 1941): 24–28.

Chaplin, Raymond E. *Deer.* Dorset: Blandford Press, 1977.

Davidson, Daniel Sutherland. *Snowshoes.* Philadelphia: The American Philosophical Society/Lancaster Press, vol. 6, 1937.

Densmore, Frances. *Chippewa Customs.* First published by Smithsonian Institution, Bureau of American Ethnology, Bulletin 86, 1929; reprint, St. Paul: Minnesota Historical Society Press, 1979.

Dewdney, Selwyn. "Ecological Notes on the Ojibway Shaman-Artist," *ArtsCanada* (August 1970): 17–28.

Drummond, Thomas. *The Canadian Snowshoe.* Transactions of the Royal Society of Canada, section II, series III, vol. 10 (December 1916): 305–20, with six plates.

Easterbrook, Gregg. "Return of the Glaciers," *Newsweek* (November 23, 1992): 62–63.

Gallagher, Winifred. *The Power of Place: How Our Surroundings Shape Our Thoughts, Emotions, and Actions.* New York: Poseidon Press/Simon & Schuster, 1993.

Gray, D. M., and D. H. Male, eds. *Handbook of Snow: Principles, Processes, Management & Use.* New York: Pergamon Press, 1981.

Halfpenny, James, and Roy Ozanne. *Winter: An Ecological Handbook.* Johnson Books, 1989.

Halls, Lowell K., ed. *White-tailed Deer: Ecology and Management.* Stackpole Books/Wildlife Management Institute, 1984.

Harrington, F. H., and P. C. Paquet, eds. *Wolves of the World.* Park Ridge, New Jersey: Noyes Publications, 1982.

Heinrich, Bernd. *Ravens in Winter.* New York: Vintage Books/ Random House, 1989.

Heinselman, Miron. *The Boundary Waters Wilderness Ecosystem.* Minneapolis: University of Minnesota Press, 1996.

Hoeg, Peter. *Smilla's Sense of Snow.* New York: Farrar Straus & Giroux, 1993.

Hoskinson, R. L. and L. David Mech. "White-tail Deer Migration and Its Role in Wolf Predation," *Journal of Wildlife Management* 40, no.3 (1976): 429–41.

Hultkrantz, Ake. *The Religions of the American Indians.* Berkeley/ Los Angeles: University of California Press, 1967.

Jennes, Diamond. *The Indians of Canada.* National Museum of Canada, bulletin 65, Anthropological Series No. 15; first edition, 1932; fourth edition, 1958.

Kappel-Smith, Diana. *Wintering.* Boston: Little, Brown and Company, 1979; reprinted 1984.

Kirk, Ruth. *Snow.* New York: William Morrow & Co., 1977.

Klein, Tom, photographs by Craig and Nadine Blacklock. *Border Country: The Quetico-Superior Wilderness.* Minocqua, Wisc.: NorthWord Press, 1988.

Klinghammer, E., ed. *The Behavior and Ecology of Wolves.* New York: Garland STPM Press, 1979.

Kohl, Johann Georg. *Kitchi-Gami: Life among the Lake Superior Ojibway.* Originally published by Chapman and Hall, London, 1860; St. Paul: Minnesota Historical Society Press, 1985.

LaChapelle, Edward R. *Field Guide to Snow Crystals.* University of Washington Press, 1969.

Lopez, Barry Hulston. "Landscape and Narrative," in *Crossing Open Ground.* New York: Charles Scribner's Sons, 1988.

———. *Of Wolves and Men.* New York: Charles Scribner's Sons, 1978.

———. "The Rediscovery of North America," *The Amicus Journal* (Fall 1991): 12–16.

Major, Ted. *Snow Ecology*. Boulder, Colo.: Thorne Ecological Institute, 1979.

Matthews, Samuel W. "Ice on the World," *National Geographic* (January 1987) 171, no. 1: 79–103.

Mech, L. David. *The Arctic Wolf: Living with the Pack*. Minnesota: Voyageur Press, 1988.

———. *The Way of the Wolf*. Stillwater, Minn.: Voyageur Press, 1991.

———. *The Wolf: The Ecology and Behavior of an Endangered Species*. Minneapolis: University of Minnesota Press, 1981.

———. *The Wolves of Isle Royale*. Fauna Series 7, Fauna of the National Parks of the United States, U.S. Department of the Interior, 1966.

Mech, L. David, and L. D. Frenzel Jr., eds. *Ecological Studies of the Timber Wolf in Northeastern Minnesota*. Research Paper NC-52, St. Paul: USDA Forest Service, North Central Forest Experiment Station, 1971.

Mergen, Bernard. *Snow in America*. Washington, D.C.: Smithsonian Institution Press, 1997.

Milne, Lorus and Margery. *The Senses of Animals and Men*. New York: Atheneum, 1962.

Moen, Aaron N. "Energy Conservation by White-Tailed Deer in the Winter," *Ecology* 57 (1976): 192–98.

Montgomery, G. G. "Nocturnal Movements and Activity Rhythms of White-tailed Deer," *Journal of Wildlife Management* 27, no. 3 (July 1963): 422–27.

Mowat, Farley. *The Snow Walker*. Toronto: McClelland & Stewart, first printing, 1975; reprint, 1984.

Murie, Olaus J. *A Field Guide to Animal Tracks*. Boston: Houghton-Mifflin, 1954; reprint, 1975.

Murphy, Cullen. "In Praise of Snow," *The Atlantic Monthly* 275, no. 1 (January 1995): 45–58.

Nakaya, U. *Snow Crystals: Natural and Artificial*. Cambridge, Massachusetts: Harvard University Press, 1954.

Nelson, M. E., and L. D. Mech. "Deer Social Organization

and Wolf Predation in Northeastern Minnesota," *Wildlife Monogram* 77 (1981).

———. "Observation of a Wolf Killed by a Deer," *Journal of Mammalogy* 66, no. 1 (1985): 187–88.

———. "Relationship Between Snow Depth and Gray Wolf Predation on White-tailed Deer," *Journal of Wildlife Management* 50 (1986): 474.

Nelson, Richard K. *Heart and Blood: Living with Deer in America.* New York: Alfred A. Knopf, 1997.

———. *Hunters of the Northern Ice.* Chicago: University of Chicago Press, 1969.

Nute, Grace Lee. *The Voyageur's Highway.* St. Paul: Minnesota Historical Society Press, 9th printing, 1976.

Olson, Dennis L., photography by Steven J. Krasemann. *Way of the Whitetail: Magic and Mystery.* Minocqua. Wisc.: NorthWord Press, 1994.

Olson, Sigurd F. *Listening Point.* New York: Alfred A. Knopf, 1980.

———. *The Lonely Land.* New York: Alfred A. Knopf, 1961.

———. *The Singing Wilderness.* New York: Alfred A. Knopf, 1979.

———. "A Study in Predatory Relationship with Particular Reference to the Wolf," *Scientific Monthly* 46 (April 1938): 323–36.

Ozoga, John J. "Aggressive Behavior of White-tailed Deer at Winter Cuttings," *Journal of Wildlife Management* 36, no. 3 (1972): 861–68.

———. *White Tail Country.* Minocqua, Wisc.: NorthWord Press, 1988.

———. *Whitetail Winter: Seasons of the Whitetail.* bk. 2. Minocqua, Wisc.: Willow Creek Press, 1995.

Ozoga, John J., and L. W. Gysel. "Response of White-tailed Deer to Winter Weather," *Journal of Wildlife Management* 36 (1972): 892–96.

Ozoga, John J., and Louis J. Verme. "Predation by Black Bears on Newborn White-Tailed Deer," *Journal of Mammalogy* 63, no. 4 (November, 1982): 695–96.

Palmer, E. Laurence, and H. Seymour Fowler. *Fieldbook of Natural History.* 2d ed. New York: McGraw-Hill Book Company, 1975.

Peterson, Rolf O. *Wolf Ecology and Prey Relationships on Isle Royale.* National Park Service Monograph Series 11, (1977).

Pielou, E. C. *After the Ice Age: The Return of Life to Glaciated North America.* Chicago: The University of Chicago Press, 1991.

Proescholdt, Kevin, Rip Rapson, and Miron L. Heinselman. *Troubled Waters: The Fight for the Boundary Waters Canoe Area Wilderness.* St. Cloud, Minn.: North Star Press, 1995.

Putman, Rory. *The Natural History of Deer.* Ithaca, N.Y.: Cornell University Press, 1988.

Quammen, David. "Tracking the Wily Gestalt," *Outside* (December 1986): 23–29.

Richardson, Larry W., with Harry A. Jacobson, Robert J. Muncy, and Carroll J. Perkins. "Acoustics of White-Tailed Deer," *Journal of Mammalogy* 64, no. 2 (1983): 245–52.

Rue III, Leonard Lee. *The Deer of North America.* New York: Outdoor Life Books, Crown, 1978; updated and expanded edition, Connecticut: Outdoor Life Books/ Grolier Book Clubs, 1989.

Savage, Candace. *Wolves.* San Francisco: Sierra Club Books, 1988.

Schwartz, George M., and George A. Thiel. *Minnesota's Rocks and Waters.* Minneapolis: University of Minnesota Press, 1954.

Searle, R. Newell. *Saving Quetico-Superior: A Land Set Apart.* St. Paul: Minnesota Historical Society Press, 1977.

Silver, H., N. F. Colovos, J. B. Holter, and H. H. Haynes. "Fasting Metabolism of White-tailed Deer," *Journal of Wildlife Management* 33 (1969): 490–98.

Skutch, Alexander. *Life Ascending*. Austin, Tex.: University of Texas Press, 1985.

Snyder, Gary. *The Practice of the Wild*. San Francisco: North Point Press, 1990.

Steinhart, Peter. *The Company of Wolves*. New York: Alfred A. Knopf, 1995.

Stokes, Donald W. *A Guide to Nature in Winter*. Boston: Little, Brown & Co., 1976.

Taylor, Walter P., ed. *The Deer of North America*. Harrisburg, Pennsylvania: Stackpole Co. and The Wildlife Management Institute, Washington, D.C., 1956; third printing, 1965.

Vickery (Huot-), Jim dale. *Open Spaces*. Minocqua, Wisc.: NorthWord Press, 1991.

Walshe, Shan. *Plants of Quetico and the Ontario Shield*. Toronto: University of Toronto Press, 1980.

Warren, William W. *History of the Ojibway People*. St. Paul: Minnesota Historical Society Press, 1984.

Williams, Terry Tempest, and Ted Major. *The Secret Language of Snow*. San Francisco: Sierra Club/Pantheon Books, 1984.

Jim dale Huot-Vickery is a native of northern Minnesota's Red River Valley. After graduating from St. John's University, he gravitated toward northeaster Minnesota's Quetico-Superior and its Boundary Wate Canoe Area Wilderness. In the backcountry near Ely established a home, Hocoka (locus of *Winter Sign*), w he has nurtured a career as freelance writer, speaker woodsman, and National Park Service seasonal rar He is the author of *Wilderness Visionaries*, a collectic biographies of wilderness naturalists in the conte America's wilderness preservation movement, ar *Spaces*, adventure narratives exploring his encou with wolves, visits to remote wilderness areas, riences as a park ranger.